DRAGON ELEGY

A MEMOIR OF SURVIVING THE CULTURAL REVOLUTION AND BEYOND

QIRU LONG WALDER

MINDSTIR MEDIA

Published by Mindstir Media, LLC
45 Lafayette Rd | Suite 181| North Hampton, NH 03862 | USA
1.800.767.0531 | www.mindstirmedia.com

Printed in the United States of America

ISBN: 979-8-9850104-7-3 (paperback)

CONTENTS

AUTHOR'S NOTE

My surname, "Long", means "dragon" in Chinese and the Chinese were supposed to be the "descendants of dragons", hence the title of the book, *Dragon Elegy*.

Also noted are the spellings of the Chinese names and places in this book. They are in the form of the *pinyin* system, which is currently used in China. In the *pinyin* system, there are four letters that are pronounced differently from their English pronunciations while the letter "g" has only one pronunciation. See below:

Letter "**c**" is pronounced "**ts**". For instance, the author's brother "Ciqing" is pronounced "Tsiching".

Letter "**q**" is pronounced "**ch**", and hence, the author's mother "Suqin" is "Suchin", her brother "Ciqing" is "Tsiching" and herself "Qiru" is "Chiru".

Letter "**x**" is close to the "**sh**" sound, and hence, the author's father "Long Xuan" is "Long Shuan" and her mother "Xu Suqin" is "Shu Suchin".

Letter "**z**" is close to the "**tz**" sound, and hence, "Nie Yuanzi" is "Nie Yuantzi".

Letter "**g**" is pronounced "**g**" only, as in "get". For instance, "genzheng miaohong" is "genjeng miaohong".

Digraph "**zh**" is close to the "**j**" sound, and hence, "Peng Zhen" is "Peng Jen" and "Zhang Lanxin" is "Jang Lanshin".

Barnaul
ganda
Soviet Union
Alma-Ata
Mon
XINJIANG
Cease-Fire Line
QINGHAI
Xining
XIZANG
(TIBET)
SICH
DELHI
Nepal
KATHMANDU
THIMPHU
Bhutan
Brahmaputra
Ganges
India
Bangladesh
DHAKA
YUNNAN
Irrawaddy
Burma
Salween
Mekong
La

LIST OF MAJOR COMMUNIST CAMPAIGNS SINCE 1949

Land Reform Campaign (1949-1952): Like the other campaigns, the land reform campaign was implemented through inciting class hatred. Poor peasants were mobilized to denounce landlords. In mass trials, land was forcibly taken away from the landlords. It is estimated that anywhere between 1 and 4.5 million lost their lives in summary executions, or died in prisons and labor camps.

Campaign to Suppress Counterrevolutionaries (1950-1953): It was launched to suppress residual opposition, such as the Nationalist functionaries, intellectuals and foreign employees suspected for their loyalty. Multimillions of those accused were sentenced to forced labor or death in mass trials. Millions were killed in summary executions or perished in prisons and labor camps.

Three-Antis and Five-Antis Campaigns (1951-1953): The former was aimed at corruption, waste and bureaucracy while the latter was against bribery, theft of state property, tax evasion, cheating on government contracts, and stealing state economic information. Hundreds of thousands of businessmen died.

Eliminate Hidden Counterrevolutionaries Campaign (1955-1956): It was launched to further purge "counterrevolutionaries". About 770,000 suspected as such lost their lives.

Hundred-Flowers Campaign (1956-1957): Affected by the chain-reaction of the de-Stalinization in the Eastern Bloc, Mao started this campaign supposedly to invite criticism. But when people spoke up and criticisms turned more pointed, the movement was suppressed.

Anti-Rightists Campaign (1957-1959): The criticisms of the party rule and policies in the Hundred-Flowers Campaign led to this campaign to purge critics. More than 550,000 of those labeled "rightists" were demoted, exiled, sent to labor camps indefinitely, or sentenced to prison or even executed while 500,000 categorized as "non-extreme rightists" and "anti-socialists" were put under lifelong surveillance.

Great Leap Forward Campaign (1958-1962): Emboldened by the Soviet Union's lead over the US in the space race and Khrushchev's goal to accelerate communism, Mao decided it was time for China to do so too. Impractical goals and malpractices led to consecutive years of nationwide famine and 36-45 million deaths.

Eradicate Four-Pests Campaign (1958-1962): It was a campaign during the Great Leap Forward. The "four pests" referred to rats, flies, mosquitoes and sparrows. The eradication of sparrows destroyed the ecological balance that further reduced agricultural outputs and added to the death toll.

Socialist Education Campaign (1963-1966): It was also known as the "four clean-ups" campaign, aimed to cleanse the grassroots level bureaucracy of "reactionary" elements. More than five million were persecuted and 77,560 died.

The Great Proletarian Cultural Revolution Campaign (1966-1976): Mao Zedong engineered this campaign to topple his archenemy, Liu Shaoqi, and cleanse the party and the nation of "enemies". It impacted everyone in the country and ended at Mao's death ten years later. An estimated 100 million, about 1/7-1/6 of the population, were implicated. Millions perished.

Destruction of the Four-Olds Campaign (1966): It was a movement during the Cultural Revolution incited by the party and carried out by Red Guards to destroy old ideas, old culture, old customs, and old habits. In this movement, things past, eye-pleasing, foreign, classic and folkloric were destroyed; over 11 million "enemy" households were ransacked, with their properties confiscated and family members beaten up and even killed or expelled from the cities.

Cleansing the Class Ranks Campaign (1967-1969): It was a campaign during the Cultural Revolution to root out every single one of the "enemies." This all-inclusive campaign resulted in 30 million persecuted, and over 500,000 beaten and tortured to death.

PREFACE

The 10-year-long Cultural Revolution is history now. However, its specter is still haunting us today. What is taking place in the US and the world is alarmingly similar to the beginning of it. Reviewing the history of Communist acts perhaps can help prevent us from the headlong descent along the same disastrous path to losing our voices, our rights, and even our lives.

Communism is never rosy as it is promised to be. Nor is it benign. Under the Communists, over 100 million people lost their lives. To strike fear into the hearts of the population, they rule by terror. They ruthlessly eliminated tens of millions of "class enemies", including their own comrades, and placed an even larger population in prisons, gulags, reform-through-labor camps, juvenile delinquent centers, and police-run work-study boarding schools for youngsters who merely committed some one-time misdemeanor. Tens of millions died there. Their lunacy starved tens of millions more to death. To keep everyone in place, they assigned each person a class label and a personal status associated with his occupation. In China, our official personal dossier called "*dang'an* (archive)" controlled our entire lives. It holds all the information about us—our background, history, official judgment about our political performance, and "wrongdoings" that included spurious accusations and hearsay. It impacted schooling, job assignment, job transfer, marriage, and advancement not only of ourselves, but of our descendants. It had legal effects that could send us to a labor camp or prison without a trial. Besides, they set up a neighborhood committee in every block to watch everyone's daily activity. In addition, the "*hukou*", a household registration system that controlled one's food and supply ration, prevented the possibility of anyone disappearing from the authorities' radar.

Out of their more than 60 classifications during the Mao years, only five groups were within the trusted "people" range, the so-called "proletariat"—Communists themselves that included all of their 24 grades of officials and military personnel, and their claimed "allied armies" ("*tongmeng jun*")—workers, poor peasants, and lower-middle peasants. At the bottom of the totem pole were the "class enemies"—landlords, rich peasants, counterrevolutionaries, bad elements, and rightists. The term "Counterrevolutionaries" included former Nationalist Party and Youth League members, government officials, military and intelligence personnel, gendarmes, police, "imperialist accomplices" and "running dogs", members of secret societies, and the "newly-bred counterrevolutionaries" while "bad elements" encompassed homosexuals, outlandish dressers, pickpockets, vagabonds, hooligans, debauchees, adulterers, and "premarital-sex offenders". Once one was labeled an "enemy", he or she would either be killed, or languish and die in a prison or a labor camp. More ingenious, the assigned label was not permanent, but subject to change, depending on our conduct and the whim of the authorities. As a matter of fact, many within the range of "people" thus became "counterrevolutionaries" or "bad elements".

Our family was within the quasi-"class enemy" range as my father had been an employee of the "imperialist-run" Chinese Maritime Customs Service. But, my grandfather's "bureaucrat-bourgeois" status could further pull us down to the "enemy" range, depending on the political situation. A quasi-"class enemy", my father was expelled from his prestigious job at the Customs and demoted to bookkeeping at a local grain bureau. We were then kicked out of our four-bedroom French colonial home and relocated into two windowless rooms. As the descendants of undesirable people, we were "born no good", "innately evil" like our ancestors, and needed to pay a fair share for our ancestors' and our own "sins". We were precluded from entering college and from obtaining any job that was desirable or considered "honorable", "sensitive" or privileged. We were only fit for the most undesirable physical labor. My brother, Ciqing, was not even allowed to become a sportsman after a background screening. For selling some used wires and waste copper picked up in a deserted area to a recycling station to fund his transistor radio project, Ciqing had a "demerit" entered in his *dang'an*. Then, during the severe famine when we were all starving, to fill our empty stomachs, Ciqing, a spirited boy still in his early teens then, dug some clams out of a lake that turned out to be reserved for ranking Communists only. With a new charge of "consecutive thefts of state properties", he was put on probation, one step short of being expelled from school. Twice, he was punished for daring to take the initiative to do something that would not constitute a "crime" in a normal society. A record like this would effectively end anyone's chance for advancement. Ciqing was not even allowed to go beyond junior high school.

With activists in every residential compound working for the neighborhood committee, nothing we did could escape their attention. Anything that displeased them was reported to the police and dealt with expeditiously. My brother, Tiemin, who, at the time quit his job as a choral member to take vocal lessons to become a solo lyric tenor, was thus sent to a reform-through-labor farm for being an "idle bourgeois descendant".

Under the Communist rule, no one was safe. No matter what his class label was, once he crossed the party line, dared to speak outside the script or lead an un-prescribed life,he would surely be punished. According to the Communist internal investigations conducted in 1978 and 1984, about 1/7 to 1/6 of the entire population was implicated during the Cultural Revolution. This ratio clearly indicated that the majority of those affected were "proletarians". All this began with Mao's personal vendetta against his archrival Liu Shaoqi, who replaced him as the state chairman and ended his disastrous Great Leap Forward that led to the severe nationwide famine and 36-45 million deaths. In this persecution frenzy, not only Liu Shaoqi, but four of his family members, 14 of his service men and countless Communist officials lost their lives, millions of ordinary people also died in vain.

Today, Communism and many Communist practices are alive and well. With the help of modern technologies, catching enemies becomes much easier. Now a social credit system that tracks every aspect of one's life is in place. The ruling class can silence you and disappear you. The population they galvanize through the media to keep themselves in power can intimidate you into submission. We now even see this take place in our beloved democratic society. If this goes unchecked, very soon, we will find ourselves living in Communist China. As Ronald Reagan forewarned, "Freedom is never more than one generation away from extinction."

What my family and I experienced during the Cultural Revolution is very ordinary, but it is precisely because of this ordinariness that allows the readers to fathom the depth of the oppressive nature of a Communist regime.

THE CULTURAL REVOLUTION ARRIVES

S pring 1966, the campaign of "cultural revolution" was growing more virulent. More people of note were singled out and condemned for "anti-Mao, anti-party, and anti-socialism" crime. It scared the hell out of people in the cultural and academic fields. Even ordinary people were rocked with angst and ominous presentiment.

I was a tenth grader at Beijing Foreign Languages School, a boarding school where students' fathers were often members of the party's Central Committee, government ministers, generals, or something. On our campus, all that some combative Communist offspring raved about was to "wage another revolution" to "beat back class enemies' onslaught against the red regime".

I was leery about the whole thing, wondering who was behind those lethal accusations lodged by some no-name critics, why a campaign was needed to take down some relatively inconsequential individuals, and what the campaign was intended to achieve. But, with my disadvantaged intellectual family background, I warned myself, stay under the radar. Do not open your mouth and err again. You can easily end up a casualty of those self-proclaimed "Communist successors" raring for revolutionary actions.

Soon, we saw the Beijing municipal government attacked for "harboring anti-party, anti-socialism elements". Before long, our beloved Mayor Peng Zhen[1], fifth-ranking official in the nation and Chairman Mao's successor apparent, was named the "backstage boss" of the "anti-party, anti-socialism counterrevolutionary black gang". More devastating, he was defined as an "anti-party, anti-socialism vanguard", which clearly indicated more and higher officials were to be singled out. At the thought of only two active members above him, Liu Shaoqi[2] and Zhou Enlai[3] left to be named, I was horrified.

Shortly, the party's May 16 Notification was leaked to us, proclaiming our nation was "in danger of seizure by Khrushchev-type usurpers". The myriad of belief-destroying events occurring in the twinkling of an eye had already knocked us off balance. With our school principal, Mo Ping, and Party Secretary, Cheng Bi, denounced and paralyzed as the "Black Gang members" by the party elite's offspring, at this proclamation, the sky seemed to have collapsed. Panic, confusion, and a sense of doom swept through our campus. Girls huddled and cried, teachers walked around dumbfounded, seeking information and assurance from one another, while Chai Feng, taking over from Mo Ping and Cheng Bi, tried frantically and futilely to calm the panicky, demoralized crowds, beseeching "unwavering faith in Chairman Mao and the Central Party Committee". It was total chaos.

Stunned like everyone else, I tried to make sense of this whole thing. Who are the Khrushchev-type figures? I asked myself. Have they been hiding there all those years? How can the party not be aware of such infiltration until it becomes so rife? How can those highly revered officials turn into "anti-party counterrevolutionary revisionists" overnight without any trace left before this? If the party is "great, glorious, and forever correct", how can any of this take place? I didn't dare to question anymore.

Faith destroyed and beliefs annihilated, with administration being dysfunctional and teachers attacked for "exercising bourgeois dictatorship", "discriminating against Communist and working-class offspring", and "shielding landlord and bourgeois progenies and giving them precedence", we, the better students, usually of non-Communist background who had defended the administrators, now found ourselves under attack, assaulted as "black seedlings" and "dog whelps of landlords and bourgeoisie help suppress the revolution" by the elite descendants. Zhang Zhongxi, the only student party member and a proper, exemplary student who was chosen to study in East Germany and arranged to leave in a month, was beaten black and blue. The attack prompted him and another female student, Shen Nailing, an "exemplary Youth League member of Haidian District" and a "Trendsetter of Haidian District on Studying Mao's Works", to denounce themselves tearfully on stage for "becoming a captive of bourgeois revisionist line and a black seedling". At this, many of us better students rushed to join the self-denunciation line. I criticized myself in a poster too. Distraught and having no one to turn to, we were desperate for guidance.

It was impossible to keep us in classrooms any longer. From that point on, school existed in name only.

On May 23, 1966, Peng Zhen was formally deposed. A new mayor was appointed. At the news, I breathed a sigh of relief, trusting with the new leadership in place, directions on how to go about the Cultural Revolution would be given and things would soon be under control.

Just as I felt reassured, on May 25, in Beijing University, some party functionary and her cohorts posted a bombastic big-character poster, ferociously accusing the administrators there of "faithfully executing the counterrevolutionary revisionist line to suppress revolutionary actions" and calling upon "all revolutionary intellectuals to unite and plunge into the fierce battle to wipe out all evil creatures and Khrushchev-type counterrevolutionary revisionists".

Mao hailed it as the "first Marxist big-character poster". It was followed by the party's incitement to "destroy whoever opposes Chairman Mao no matter how high his position is". At this, the whole nation found its direction. At once, students from colleges to primary schools, staff members, government cadres from top to bottom in every branch, factory workers, peasants, and personnel from the military and public security organs all rushed to attack their administrators and whomever they suspected to have opposed Chairman Mao. The cultural revolution within the cultural and academic fields was now turned into a nationwide "Great Proletarian

Cultural Revolution" that would "wring everyone's soul" and "pound all and clean up all", led by Chen Boda[4], Kang Sheng[5] and Mao's wife Jiang Qing[6].

Once the forbidden zone was opened, there were no longer secrets within the party. A profusion of secrets were revealed about the party's inside stories and officials' shocking corrupt personal lives contrary to the "forever-upright" image the party had created for itself.

Aghast at what I learned and convinced that there was indeed a fierce two-line struggle within the party from the top to the grass-roots level, and proved to have been on the wrong side of the line, I now joined the Communist offspring and others to criticize the administrators and teachers, mimicking whatever accusations we read from the big-character posters posted at the colleges we visited to stay in line with the trend. But we were taunted, pushed around or beaten as "opportunists", "fence-sitters" and "double-faced cowards" by the Communist offspring.

Validated by Mao's and the party's endorsements of the actions against the administrators, the self-proclaimed "born-revolutionary" Communist offspring at our school turned more righteous and violent. At the party's call on June 1 to "sweep away all forces of evil" and to "destroy the old and establish the new", they rounded up Principal Mo Ping, Party Secretary Cheng Bi, other administrators, teachers, and school aides having some "undesirable" background or "suspicious" history, and placed them in solitary confinement, torturing and savagely beating them up to exact confessions for their presumed "crimes". They also punished them with dirty, heavy labor, and humiliated them with parades in grotesque outfits, erratically cut hair, dunce caps and heavy wooden placards with worn shoes, dirty socks, used cans, pots and pans around their necks. Our English teacher, Mr. He Huisheng, an overseas returnee who had served as the English interpreter in Mao's meeting with the Russian head Voroshilov in 1958; Mr. Lin Yi'an, an "uncapped rightist" demoted from Foreign Affairs Ministry like Mr. He; Mr. Yan Guisen, our Chinese teacher singled out as a "historical counterrevolutionary"; Mr. Zhang Lanxin, our history and homeroom teacher with a landlord family background; our beloved gym teacher, Mr. Hong Jinlong, another overseas returnee, all were taken into custody.

⌒⌒

It turned out that Mao, who was sidelined and ceded the state chairman position in humiliation to Liu Shaoqi, his archenemy, for the 40-million deaths caused by his Great Leap Forward (1958-1962), was behind all of this. With the removal of Liu Shaoqi's right-hand man Peng Zhen and other key figures, Mao was now within sight of vanquishing his nemesis.

With Mao mysteriously unavailable, Liu Shaoqi was left to struggle in the mine with no escape. To quell the anarchic, violent situation, at Mao's approval, on June 3, Liu Shaoqi decided to distribute work teams to universities and troubled secondary schools in Beijing.

At the news, I once again felt relieved, believing the anarchic state would be finally brought to an end.

On the morning of June 8, before the work team was to arrive, I noticed dozens of elite offspring rode out of school on their bicycles. Upon their return, all ranking officials' offspring unanimously donned hand-me-down faded green army uniforms, the typical outfit of Communist offspring before the Cultural Revolution, and red cotton armbands printed with "Red Guard" in yellow ink. They looked and acted as if some secret sacred mission was bestowed upon them. I was totally unaware that around that time, many contingents formed by officials' offspring in other elite secondary schools throughout Beijing also adopted the same name with their members all arrayed the same way. Perplexed by Red Guards' incomprehensible acts, I anxiously awaited the work team's arrival to guide us out of this chaotic, baffling state.

At dusk, the work team dispatched by the Central Communist Youth League Committee finally entered our school. Enthusiastically and emotionally, we greeted them like long-awaited saviors. We'd rather believe the party was still as intact and correct as it had ever been.

At the school-wide meeting convened in the auditorium that night, the head of the work team immediately endorsed Red Guards' actions, justifying their violence as an "inevitable outcome of masses' movement", and citing Mao's words, "If a good person is beaten by a bad person, it is a glory! If a bad person is beaten by a good person, he rightfully deserves it!"

On June 10, we were taken to the Central Communist Youth League to attend an orientation meeting for troubled secondary schools in Haidian District, where many elite offspring were concentrated and where unrest originated, on how to go about the Cultural Revolution. With leadership in place, situation analyzed and direction pointed out, we felt reassured and relieved.

On June 13, school was officially suspended to solely make the Cultural Revolution.

With the *dang'an* (official personnel-dossiers) and the mandated written self-disclosures, the work team secretly classified administrators, staff members, school aides and students as "leftists", "middle-roaders" and "right-wingers" according to their class origin, history and political performance. A Revolutionary Committee was formed with selected teachers and student loyal to authorities. Zhang Zhongxi, the obedient boy, was chosen as the student representative. The wild attack turned into a planned and organized one. Every day, the work team cast out some information about certain individuals to lure out more "self-exposed class enemies" in the masses' mad disclosures of each other. Fearing to be singled out as a new target, we all rushed to denounce the targets blindly and went on with our self-criticism of any of our association with the targets in order to clear ourselves. Very soon, Mo Ping and Cheng Bi were declared "traitors" and "executors of the counterrevolutionary revisionist line", and removed from their posts. Concurrently, many teachers, administrators and school aides were labeled "class enemies", "phony leftist but bona fide rightists" or "counterrevolutionaries".

To our incomprehension, the Red Guards barricaded themselves and set up a different camp, unanimously opposing the work team. They accused the work team of "executing the counterrevolutionary revisionist line, exercising counterrevolutionary bourgeois dictatorship and surrounding themselves with dog whelps, bad people and counterrevolutionary elements to suppress revolutionary offspring and revolutionary actions and divert the general direction of the struggle". In spite of the work team's repeated pleas for them to "return to the right track", they continued to wreak havoc and beat up people siding with the work team. Even when they were declared "counterrevolutionaries" by the work team, they showed no fear. On the contrary, more and more middle- and lower-ranking Communist offspring gathered under their banner. Even Communist offspring from the elementary section already dismissed for home returned to join them.

Baffled by their inexplicable unanimous sudden change of stance, I wondered what they attempted to accomplish. Evidently, something mysterious beyond our knowledge was going on. Since May, I had noticed the official offspring's frequent secret contact with the Communist offspring from other schools. I had no idea that Mao's wife, Jiang Qing, was behind the scene in all of the "spontaneous actions" through the liaison men she dispatched—turning against the school administration, uniformly renaming their organizations to "Red Guards", and opposing the work team.

Unable to break the Red Guards, on July 16, the new Beijing administration decided to divide the students in troubled secondary schools into three parts to quell further unrest: The Red Guards and students reliably obedient to authorities would remain at school to continue with the revolution; the students deemed harmless were assigned to guard the school to prevent the Red Guards from further contacting people from outside the school; and the "unreliable" ones were to be sent away for military training at a military base on the outskirts of Xingtai, a city some 220 miles (354 kilometers) southwest of Beijing.

A political laggard, I was among those sent away, leaving behind many unresolved questions—Mao's conspicuous invisibility at a time when we needed his instructions most, the mysterious reorganization of Communist offspring's squads right before the arrival of the work team, their incomprehensible actions against the work team, and secretive daily contact with Red Guards from other schools.

Marching and drilling in the morning, and studying Chairman Mao's works in the afternoon daily like the soldiers on an isolated military base with no newspaper, radio or outside contact, we had developed a false sense of normalcy. After 13 days of training, we were abruptly recalled from our military training on the afternoon of July 29.

Military personnel trucks dropped us off at Ganjiakou at about 8 p.m. From there, we would march for about 15 minutes back to school. With our bedrolls on our backs and toiletry bags in our hands, we marched to our school while singing revolutionary songs, totally unaware that Liu Shaoqi was to be purged.

As we were approaching the school campus, we could hear Mao's quotations blasting out of the school's loudspeakers one after another:

"The thousand strands of Marxism can be summed up in one sentence: 'Rebellion is justified.' Based on this principle, revolts and insurrections come along, and socialism is made."

"Revolution is not inviting someone to a dinner party; nor is it writing an article… It is a riot, an act of violence by which one class overthrows another."

"We must strike the class enemies down to the dust and stamp a foot on them to make sure they will never be able to turn over."

"Communism is not love. Communism is a hammer which we use to crush the enemy."

Immediately alarmed by the not previously cited Mao's quotations on violence against class enemies, we stopped singing, marching back to school silently. Obviously, something drastic was taking place.

On campus, we, the silent, orderly and disciplined returnees found ourselves an incongruous sight in a wild, anarchic scene, looking surreal, outmoded, and embarrassingly comical in the sea of Red Guards who were all geared up with faded green army uniforms and red silk armbands printed with "Red Guard" in black ink. Legions of them were from other elite schools to lend their support for the Red Guards in our school to suppress the "dog whelps' savage onslaught and class vengeance". We were raucously taunted by them as "dog whelps" and "progenies of landlords and bourgeoisie".

From the big-character posters and slogans posted on the walls, I became aware that the work team had been removed the day we were summoned back. The school was now under the total siege of the Red Guards, with the gatehouse, administrative offices and broadcasting all under their control.

At the dismissal, I returned to the dormitory to unpack. Along my way, I saw debating crowds and shockingly violent posters and slogans posted everywhere, covering almost every inch of reachable surfaces of the school buildings: *Long live the proletarian dictatorship! Long live the proletarian class line! Father a hero, son a true man; Father a counterrevolutionary, son a bastard! Suppress counterrevolutionary dog-whelps! We will not permit progenies of landlords and bourgeoisie to retaliate! Only the leftists are entitled to rebel while the right-wingers are forbidden to overturn the sky! Sweep away all forces of evil! It is righteous to rebel against the counterrevolutionaries; It is justified to carry on the revolution! Whole-heartedly support the Central Party Committee's decision on removing the work teams! Anyone suppressing the students' movement will come to no good end! Smash his dog-head if one dares to oppose Chairman Mao and the party! Protect the Central Party Committee headed by Chairman Mao with our lives!*

At these ghastly posters and the disturbing violent messages, my heart pounded. I sensed our life as non-proletarian offspring was going to be fundamentally changed for the worse and that someone high above was about to be singled out. But who is the one that "suppressed the students' movement"? I asked myself. I had no idea that these ominous words came from Mao and that on the same day of our return, Liu Shaoqi had publicly criticized himself in front of Red Guards and college revolutionary activists for dispatching work teams, a decision that Mao had approved, and that Mao had sealed Liu's fate that day by branding him a "counterrevolutionary-all-along", at backstage.

I couldn't wait to find out what was going on. As soon as I finished unpacking, I returned to the campus and blended myself in the debating crowds to obtain more information.

The debates were about whether family background and political outlook correlated with each other, nothing to do with the large political picture. After managing to put in a word, I turned to leave— There was no point in this debate since we had long been branded "dog whelps of landlords and bourgeoisie". But, as I turned, I found my way out blocked and myself encircled by seven or eight overbearing male Red Guards from other schools, arm-in-arm. Apparently, my remarks provoked them. It was a hot night. The circle was so tight that I felt their body heat and hot breaths.

"What family are you from?" They asked threateningly. "What does your father do?" "Is he a revolutionary or a counterrevolutionary?"

At their hostility, I hedged, "He teaches at college."

"You fucking bourgeois dog-whelp! We detected it from the very first sight!" "You are a fucking born-opportunist!" "A fucking fence-sitter!" "A double-faced coward!"

I was shocked. Such language was unheard of before we left the school. Just as I was in disbelief, I heard a shout from behind, "What do you think of the Cultural Revolution?"

I turned to him and hastened to say, "I will respond to Chairman Mao's call and plunge myself into revolutionary actions."

More swearing followed at my response, "You are a fucking tricky dog-whelp!" "A fucking born-hypocrite!" "A phony revolutionary, a bona fide counterrevolutionary!"

"What do you think of the antithetical couplet?" One of them shouted out a question.

Knowing he meant the one that said "Father a hero, son a true man: Father a counterrevolutionary, son a bastard", I responded by repeating what had been taught to us before the Cultural Revolution, "I don't agree with it. One cannot choose his family, but he can choose his own path."

They hurled invective again: "You fucking sly! Stop deceiving us with your sophism!" "Dictatorship to you dog whelps!" "Suppress all counterrevolutionaries!"

"Behave yourself," the one standing in front of me berated me. "You have proved bourgeois blood is inside you. You were born tricky and dishonest. Your only way out is to subject yourself to the proletarian dictatorship. You dog whelps are forbidden to speak out or move about!"

In their triumphant moment of raucous swearing and jeering, I dug my way out.

On the campus, menacing slogan shouting and songs composed by Red Guards were heard here and there consecutively: *"If you want to make revolution, come over; if not, get the fuck out!" "The party is our blood parents. If anyone dares to attack the party, we will smash him to Hell! Kill-kill-kill-kill, kill!" "Father a revolutionary, son a true man…!"*

In front of the auditorium where the Red Guards' rally was to be held, hundreds of Red Guards from other schools were waiting. With all of them in uniforms and armbands, singing revolutionary songs and shouting slogans under their red silk banners, it felt like a miniature of rallying cries of Hitler's Third Reich.

At nine o'clock, the Red Guards' rally began. Slogan shouting and songs ushered in a screaming speech given by a well-known super-active female Red Guard from Beida Fuzhong (secondary school affiliated with Beijing University). After citing "beloved" Jiang Qing's words "Those who want to make revolution, come over; those who don't, get out", she called on the Red Guards to "suppress dog whelps and all forms of counterrevolutionaries with Red Terror and proletarian dictatorship" and "smash them to hell". At this, Red Guards jumped onto the stage one after another to shout themselves blue with profanities against "dog whelps" and declared "imminent proletarian dictatorship on dog whelps". In each of their speeches, they cited Mao's quotations to justify their soon-to-be-taken actions: "Revolution is not inviting someone to a party… It is a riot, an act of violence by which one class overthrows another." "We must strike the class enemies down to the dust and stamp a foot on them to make sure they will never be able to turn over." "In righting wrongs, we must exceed the limits. By not exceeding the limits, we will not right wrongs."

The rally ended after 11. With Red Guards groups from other schools departing one after another, the campus finally quieted down at midnight.

Knowing some drastic measures would be taken against us, I returned to my dormitory heavy-hearted, wondering what the Red Guards could do to us. In a school with 82% of Communist offspring and 10% working-class offspring, those of us non-proletarian descendants were sure targets.

The next morning, at five o'clock, a thunderous "Red Guards Commands" bursting out of the loudspeakers woke us up. It declared that "from this very instant on, all dog whelps are put under proletarian dictatorship, forbidden to leave the campus without permission, forbidden to form counterrevolutionary alliances, forbidden to wreak havoc or make mischief, and forbidden to speak out or move about". It also warned that "further revolutionary actions are to be taken" against us and that "anyone daring to defy the commands shall be eliminated on the spot". It was broadcast from time to time throughout the entire day.

News about violence and deaths in our school and elsewhere reached us by word of mouth: some students were beaten to a pulp; the Red Guards in our school had bludgeoned our school gardener and a local "landlady" to death. A quiet girl, our classmate and dormmate, was said to have contributed the most lashes to the demise of the woman. At the news, we were seized with waves of terror, keenly aware of our proximity to mortal danger.

Before noon, a new contingent called "Red Peripheries" was formed by students of other proletarian backgrounds to distinguish themselves from us "dog whelps" and to identify themselves as being affiliated with Red Guards, legitimate in making the revolution. With this formation, we were made especially conspicuous on the campus. We needed to be more vigilant. We could be singled out for assault by either of them with no provocation.

We holed up in our dormitory. When the peak hour for lunchtime was over and the campus quieted down, the few of us banded together to make ourselves feel safer and headed for the dining hall.

On our way, we noticed new alarming posters and slogans all over the campus: *Long live the Red Terror! Down with all progenies of landlords and bourgeoisie! Dragons give birth to dragons, phoenixes beget phoenixes while rats can only produce hole-digging litters! If dog whelps dare to speak out or move about, we will smash them to hell!* To avoid trouble, we took a side route, but still found ourselves cursed and spat upon by the few Red Guards passing by.

Having learned the Red Guards were guarding the passageway to the dining hall and forced "dog whelps" to crawl under a tunnel of crotches and that Chen Dong, a senior student who defied the humiliation, had been savagely thrashed and had to be carried off, we slipped into the dining hall through the back door.

There was hardly anyone there. We hurriedly purchased our meals for a few days' consumption and left there right away.

On our way, we unfortunately encountered a group of our classmates, the newly formed Red Peripheries.

"Stop here, you dog whelps!" One of them shouted, "Don't you know you dog whelps are forbidden to bind together to form counterrevolutionary alliances?"

Another singled out a classmate in our group, "Lu Panpan! Why did your dog parents name you 'Panpan'?"

"Pan" means "expecting" in Chinese.

"What did they expect?" In a mocking tone, another classmate took over, "The return of Chiang Kai-shek's Guomindang (Nationalists) regime?"

"Expect to be liberated by Chairman Mao and the party," clever and quick-witted, Lu Panpan blurted out a ready riposte.

"Bullshit! Your father worked for a Guomindang newspaper. How could he expect to be taken over by the Communists? When were you born, before or after the communist takeover?"

"Before."

"What date?"

"December 26."

"How dare you tarnish the image of our great leader Chairman Mao by claiming to have the same birthday?" a female Red Periphery screamed.

"December 26, 1948 was my birthday."

"Shut up!" One barked, "Wait till we check it out!" Turning to us, he warned, "You dog-whelps are forbidden to speak out or move about! Watch out and behave yourselves!"

They finally moved on.

With trepidation in our hearts and the broadcast going on ceaselessly, it was impossible to fall asleep at night. When it began to quiet down sometime after 11 p.m., I finally drifted into sleep only to be awakened by a blaring "Red Guards Command" that we, the "named dog whelps", were to "report to Red Guards' headquarters at 12 a.m. sharp" and that "anyone daring to show up late shall be thrashed or exterminated on the spot".

To be woken up in the still of the night by the barking order out of the loudspeakers was enough to cause anyone's heart to pound. Hearing our names broadcast out as "dog-whelps" faced with the imminent danger of being beaten up or killed was simply terrifying.

At the few minutes' allowance, we scrambled to our feet and scurried to Red Guards' Headquarters while buttoning ourselves along the way.

Hearts still pounding from rushing and fright, we found ourselves among the scores lined up in front of the Red Guards' Headquarters, ordered to disclose three generations of our family background, which meant, any member in the family within three generations categorized as an "enemy" would warrant us a severe beating at the least. With Red Guards pacing around us, snapping their leather belts at the most unexpected moment from time to time in our faces and at our backs just inches away, none of us revealed anything detrimental. Obviously, many of us took a chance. I told them my father was a "teacher" and my grandfather was a "clerk". Another round of denunciation, belt lashing and warnings finally brought an end to this terror.

Returning to the dormitory, not yet recovered from the fright, I was unable to sleep, worried about the consequences if my grandfather's real "top-enemy" category of "bureaucrat-bourgeois" was found out by the Red Guards. Eventually, I succumbed to fatigue and fell asleep.

No sooner had I fallen into deep sleep than I was woken up by violent kicking on the door and the switched-on light. An ear-splitting swish of a leather belt brought me to my full awakening and comprehension. Our Red Guard roommates returned.

"Fuck!" a normally pleasant girl barked out. "While we are busy making revolution, dog whelps are sleeping like dead dogs!"

Half-naked in the most defenseless position, I held my breath, lying still in bed like everyone else.

Fortunately, it was the end of a long day for them. After a fit of swearing and threat, they retired to their beds.

Knowing the danger was real, the next day, I moved out quietly without daring to take my bed-set.

I had no idea where my roommates were. I made my hideout on the top floor of a dormitory building vacated by elementary students. I could observe the situation from behind the closed window. I spread some newspapers on a dusty bunk bed. I already ran out of stored buns, hesitant about the trip to the dining hall. I didn't even feel hungry.

In my isolation, I was anxious to find out what was going on. At dusk when the Red Guards were away to make revolution elsewhere, I went out to breathe the fresh air and steal a look at the big-character posters to keep myself informed and rushed back before it became completely dark. At night, with no one around and no light turned on, the deserted pitch-dark three-story building felt like a haunted place. But what was even more petrifying was the outside, the human-shaped ghosts. I was fully clad, pricking up my ears, startled by any slightest noise, lying wide awake with my imagination running wild until I succumbed to fatigue.

KILLING BEGINS

On August 1, Mao rendered his "fieriest support" for Red Guards' "righteous actions against the landlord class, bourgeoisie, imperialists, revisionists, and their running dogs". At Mao's affirmation, Red Guards immediately extended their revolution thus far largely confined within campus and local areas into the greater society.

Their change of course gave us "dog whelps" a modicum of relief. We were to be dispatched to a farm on the outskirts of Beijing to "be reformed-through-labor". In my class, Weng Rulian, Shen Yuan, Wang Qian and I—all having some sort of "intellectual" background—were among the team.

With no specified length, our exile from Beijing could be indefinite. Permitted to go home to get the needed money and grain ration coupons, I was on my way.

I had not seen my family in weeks. To get a seat for the long ride, I reversed my route by riding to the trolleybus terminal by the Beijing Zoo.

The moment I stepped out of the trolleybus at the terminal, I was startled by a terrifying commotion of savage thrashing and raucous swearing nearby.

Straight ahead, within a circle of onlookers, several Red Guards were ferociously beating up a rustic-looking teenage boy who wore a green uniform of another shade, which indicated he didn't belong to the privileged lot. Some were whacking him with their leather shoes while others were flogging him with two-inch wide brass-buckled leather army belts. At each head-splitting blow, the boy howled. Blood was streaming down his head and face.

Though violence was prevalent then, it was the first time that I witnessed such a brutal, sadistic act. I shuddered at the ghastly sight, blinking and flinching at each piercing lash. A circle of onlookers had gathered, looking on intently and silently. But no one interfered. Although my heart palpitated with fear, disturbed by no one coming to the boy's aid, I couldn't help but intervene.

"Stop beating him," I implored. "Don't you see the shape he's in? You are going to kill him!"

With one full-forced bashing of the boy, a Red Guard roared, "He's a fake Red Guard, a fucking thug! He deserves a good beating!"

"He's a pickpocket too!" Another bawled as he whipped open a gush of blood.

I quailed at the sounds and the spurting blood, but I managed to add, "You should send him to the police and let them handle it!"

"Mind your own fucking business! He poses as a Red Guard, discrediting the genuine ones. He deserves to be beaten!"

At a time when violence was justified and killing was condoned in the name of revolution, Red Guards were on a free pass to beatings. Envious of Red Guards' privileges, some boys from the urban poor dressed themselves up as Red Guards with the uniforms they obtained from their friend or relative from the production and construction corps—often disguised reform-through-labor camps. This travesty was met with Red Guards' violent objection. Later on, Red Guards' undue violence against the so-called "hooligans" caused urban young riffraff's resistance. With the uniforms they obtained, they organized themselves and fought back, which led to deadly clashes between the two gangs.

The boy now had fallen to the ground, writhing on the bloody pavement, unable to pick himself up. But the Red Guards had no intention to stop. It was just a matter of how much longer the boy could cling onto his life.

At this gory, macabre scene, my whole body shook and my stomach churned. Unable to stop and bear it any longer, I left the site.

Returning home, I found our cozy home suddenly appeared desolate. Mother and I were the only two at the dining table. Father was under intense interrogation at his college for having worked for the "prerogative imperialists-run" Customs, allowed to return home only occasionally. My brother, Tiemin, was reforming in a labor camp for being an "idle bourgeois descendant". My sister, Qijuan, and my brother, Ciqing, seldom came back. All of us were struggling to adjust to this crazy, overwhelming situation on our own.

To make Mother less worried, I didn't tell her I was put in a reform-through-labor team, but simply informed her that I was to be sent to the countryside to work in the fields, perhaps for a while.

The next morning, I returned to school and found that along with us scores of "dog whelps", a number of less problematic teachers were also placed in this team to be taken to the same commune, including our teachers, Mr. Hong Jinlong and Mr. Zhang Lanxin. Scores of Red Guards were dispatched to supervise us.

At the farm, we were lodged in a mud house on an end-to-end long *kang* (northern peasants' heat-able brick bed) with a Red Guard flanking our sides and a personal space of about 30 inches (some 70 centimeters) wide, packed like a sandwich with alternate layers. This arrangement was clearly made to intimidate us, deny us the little comfort of sleeping next to our own kind, and prevent us from "forming counterrevolutionary alliances".

Every morning at daybreak, before being herded into the field, we would stand in line to read aloud what was called "Chairman Mao's supreme instructions" from the "*Hong Bao-Shu*" (*Precious Little Red Book*), and begin our 12 to 13 hours of workday to harvest the crops or hoe the harvested fields loose, free of roots and rubble. To avoid trouble, no matter how exhausted or aching we were, no one raised his head or stretched his back. At the end of the day, we would feel the aches all over our bodies and our faces swollen from bending all day.

We were allotted a ladleful of cornmeal gruel and half of a fist-size coarsely ground plain cornmeal bun with a slice of pickled turnip for breakfast, and two cornmeal buns with a ladleful of meatless and almost oil-less vegetable for lunch and supper, far from enough for our intense, demanding physical labor. We were hungry all the time.

Dictated by our subhuman status, we remained quiet. At night, even when the Red Guards went into the village to denounce and beat up ex-landlords and ex-rich peasants, we didn't have much to say to one another. All were overwhelmed by hopelessness and uncertainty.

Since we didn't cause any trouble, we were largely left alone, as the Red Guards had more important targets in mind. It was a Red Periphery that treated us harshly. Left out of the Red Guards' actions and stuck with us "dog whelps", she harassed us all the time to demonstrate her superiority over us, chiding us for writing letters to our "dog-mama", for keeping "counterrevolutionary diary", and for our "incorrigible bourgeois habits". Everything we did or didn't do was condemned by her. We were forbidden even to say a few trifling words to one another. The sight of our existence alone irritated her to no end.

One night I was awakened from my deep sleep to some whimpering utterances, "Mama, mama, please come and save me... Take me out of here... Please hurry... I'm dying..."

It was from Yang Yuhe, a girl who slept a person away from me. Evidently, the distress she was experiencing during the day that was suppressed was activated in her sleep and manifested itself as a dream. The stillness of the night made the sad utterances betrayed only by dream sound especially poignant. It dredged up my own latent grief.

"Damn you." Immediately awakened to her class consciousness, the Red Periphery who slept between me and Yang Yuhe broke the silence and cursed, averring with Mao's quotation and official line, "'The day of joy for the people is a day of woe for the counterrevolutionaries'. This is the proletariat's world that makes sure your kind suffers. Your dog-mama won't be able to come here to save you. You 'class enemies can only hide in a dark corner and weep all alone!'"

At hearing we "class enemies" didn't even have the right to cry in our dream, I was even more dejected.

Those days were excruciatingly long and hard. Every day we spent there was a constant reminder of our subhuman status. There was not any hope ahead of us. Red Guards came and went switching among themselves, but we remained. After two weeks of reform-through-labor, on the evening of Aug. 17, we were hastily taken back to school, evidently thanks to some sudden happenstance.

Back at school, new big-character posters and slogans immediately caught my eye: *Long live the Red Terror! Long live the Red August! Suppress all dog whelps! Down with all hooligans!* At these ghastly sights, I was at once geared up, sensing Red Guards' actions had turned up to a new level and that things had become more unfavorable to us non-proletarian offspring.

While we were away, a multitude of events had taken place: On Aug. 5, the party revoked Liu Shaoqi's June-20 Decision on curbing violence. At once, violence on campus escalated. That very afternoon, a vice principal and a teacher were beaten to death by Red Guards from some elite secondary schools. More violence and deaths followed. A beautiful, all-around gold medalist for her academic achievements from Qinghua Fuzhong, was beaten up for being a "black seedling" and a "dog whelp"—Her father also worked for the "imperialists-run" Customs. Unable to bear the persecution any longer, at a chance, she escaped and dashed toward a fast-approaching train. She survived, but was left with two fingers missing and a foot-long scar in the face and head, a lifelong disability and a psychological wound that would never heal. On Aug. 8, the Central Cultural Revolution Group issued the Sixteen-Point Resolutions to legitimize and protect the masses' revolutionary actions, emphasize the need to firmly execute the party's class line, call on the revolutionaries to replace "old ideas, old culture, old customs, and old habits (the *Four Olds*) " with "new ideas, new culture, new customs and new habits", and "denounce and crush the principal enemies—capitalist roaders, counterrevolutionary bourgeois academics and authorities, bourgeois rightists, and counterrevolutionary revisionists". Like the previous vague terms such as "newly-bred counterrevolutionaries", "bad elements", and "rightists" that felled millions of lives for their speeches, behavior "crimes", suspected "thought crimes" and "face crimes", these new terms were also broad-brushed, subject to free interpretation. It gave Red Guards the leeway to take down whatever and whomever they considered "bad" and "counterrevolutionary", beyond the original relatively well-defined "enemies"—landlords, rich peasants, and historical counterrevolutionaries. On Aug.13, in a joint action, Red Guards from my school and other elite secondary schools had taken over the Central Committee of the Youth League. That same day, in Beijing Workers' Stadium, Red Guards held a city-wide struggle session against "hoodlums", singled out for some mere momentary dishonorable acts. It was attended by Li Fuchun, a vice premier, and some other key figures, on behalf of the party's Central Committee. In the presence of high officials, Red Guards violently abused and beat up the singled-outs. City-wide, many "hoodlums" had been beaten to death.

I gasped at the rapid development. Who doesn't have some fault or enemy that can lead to this? I said to myself. We can easily become the next target.

What we didn't know was that we were called back for Mao's gigantic review of a million Red Guards at Tiananmen Square the following day.

The next morning, at daybreak, loudspeakers woke us up with the broadcast that our great leader Chairman Mao would grant us a review that morning. At the unexpected exciting news, we at once jumped up, cheering and hurrahing, wild with joy.

We arrived to find ourselves among the sea of jubilant Red Guards and students from other secondary schools in Beijing on the gargantuan square and along the broad Chang'an Boulevard.

When the music "The East Is Red" burst out of the loudspeakers installed in the square signaling Mao's emergence, we immediately began chanting "Long Live Chairman Mao" rhythmically with all our might, leaping and waving our *Little Red Books* in frenzy as if seeing God, although we saw nothing, not even a speck. Like others in the deafening crowd who tried with all their might to prove their feverish revolutionary zeal and unquestionable loyalty to Mao, I robotically chanted, bouncing up and down waving the *Little Red Book* at our idol, not daring to appear any different, not even knowing how I truly felt. In the vast sea of collective force—the mass hysteria, we had lost our own thoughts, our own feelings and our own identities.

From the anchorman's reporting, I was dismayed to learn the normally second-place public figure, Liu Shaoqi, was bumped to eighth place, behind many newly promoted figures in the Central Cultural Revolution Group.

In a frail, unsteady voice, Lin Biao[7], now the second-place figure, read his speech, calling on the revolutionaries to "smash enemies of all sorts" and to "destroy the *Four Olds*". Then Zhou Enlai gave a speech on following Mao and carrying the Cultural Revolution through to the end.

With Mao granting 1,500 elite Red Guards a close review, the message couldn't be clearer. In his few words with the female Red Guard who put a Red Guard's armband on his arm, he made his message further palpable, advising her to "resort to force" instead of being "urbane" as her name indicated.

The next morning, we were vying to read the newspaper accounts about the event. My heart sank at the picture showing Mao and the new figures from the Central Cultural Revolution Group all in army uniforms and in festive mood while Liu Shaoqi standing alone in his civilian clothes, looking forlorn, and Zhou Enlai, also in civilian clothes, waving Mao's *Little Red Book* nervously.

That same day, at Mao's endorsement of Red Guards and his advocacy of force, Red Guards organizations sprang up throughout the nation with youths of other proletarian backgrounds, all mobilized to smash the enemies within and outside the party and to destroy the *Four Olds*. With directions given by the Central Cultural Revolution Group, all actions taken in the name of revolution legitimized and protected by the Sixteen Points, and funds provided by the State Council for the elite groups in Beijing, they promptly went on their missions to crush all "enemies" and to destroy all symbols of "vices" in their way.

They rushed to change their own names to *Yaowu* (resorting to force), *Wenge* (Cultural Revolution)..., and the names of schools, businesses, hospitals and streets to *Red Guards Combating School, Anti-Imperialist Hospital, Anti-Revisionist Road, Revolution Eatery,*

New-Protocol Barber Shop... My school thus became the *School of International Communism.*

They forbade anyone to wear "outlandish bourgeois" clothes, forbade businesses to serve bourgeoisie or cater to "bourgeois" life style, demanded banks to confiscate dividends, cancel depositors' interest and freeze deposits, and forbade anyone to retain any properties previously allowed for private use. They decreed the current National Anthem be replaced with one that would only eulogize Mao and the party and place Mao's image and instruction at the entrances of every school, business, and public place. They also demanded the traffic lights be changed from green to red (symbol of revolution) for "go" and red to green for "stop", which was timely stopped by Zhou Enlai before major accidents occurred. In their wild search for targets to strike down, my classmate, a girl, led a group of Red Guards to *Chen Zhenchang* to vandalize the brassiere tailoring store and denounce the former owner whose store had long been appropriated in the Nationalization in 1955, for the business' "indecent, pornographic, bourgeois" nature. One group took Hu Qili, the third hand of the Central Communist Youth League, to our school and denounced him as a "capitalist roader" "executing the Counterrevolutionary Revisionist Line". Another group carried their revolution to Babaoshan Revolutionary Martyrs' Cemetery to smash the tablet and grave of Qu Qiubai, an originally designated "revolutionary martyr" but now a newly discovered "enemy" and "traitor to the revolution".

Red Guards formed check points throughout major sections and crossroads in Beijing. They stopped anyone who didn't carry Mao's *Little Red Book* and anyone who looked different, dressed or behaved differently. The luckier ones could escape with damaged clothes, destroyed shoes, irregularly shaven facial hair and long hair. The less lucky ones would find their skin or scalp sliced off, themselves beaten, rounded up and even killed. The night curfew imposed by Red Guards made the scene even more ghastly. Armed with brass-buckled leather army belts and baseball bats, they stopped and questioned anyone who dared to come out or pass by. Anyone who was seen as an affront to their authority would face the danger of whatever might come his way.

Competing to be the most revolutionary trailblazers, Red Guards expanded their undertaking by the hour. They eradicated anything that was not Communist-related and anything that was eye- and ear-pleasing, foreign, classic and folkloric. Inestimable priceless paintings, artifacts, books and records, historical and memorial sites, historic monuments and relics were burned or demolished. Not even flowers, plants, and tombs could escape their attention. They exhumed the remains of emperors, historical figures, heroes, scholars and foreigners and scattered the remains or burned them. Before long, they outlawed all religions and vandalized all religious edifices, destroyed religious symbols and icons, burned Bibles, Sutras and Korans, and assaulted nuns and monks to force them to renounce their beliefs. They also went to current and historical sites of foreign firms, past and present legation sites, and held demonstrations outside, denouncing the subjects in absentia for "looting" and "cultural invasion" of China.

Afraid to become the target of Red Guards, people who owned some spare rooms previously allowed for private use or objects that could be construed as *Four Olds* joined the rush to relinquish their right to such property, and to destroy and discard their personal possessions, priceless or otherwise. My maternal Uncle Ke in Wuhan slipped his family's few cherished possessions and pieces of jewelry into the Yangtze River one night. At the time, sanitary workers often found rejects such as images, icons, artworks, artifacts, books, records, photos, manuscripts, research papers, musical records, gold, gems and jewelry in garbage dumps and sewers.

In no time, they carried their revolutionary actions from the streets to the homes of the "enemies". They broke into private residences, beat up the "enemies" in their own homes, confiscated their possessions and property, relocated them to a small place, and, in some cases, deported the entire family out of the city or simply eliminated the entire family. Within two days, residence after residence of the "enemies" was ransacked and sealed off.

Slogans that intimidated and glorified violence and killings were seen all over Beijing: *Long live the Red Terror! Long live the Red August!*

Long live the August Tempest! Eliminate all class enemies! Some were even written with the blood of the "enemies" killed on the spot.

In the frenzy, in my school of some 400 secondary-school students, exclusive of the primary-school section, five people had lost their lives thus far: Besides the school gardener who was "eliminated" a little earlier, Liu Guilan, a school aide in her early-20's and the mother of an infant, was thrashed to death with belts and a water hose as a "landlady", an absurd accusation for her age—At the census conducted in 1953 to categorize everyone's class status, she was only a child. An administrator, Zhang Fuzhen, was also beaten to death. Yao Shuxi, another administrator tortured and beaten up for having a capitalist family background, took her own life. Mo Ping, our principal and a veteran revolutionary categorized as a "traitor" and a "capitalist roader", also committed suicide. On top of the deaths they caused in our school, some Red Guards were said to have beaten several to death outside the campus in one day.

In Red Guards' pursuit of class enemies, students who were special, different in some way or had an "undesirable" background, "clerk", "intellectual" and "small business owner" included, also lost their lives, beaten to death or committing suicide.

Red Guards' movement was raging like a wild fire. They were too engaged in their goal to "kill, kill, kill and kill until the entire world is all red" to pay attention to us "dog whelps". At the Red Guards' maniacal actions, I was very worried about my family. On Saturday afternoon, two days after Mao's review of the Red Guards, I sneaked out of the campus.

Into our lane, as I was approaching my acquaintance Lu Ruyao's home, I was startled by the commotion coming from their yard. With their gate wide open, I could see Red Guards hurling things and the Lus' family members cowering in the yard. The Lus were the relatives of Yue Songsheng, the original owner of a large traditional herb medicine company *Tongren Tang* who was beaten to death later. Seized with sudden fear, I sped up, left the site of trouble and headed home.

Lu Ma was the only one home, looking anxiety-ridden. In a while, my sister Qijuan returned.

Visibly shaken, the moment Qijuan stepped inside, she said to Lu Ma, "Lu Ma, I just witnessed a beastly beating. There's no chance the woman beaten is going to survive. It was terrifying. I'm afraid they will come to us soon. Hurry up and get ready before they come. There's not much time left."

This said, Qijuan hastened to look around and began tossing our photo albums and Father's books in foreign languages onto the floor. "These should not be kept any longer," she said. "Burn them!"

Before Lu Ma carried the gathered discards in the aluminum washtub to the yard to burn them, my sister hurriedly stopped her, "Wait a minute." Hurriedly leafing through the photo albums, she picked out a coffee-colored picture of her taken in our Westernized home in Shanghai that showed her in complete Western attire from head to toe like a Western doll, with curled hair and in a lovely peter-pan wool cashmere knit dress, leather Maryjane shoes and tights. "Burn them," she said. "Nothing should be spared."

Already averse to my sister's decision to destroy our parents' personal possessions without consulting them first, at her act of picking out her own picture that could produce a similar harmful effect, I was appalled by my sister's inconsistency. She was the only one considered to be close to our parents. Now she took such liberties to decide for them to destroy all the memories without any sentiment or hesitation. Yet in the same breath, she took the risk salvaging and preserving her own picture.

Disturbed by my sister's fervor to wipe out traces that could reveal our identity, I protested, "No! We don't have the right to destroy them. They belong to our parents and grandparents. Besides, these are the only family mementos we have!" I stepped ahead to pick the albums up.

"Leave them there!" my sister screamed. Turning to Lu Ma, she said, "Lu Ma, don't listen to her. She's just a senseless child. What's the use of keeping those old photos? They can only reveal our background and cause us trouble. Burn them!"

My sister was not entirely wrong. At the time, one telling photo could lead to death, let alone the revealing albums we had. Without seeing what was inside, just their large dictionary size and their embossed ornate appearances alone were enough to decide our class origin and warrant our physical destruction. The pictures of our family alone could reveal our upper-middle class social status and our completely Westernized life style before the communist takeover, not to mention those taken during my grandparents' Tianjin years in their well-appointed sumptuous French home tastefully decorated interiorly and exteriorly that clearly indicated my grandparents' former social standing, their living standard and life style. My sister's words counted. Her role in the family had swiftly ascended due to her political standing.

Lu Ma carried the to-be-burned into the yard. But, despite the burning of other things, the albums refused to burn.

"Chop off the covers with an ax and douse the leaves with gasoline," urged my sister.

These done, the albums soon caught fire.

Watching the albums consumed by flames and reduced to ashes little by little, I gnawed at the loss of our heritage and of the records of our family expunged by its own offspring. With the strike of a match, not only were the memories of three generations and the family history annihilated, but the rare, precious historical records of recent eras were extirpated in my sister's act. Our past was gone without a trace.

Initially, it was a trend to take the initiative to destroy personal possessions in public to avoid further trouble. Lu Ma's burning, perceived as a "revolutionary action" at the time, passed without much notice.

At dusk, my parents came back one after another.

In contrast to what was taking place outside and the trepidation we each had, our home was eerily quiet. At the dinner table, Mother, Father, my sister and I had a silent meal as if this were our last supper together.

Concerned about my paternal grandmother, after dinner, I went to her home in the same compound and found her reading the Bible at the bay window by a dim table lamp. Fatal solemnness had added to her poised manner that indicated she was ready to meet her fate. Sitting in the dark corner watching her dignified tragic profile, I was overwhelmed by premonition.

In a while, Father entered. After a brief greeting, Father suddenly dropped to his knees in front of my grandmother. With his head lowered, he uttered in an almost inaudible voice, "Mother, please pray for me."

Startled by the unusual display of weakness, my grandmother tensed up. "Steady, Son," she said. "I will pray for you. God bless you and all of us."

Father arose. When he turned, he caught sight of me. "Oh, you're here," he equivocated. "There's nothing to worry about…"

He hurried away.

Choked up with emotions at what I saw, I tried to hold back my tears, even more aware of the inescapable fate awaiting us.

Returning home, I overheard Mother's talk with my sister.

"Qijuan," she said. "The account-clearance has spread into our lane. The Lus' home was raided today. I'm afraid it's going to be our turn soon. Will you please take the jewelry package with you and hide it in your home? Your husband is a revolutionary officer. They can't search your home."

The volleyball-size package of quality jewelry of gold and precious stones contained Mother's life-time collection, inherited and given by Father for holidays, birthdays and wedding anniversaries, perhaps worth hundreds of thousands of dollars today. It was impossible to bury it since our neighbors were watching us closely. It was their chance for revenge. They were waiting quietly for our fall. My sister's husband was a naval officer protected by the decree—No one was permitted to attack the military or military personnel in any way. Other than my sister's home, there was no place to hide the package.

"No, no!" Immediately, Qijuan objected, "I can't! I myself am barely surviving. I'm not going to incriminate myself and my husband." Pausing momentarily, she hastened to add, "By the way, if there's nothing unusual, I won't come home anymore."

This said, Qijuan left. Since then, she no longer came here.

Qijuan might be cynical, but she had a point. At the time, anyone could be singled out at any given moment. Today's "honorable revolutionary" could be reduced to "enemy of the revolution" tomorrow. Qijuan's husband turned out to be only safe for the moment.

Within a few days of Mao's incitement to violence, in the urban part of Beijing alone, hundreds of people had been beaten to death, thousands of homes had been ransacked and thousands of legal residents had been expelled from the city.

On August 22, Mao decreed that the police "must not interfere with Red Guards' revolutionary actions". Xie Fuzhi[8], Chief of Police, Mao's flunkey and China's Dzerzhinsky who had said it was "no big deal if Red Guards beat bad people to death", promptly instructed the police to join Red Guards' revolutionary actions by supplying them all the information about residents and assisting them in their revolutionary actions. Deportation was thereby officially taken over by the police. The wild actions taken by Red Guards were thereupon turned into institutionalized state-sponsored terror.

With information provided by local police and neighborhood activists, all of the "enemies" were to be ferreted out one after another, including the "*louhuas*"—the ones who escaped from being classified as certain "enemy" category at the beginning stages of the regime: *louhua* landlords, *louhua* rich peasants, *louhua* counterrevolutionaries, *louhua* bad-elements, *louhua* rightists, *louhua* capitalists, *louhua* of everything… With the reopening and reexamination of the already microscopically examined, handled and tried cases at the takeover and at each of the previous campaigns, the already sufficiently punished and mercifully spared were now faced with their inescapable fate. With Red Guards clearing accounts street by street, door to door to root out every single one of the "enemies", it was inevitable that all that had some problems would be in trouble.

A vast population was affected by the broadened intensive hunt for enemies since almost every family had a relative somewhere who had served some firm, organization or institution in some capacity before the communist takeover that warranted scrutiny. If one was singled out, the entire clan would be endangered. My former schoolmate and friend, Yang Ju, a sweet, pretty girl whose father had been a county magistrate in the Nationalist government but had passed away before the communist takeover, was thus turned into a "*louhua* landlord" and "*louhua* counterrevolutionary" family member. She and her mother, a school teacher, were stripped of their citizenships and banished to their origin in Nanyuan County for the masses there to deal with. Lao Yang, my friend and teammate in the reform-through-labor team, was also deprived of citizenship and sent back to the countryside together with her ailing aging parents as a member of a family of a "*louhua* landlord".

With more people labeled "enemies" every day, more persecutions, ransacking and killings were on the way. In the revolutionary frenzy, over 11-million households were ransacked; a hundred million people were implicated.

As Hong Kong was promised with 50 years of autonomy at the Communist takeover in 1997, Mainland China was also guaranteed with a "coalition government" at the takeover. But after the regime was consolidated, it was turned into "people's democratic dictatorship". Now without much notice, it was formally changed to the "proletariat's comprehensive dictatorship".

CAUGHT IN THE MAELSTROM

August 23, the party's principal mouthpiece, the *People's Daily*, extolled Red Guards' "great actions". At this, a foreboding arose in me. Worried about my family at the free pass to more lunacies, I slipped out of the school in the afternoon.

In our alley, I spotted two army personnel trucks and a jeep parked near our home and a few young men with a red brassard printed with "Revolutionary Rebel" guarding our gate. I was chilled. No doubt they came after us. They stopped me at the gate.

"Are you Long Xuan's daughter Long Qiru?" One of them asked. At my affirmation, he said, "Long Qiru, listen carefully: We represent the revolutionary rebels from your father's college. Due to the nature of his crimes, we are here to search your home and confiscate your properties. Watch how you act during our revolutionary actions. Nothing will escape the masses' supervision. Is that clear?" At my nod, they let me in.

I couldn't wait to see what was befalling my family. Into the compound, I at once sensed the unusual tense atmosphere: There was no one around; every door was shut; all the curtains were pulled down. At our own yard, I saw Lu Ma surrounded and questioned by several young men. At the sight, I felt terrible about getting her into trouble because of us.

"Confess!" A crude-looking man shouted at Lu Ma, "What's your relation with Long Xuan?"

Apparently, this man's notion came from a movie called *Secret Post in Guangzhou*, in which a hidden Nationalist agent disguised herself as a maid to give orders to the family she served. Back then, the overwhelming majority of college students were "proletarian descendants" who had little exposure to or understanding of people and the world outside their own social stratum but what the party exposed them to, which was a fundamentally misrepresented picture purposefully distorted to the Communists' advantage.

I was shocked by this asinine question. Anyone who had a bit of discernment could tell Lu Ma was a hired hand, a country folk trapped in her own simple world just by her unaffected, elementary look alone. The connotation of "relation" suggested here was simply beyond her scope of comprehension.

While I was worried about where this sheer ignorance was leading to, I heard Lu Ma raise her voice in frustration, "I don't understand you!"

"None of your tricks," another man took over. "What did Long Xuan order you to do?"

Looking even more frustrated, Lu Ma objected, "What are you talking about? It's *Taitai* (madam) who tells me what to buy and what to do every day."

"Stop feigning dumb! Long Xuan has confessed. If you don't confess and disclose your counterrevolutionary ties and counterrevolutionary crimes, you will be handed over to the masses and subject to the masses' dictatorship!"

"Masses' dictatorship" meant terror produced by the masses purposely released by authority against an individual that could result in unbridled violence and even death.

"I don't understand a word of what you said!" Lu Ma protested, visibly shaking.

"What's your class origin?" another man inquired.

Even more flummoxed, Lu Ma said, "C-class origin? What is that? I don't know what you are talking about!"

Enough, I said to myself. Poor Lu Ma, who devoted her entire life to serving us, is taking the heat for us. What's happening to my family has nothing to do with her. She shouldn't bear the responsibility and suffer for us. I sped up to them and cleared my throat to draw their attention.

They all turned to me now. Approaching me was a bespectacled, reasonable-looking young man, apparently the leader of the group whom we later found out to be the son of Nan Hanchen, director of the State Committee of Foreign Trade and Economy who killed himself shortly. "This must be Long Xuan's daughter Long Qiru," he said. At my acknowledgement, he continued, "Long Qiru, judge the situation correctly. Draw a line between you and your exploiting family. Disclose and denounce your parents thoroughly. Our party's policy is 'leniency for confession and severity for resistance'. Now disclose your father's counterrevolutionary crimes to us."

As if to add to the point his leader made, the coarse man got in and barked at me, "Long Qiru, if you dare to play tricks and turn against the revolutionary rebels, you will meet no good end like your parents!"

Just at this moment, Mother's voice came from behind. She was back from work. "What's going on, comrades?" she inquired as she was fast approaching and examining the situation unflinchingly. In front of the adult male rebels, she was her usual self—graceful, dignified and well composed.

"Xu Suqin," the crude man barked. "Stop playing games. You know clearly why we are here and what your counterrevolutionary crimes are!"

"What 'counterrevolutionary crimes'?" Mother answered coolly, "We are not 'counterrevolutionaries' but working class people like you…"

"Shut up!" Pointing his finger at Mother's face inches away, the man roared, spittle spraying, "Class enemies have no right to speak! You are forbidden to insult us working class people!"

In subtle despise, Mother calmly tilted her head away from being sprayed upon.

Pointing to Lu Ma, the man continued, "What's her class origin? Is she a 'fugitive landlord' who fled the Land Reform campaign (1949-1952)?"

"She's a working class member, as you can see yourself. She's illiterate." Mother answered calmly, "She works for a living. She's been working for us ever since the war resisting the Japanese invasion (1937-1945), long before the communist takeover."

Mother was lying to protect Lu Ma. In reality, Lu Ma was classified as a "rich peasant" simply on account of the two years of living and working as a child bride in the household she was betrothed to and ran away from. When she left that household, she was only 17.

"Cut the crap!" The man roared, "Don't think we don't know your history. You and your husband are enemy agents taking orders from her!"

At this absurd claim, the leader raised his hand and stopped him. Turning to Mother, he stated, "Xu Suqin, you know our party's consistent policy: leniency for confession and severity for resistance. Make no mistake about it. If you dare to put yourself in an antagonistic position, you will come to no good end. Now, take the initiative, confess your crimes, and voluntarily turn in all counterrevolutionary evidence and belongings you obtained from exploitation. If we find them, you forfeit the chance of being treated leniently."

"We have nothing to confess," Mother answered flatly. "We are not 'counterrevolutionaries' but working class people like you. We have no possessions of those sorts you referred to. Everything we have in our home was purchased with our own salary. Both my husband and I work for a living. We live on salaries. How can you accuse us of 'exploitation'?"

In times of danger, we all looked up to Mother, pillar of our family. When we were rattled by the worsened situation, it was mother who injected us with her steeliness. "Nothing is to be feared," she said. "The falling of the head leaves but a scar the size of a rice bowl." Without Mother, we wouldn't know how to face the situation. Given the frenzy of the times, her risky act could provoke violent reactions that might result in death. At her response, my palms went moist. In reality, we had been property owners of some 40 rooms bestowed by my grandfather to help Mother sustain when she arrived in Beijing from Haikou with the three elder children in 1953. But they had all been confiscated two years later in the Nationalization in 1955. Surmising they didn't know at the moment that we had been property owners, Mother was taking a chance.

At Mother's daring retort, the earthy man flared up again. "Damn it," he muttered, rolling up his sleeves and approaching Mother menacingly. "In this position, this sly vixen still dares to resist. Let me work the bitch over!"

Just as he was about to reach Mother, the leader stopped him. Mother headed off a seemingly unavoidable danger. Turning to his men, the leader commanded, "Let's proceed with our revolutionary action."

At his order, the men ripped through the whole house, overturning mattresses and cushions, emptying suitcases, and rummaging through chests, cupboards, and drawers. Our home was instantly turned into a huge mess.

At each of the objects taken out that looked unfamiliar to the crude-looking man, he would groan out some angry, disparaging remarks. Mother's exquisite, elegant wool, velvet and silk georgette and satin qipaos (figure-hugging Chinese dresses), high-heel shoes, stockings, girdles, silk satin undergarments, and fur coats purchased before the communist takeover; Father's collection of old Swiss watches, ties, three-piece suits, dress shoes and wool-cashmere herringbone topcoat, record player, Zeiss cameras, Royal English typewriter and six-speed Raleigh bicycle; our suitcases, portmanteaus, old-fashioned ice-fed refrigerator, brocade bed sets, wool blankets, goose-down comforters, and vases…, everything he saw irritated him.

When they discovered the volleyball-size package hidden at the bottom of a suitcase that contained the jewelry and bank accounts, they looked stunned.

With a gaping mouth, the peasant-looking man stuttered, "Where did you… get this much… jewelry?"

"Through decades of accumulation of inheritance, gifts and purchases," Mother replied, not looking at him.

"Rubbish!" The man bellowed, "It was from generations of exploitation of us working class people! What about the bank accounts? How could you have such large savings while we working class people could barely make ends meet?"

"We have double incomes. Both my husband and I are wage-earners. And my husband earned remunerations for his spare-time translation work too."

"That's capitalist road!" the man bawled. Pointing to Lu Ma, he questioned again, "What about her account? How could she have such a large sum of money? Is that your money you transferred under her name to deceive us?"

"No. That's hers. She has worked for us for three decades and gets paid every month equal to what an average worker makes. She lives and eats with us for free. Besides, she hardly spends any money."

Needless to say, the jewelry, the bank accounts and the government bonds mandatorily purchased for a decade to "assist socialist construction" were all confiscated.

With more things taken out and heaped up, the men began to remove from our home anything that looked fancy to them. Our door was left wide open with the scene exposed to our neighbors.

When the two vehicles already perilously piled up could not contain anymore, the looting was brought to an end. With a list of the confiscated items issued to us, they took off, leaving behind a litter of things they left out along their path. Uncle Six's home was also raided on the same day by the same group, with his piano, sofa set, furniture, bank accounts, TV set, cameras and other valuables hauled away.

From that day on, we became a "*chaojia hu* (ransacked household)", explicit "class enemies". Whenever I came back home, I would meet with the neighborhood activists' disgusted eyes and silent contempt. Aunt Zhang, the housewife from across the yard who used to be friendly with us and whose husband had chatted with Mother in confidence during the man-made famine (1959-1962) about buns made with human flesh, had put on a Red Guard's brassard and belt, righteously displaying her disdain for us. One chilly morning, I bumped into her in the narrow passageway in our yard and noticed that under her blue Mao uniform stuck out the collar of Mother's *qipao* that she dug out from the litter left by the rebels.

In hindsight, we were lucky to have been raided by college rebels instead of Red Guards since college students were more educated and more reasonable. They didn't smash anything or beat us up except hurling into their truck hundreds of Father's classical musical records irreplaceable at the time. Had we been ransacked by Red Guards, with Mother's daring act, she would have no doubt been beaten up or even lost her life on the spot.

Actions authorized and affirmed by Mao and the party, Red Guards were on a persecution and killing rampage. With their school rooms filled with enemies from their own schools—administrators, teachers, school aides and students, local theaters, stadiums and malls were used to contain and beat up the "enemies" they rounded up from elsewhere. Jixiang Theater, occupied by the Red Guards from Boys' Secondary School No. 6, was now turned into a bloody sports ground with a daily death toll, bearing a reputation of "going in alive; coming out dead".

According to official statistics in Beijing's rectification report on November 5, 1985, in August in Beijing, 10,275 were beaten to death; 92,000 households were ransacked; and 125,000 households were expelled. Even in Daxing, a rural satellite county of Beijing, in five days, 325 people were eliminated as unwanted "class enemies", including a month-old infant, a female octogenarian and loads of deportees freshly out of Beijing clubbed to death on the spot upon their arrival at their origin. Twenty-two families were thus stamped out. At the state-sponsored terror against "class enemies", the entire nation was turned into a persecution and killing ground.

With those killed in such a short period and afterward dumped into crematoriums to be burned, the crematoriums were kept busy beyond their normal capacity. My brother Ciqing, who worked near Babaoshan Crematorium, told us that for many months to come, people working and living there complained about headaches, respiratory problems and other illnesses caused by the piled-up decomposed bodies and from breathing in noxious odors, fumes and soot permeated in the air from the ceaseless cremation.

Since August 22, Father had been formally taken into solitary confinement, not allowed to come home anymore. As early as May, he was already accused of being a "counterrevolutionary academic", a "historical counterrevolutionary", a "British-American imperialist flunky", and an "imperialist running-dog" for his history of working for the "imperialist-run" Customs. Now as the investigation intensified, a case was framed against him. He was charged with the crime of being a "Japanese puppet", a "traitor to the nation", a "Japanese collaborator" and a "Japanese agent". Even his casual remarks made before the Cultural Revolution about Yasuji Okamura, the head of the Japanese invasion army of China, was used as "proof" of him being a "Japanese agent".

The Japanese took over the Customs Inspectorate, located in Shanghai's International Settlement at the Bund, after the Pearl Harbor attack on December 7, 1941. They interned Sir Fredrick Maze, inspector general of the Customs, and other top-tier Customs officials. Under Japanese pressure, the British officials collapsed and ceded the newly collected tariffs to the Japanese. Maze was dismissed by Wang Jingwei, the head of the puppet government. Kishimoto Hirokichi, a Japanese commissioner at the Customs, was placed in the position. The Customs was thence put under Japanese nominal control.

Deeply disappointed, Chiang Kai-shek declared the Customs bogus. In 1942, he ordered the inspectorate to be established in Chongqing, the wartime capital. With revenues mainly from coastal branches, and "no staff, no archive and no money, not even paper, furniture or typewriters", there "didn't seem to be sound rationale for the newly established Customs to exist", as was pointed out by Dr. Robert Bickers, director of the British Inter-University China Center and professor of history at Bristol University overseeing the research project of the Chinese Maritime Customs.

With only senior staff of the Customs ordered by the Nationalist government to leave their posts and report to Chongqing by 1943, thousands of coastal employees—top performers of the Customs—found themselves completely left on their own at their own risk. Under tight Japanese surveillance with their photo IDs posted at various check points and job prospects dim during wartime, they were left with little choice. At the time, Father had been transferred from Shanghai to Qingdao Branch. Like others, he stayed on his post— He had a family of five to support.

When the war was over, all the coastal employees who stayed put in the enemy-occupied coastal branches, including foreign employees, were under moral investigation. Except four who were charged with treason, including two foreign nationals, the vast number of employees, Father included, were pardoned, retained and demoted as "working under duress". He was dispatched to Haikou, a southernmost coastal branch.

With the case closed, and sufficiently punished, those employees however found their cases reopened at the communist takeover. Not only they themselves were repeated targets of Communist campaigns year after year, but their family members were also impacted. Like all the offspring of the "undesirable" punished for their ancestor's "crime" and denied all chances of advancement, my older elder brother Tiemin, a professional lyric tenor who quit his choral member job to take vocal lessons to become a soloist, was sent to a reform-through-labor camp for being an "idle bourgeois descendant"; my younger elder brother Ciqing, a state-certified Grade-Two ping-pong player, was rejected by the army's ping-pong team after background screening. Then he was punished for selling picked-up scrap iron and used copper wires to a recycling station to fund his transistor radio project. During the severe man-made famine when we were all starving, to fill our empty stomachs, he dug some clams out of a lake that turned out to be reserved for high Communists only. With a record of "consecutive thefts of state properties", he was stopped from advancing beyond junior high school.

Now with the case reopened, a special-case group was established nationwide to investigate all former Customs coastal employees. With the Customs' roster and archives combed through, every single one of those employees was tracked down and put under solitary confinement to go through round after round of interrogation with mental and physical tortures, and public struggle sessions to extract the needed information to nail the presumed crimes of his own and others.

Held in seclusion, not knowing what upper hand the other person may hold against him, this person may panic and strike first to gain initiative. In a case with thousands investigated, if one link was broken, the entire chain would be incriminated. Tens of thousands would be implicated. All of his associates would also be in trouble, including their families, relatives and acquaintances. Under pressure and coercion, many people buckled and confessed to things that had never happened. Some even fabricated things against others in an attempt to save themselves from further tortures. There were incredible fabrications of all kinds. But, in an insane era when the entire nation was in a persecution frenzy, no matter how tenuous and absurdly incredible the information they obtained was, it was given credence anyway.

Father, however, a wrongly-perceived "coward" for bowing to anyone who looked like a proletarian, endured this trial. He never betrayed his conscience. No matter what pressure he was under, he never made any false accusation to implicate any of his former colleagues, not even the newly incarcerated Zhang Leng in a sealed case as a "Japanese collaborator and agent". He would rather be beaten and bear the trouble himself than violate his principle. He took the risk and pains to absolve anyone investigated through him by piling up good things about him, such as, so-and-so "showed patriotic feeling against the Japanese invasion", such-and-such a person "grumbled about the Nationalist regime", and another person "supported the communist takeover". When many people in trouble chose to preserve themselves by implicating others, my "cowardly" father turned out pure, noble and true to himself, a much better human being than many decided by the Communists to be a "good" person and a good person of normal times.

At the time, Mother had not been singled out yet. But she knew it was just a matter of time. Our next-door neighbor, Guo Lilan, her friend and high school classmate at the missionary school, had been taken from her home recently by state security agents for allegedly being an "imperialist agent".

An aloof, delicate and graceful-looking woman, Guo Lilan was extravagantly attired even when the nation had conformed to the proletarian life style, coming and going under a vintage parasol in eye-catching, figure-hugging *qipao* and stilettos, leaving a whiff of expensive perfume trailing her path. Divorced a long time ago, she had some male foreign friends in the early 1950s when control was relatively loose. Her foreign ties and perhaps even her English-speaking background were probably the causes of her woes.

At her friend's arrest, Mother was alerted to the imminence of her own anticipated fate. Although she had never made known her ability to speak fluent English and French, she knew she could be faulted for a number of other things. An exquisite beauty and a fastidious dresser, at 50, Mother still looked stunning. This and her uncompromising personality were enough causes for persecution, let alone her status as an ex-property owner.

It hardly took any time to have Mother's concerns turned into a reality.

One day, at a struggle session, Mother's colleague and friend, Li Ruisen, a charming, vivacious and insouciant divorcee from a wealthy family, was singled out as a "bad element" on account of her background, personality, accouterment and life style.

At that moment, someone in the crowd shouted out, "Xu Suqin, come out and stand with Li Ruisen to be denounced!"

Mother at once shot back, "What's my crime? Why should I stand out?"

Long awaiting Mother's downfall for whatever reason, at Mother's daring act, the masses growled, "How dare you resist the proletarian dictatorship?" "You are a bad element!" "A property owner exploiting the working classes!" "The witch is defiant and unrepentant!" "Strike the sly vixen down!"

At the shouts, several women jumped up and pulled Mother out. They dragged her by the hair and arms to the front stage, and forced her to kneel. But Mother refused. She was slapped and kicked. But she was unbending. Violently kicked from behind, she fell down. Despite her repeated attempts to rise, she was held there firmly. In the storm of slogan shouting and physical abuse, Mother saw herself immediately turned into a "class enemy". Despite the escalated violence against her, she refused to admit to any wrongdoing.

At dusk, Mother returned home. Disheveled, she looked like an insane woman. Her hair was chopped short in some spots, completely shaved off or left straggling long in other spots. Her normally well-pressed, well-starched crisp clothes were turned into a dirty, wrinkled, shapeless mess.

Seeing our proud Mother humiliated and reduced to this sad state, I was in tears. Obviously, she had just been denounced and physically abused at a struggle session. Knowing how proud Mother was, I withdrew to a dark corner to grieve on my own.

In a moment, Mother stepped in. Clearly, she wanted to speak to me. As she came face-to-face with me, I noticed her blood-shot eyes and bruised, puffy face.

"Xiaomei (Little Sister)," she said. "Beginning tomorrow, I will be placed in solitary confinement too. Things don't bode well. I don't know what's going to happen to your father and me. Nowadays sons and fathers are trying to kill each other while husbands and wives are turning against one another. Anything can happen. Husbands and wives are but birds sojourning in the same woods. When their lives are threatened, they flee for their own lives." At the prospect, Mother suddenly burst out into a sob and held me tightly in her arms. "Xiaomei," she cried. "We may never see each other again. Promise me no matter what happens, hold onto your life and try to survive on your own and live on."

It was the first time that Mother was physically close to me. At the petrifying prospect of struggling entirely on my own in this upside-down world as a 16-year-old girl to deal with the things that were going on at a force, pace and scale that even adults were unable to comprehend or cope with, my heart squeezed. Dazed and overwhelmed, I was strangely remote, unresponsive to Mother's emotions.

The next day, Mother was gone.

Without my parents, it was no longer a home. No one came back anymore. There was only Lu Ma and I facing each other without a word. Lu Ma wept all the time, worn out by the thought of what would become of us tomorrow when the money Mother left us was used up. Her eyes were always red and puffy. Whenever she saw me, she would shed more tears.

Faced with the uncertainty of our future, I was in a trance, with no tears or thoughts, except a lump in my chest all the time. All this was like an endless nightmare to me.

At last, my sister Qijuan showed up. She snuck in one night, looking like a scared, fidgety mouse. She was in a big rush, not even having the time to sit down. Instead of comfort and assurance, her visit produced a sense of extreme insecurity and brought us back to reality.

"Xiaomei," she whispered in an almost inaudible voice as if worried about being overheard by the neighbors from across the yard. "We shouldn't come back to this home anymore. It's too dangerous! We don't know the nature of our parents' problems and what their crimes are. We don't know what's going to happen next. Look for a place and hide yourself there. Don't come back here anymore!"

Turned off by my sister's doubts about our parents and her self-concern, I couldn't help contradicting her, "If you don't even trust your own parents, whom else do you trust?"

"That's right," seemingly unblinking, my sister hastened to say. "I don't trust anyone. One has to look out for his own interest first." Taking out 10 yuan, she went on perfunctorily, "I'm unable even to fend for myself. Here's 10 yuan. Let's flee for our own life separately!"

With this, Qijuan hurried away. Her visit lasted for no more than 10 minutes.

My sister and her husband's home was big enough to accommodate me as a temporary refuge. But she didn't make the offer. Instead, she told me to "look for a place to hide". Where could I find such a place at a time when one's own sister even refused to shelter him or her? Financially, my sister could afford to spare more, but she didn't. Ten yuan was about 5% of their combined monthly income, equivalent to 2 dollars at the time. With this amount, I would be able to get by on one plain steamed-bun a day for half a year. How would I live on after the money was used up? Whom else could I turn to for help at a time when even one's own sister would turn him or her away? My sister didn't care. Sink or swim, it was entirely my own business.

Taking in my sister's advice, I stayed at school and returned home occasionally just to find out further information about my family. Going back home gave me a momentary sense of belonging, albeit no longer a real home.

Not long after the ransacking, Uncle Six, Houde, a handsome, brilliant man, was taken into police custody as a "historical counterrevolutionary" again. Since his late 20s, he had served years in prison at the communist takeover simply for being a surgeon and a gynecologist of colonel rank in the Nationalist army. His own son, then a tender boy of 3 or 4, was constantly shoved around, cuffed and kicked as a "dog whelp" by bigger boys in the neighborhood. The only protection my grandmother could provide was to allow him to plunge himself between her knees and cry.

Faced with the state-sponsored terror against its own citizens, my grandmother, a strong woman, despaired. Coming from an affluent family, receiving a Western missionary education and speaking flawless English, my grandmother, wife of a "bourgeois bureaucrat", had witnessed the moribund Qing Dynasty, the chaotic Warlord Period, the burgeoning Nationalist era, and the barbaric Japanese invasion. She had experienced and seen plenty in life, but never had she experienced anything like this, "not even during the wartime", using her words. As a child, she rejected foot binding and demanded to attend *yang xuetang* (missionary school). As a young woman, she advocated social reform and women's emancipation at a time when most women were confined to their own domiciles. A strong character, she would allow nothing to demean her or wear her down. The last thing in this world that she could afford to give up was her dignity. One night, after praying to God as she routinely did, she swallowed an entire bottle of sleeping pills and rested in peace forever. She was gone, carrying with her memories of three-fourths of a century's history of a nation.

Not long after my grandmother's death, one night when I was home, my sister came back to clear out her belongings.

In a moment, we heard some faint, timid tapping on our door. My sister opened the door. It was Uncle Six Houde's wife and their son. With only her head sticking out, my sister whispered a question, "Aunt, something the matter?"

"Qijuan," Pointing to her son, my aunt said. "Will you please take care of this child? His father is arrested and his grandmother is gone, leaving the two of us to struggle. I'm afraid I may get into trouble too. This child is the Long family's flesh and blood. If I'm gone, will you please take him in and save him?" She began to whimper.

At this, the little boy wailed. My aunt immediately covered his mouth to muffle the cry.

"No, no!" My sister responded instantly, "We aren't able to take care of him. We have a lot of our own troubles. We can't afford more!" This said, she promptly shut the door.

It was too disturbing to look and listen. At what I just witnessed, I acutely grasped that in times of danger, one was on his own.

News got around about our relatives.

With the information provided by the police and neighborhood activists, a group of female Red Guards from an elite girls' secondary school had taken their revolutionary actions into the home of my grandfather's current legal widow, originally his fifth wife, Lu Shi, the daughter of Lu Runxiang, number-one scholar in the imperial examination for civil service (abolished in 1905) and prime minister of the late Qing Dynasty (1636-1912). A harmless, apolitical old woman who didn't even know what era she was living in, she was ruthlessly eliminated in her own residence as a "rotten diehard of bureaucrat-bourgeois class", an "evil feudal leftover", the "widow of an arch-counterrevolutionary bureaucrat", a "fierce class enemy" and a "counterrevolutionary through and through defiling our great leader Chairman Mao and the party" for not having a Mao portrait in her home and not posting on the wall Mao's "sacred letter" to my grandfather and the citations issued by the Communist government for my grandfather's deeds.

Lu Shi's son, Wenli, a harmless man assigned to collect garbage and frequently harassed and detained by the police for years before the Cultural Revolution as a "decadent offspring of a bourgeois bureaucrat", was kicked out of his own home and became homeless. He was taken in and out of Fangshan Mental Hospital many times. Years later, still in his 20s, Wenli succumbed to years of deliberate tortures and died in this so-called "mental hospital". The Cultural Revolution provided an excuse to finally do away with this "insane, evil young diehard". Lu Shi's daughter, Jingbei, who was assigned a job as a textile worker, married another worker. When the Cultural Revolution arrived, she cut herself entirely off from her own family.

With the whole compound looted and sealed off, the Cultural Revolution brought the official death to a family already at its last gasp.

Like everyone else having a good side and a bad side, my grandfather, Long Xiang (1882-1961), deserved some fair judgment rather than vilification. He served as presidential secretary, presidential consultant and state financial consultant under Li Yuanhong (1864 -1928). At the time (1912), the nascent republic was in dire need of directly taking control of the nation's economic lifeline because the revenues collected by the Maritime Customs were deposited in foreign banks to pay off the interest accrued from the indemnities incurred from wars. My grandfather was trusted with the tasks of taking hold of the revenues generated from imports and exports via overland trade routes, and later, seeing to the development of Zhangjiakou into a large commercial trading city. Disenchanted with the lasting Civil War amongst warlords, in 1924, my grandfather resigned from all of his posts. In 1928, the Northern Expedition, led by Chiang Kai-shek, finally ended the Warlord Period and unified China. In need of capable hands, Chiang Kai-shek paid a personal visit to my grandfather at his home, sincerely inviting him to assume some post in his Nanjing government. Unable to resist for too long, my grandfather conceded and took up secretary-general position at the Ministry of Internal Affairs. In 1929, he was transferred with the same position to the Control Yuan, one of the five government branches that monitored the other branches of the government. Two years later, he resigned from all posts once and for all, devoting his time to scholarly works, and had books published that encompassed Chinese classics, finance, governing, and histories, geographies and annals of China's borders, coastlines, and oceanography of outer-boundary territories. When the Japanese invaded China and repeatedly coerced him to assume office, he resisted the pressure and refused to take up any post. When Beijing was besieged by the Communists between December 1948 and January 1949, supply lines were cut off; garbage and sewage were piled up. To resolve the crisis, frenzied activities were taking place behind the scenes and in the open. My grandfather was a signee in a 100-personages petition initiated by Liang Shuming[9], He Siyuan[10] and Zhang Dongxun[11] to urge General Fu Zuoyi to surrender in order to save lives, avoid bloodshed and war damage to this historic city, which contributed to a bloodless transition. When Mao called to "liberate Taiwan", he dedicated him a book he wrote on the histories, geographies, and annals of Penghu Islands (Pescadores Islands), an archipelago of 64 small islands between Mainland China and Taiwan, for Mao's reference. This and the large quantities of valuable historical records and rare books he donated earned him commendations from Mao and the Central government for his "patriotic deeds". My grandfather luckily passed away before the Cultural Revolution, but his survivors paid the price with their lives for his "crimes" of serving the Nationalists.

In Shanghai, where my aunt Houying and her family lived, Red Guards had ransacked over 150,000 households and seized 32 tons of gold at the time. My aunt's home had been looted four times by four different groups of Red Guards. With their gold bricks confiscated and household stripped almost bare, they were left with little means to live on, given that one son was sent to a farm to raise pigs and the other, banished to collecting garbage. They were forced into two small rooms in the attic to let other families move in and occupy major sections of their own three-story home. My aunt's husband, an investor who had already been haunted to clinical depression by the Nationalization in 1955 at the invalidation of his shares as a large shareholder of Shenxin Textile, was taken into police custody as an "active counterrevolutionary" for daring to utter opposition against the looting.

꩜

One morning, I was summoned to the Red Guards Headquarters at school and ordered to go to Father's college.

When I arrived there, I was told to wait in the lobby. In a while, Father unexpectedly appeared under the escort of two rebels. With his head kept low as was demanded of a "class enemy", he was unaware of my presence.

I had not seen Father in weeks. His usually clean-shaven cheeks and jaw were now entirely covered with facial hair. He looked thin and unwell. His originally fitting clothes now looked loose on him. Pinned on his left breast pocket was a white label with "Counterrevolutionary" written in black on it that bore a red cross symbolizing his death penalty. Upon seeing the obvious changes in him in just weeks, my eyes went moist.

Apparently, Father had no idea where he was being taken. The moment he caught sight of me, he was startled. Obviously ashamed of appearing in front of his own daughter this way, he immediately attempted to insert the labeled flap into the pocket.

"What are you doing? Leave it on display!" An escort growled and wrenched his hand down.

At seeing him treated this way, my eyes began tearing.

"Long Qiru," I heard the leader say. "Here's a chance for you to prove your revolutionary attitude."

Knowing I was expected to perform, I approached Father and managed to tap him in the cheek as a gesture of slapping only to be betrayed by my own weak neutral utterance, "Long Xuan, what have you done to deserve this?"

Father immediately raised his fist and shouted, "Down with Long Xuan! 'Revolution is not inviting someone to a dinner party, nor is it writing an article... It is a riot, an act of violence by which one class overthrows another.' Comrade Long Qiru, you must not be soft-hearted toward class enemies. You must draw a line from all counterrevolutionaries, including your blood relatives."

"Take him back," the rebels' leader bellowed. "He's playing counterrevolutionary tricks and spreading counterrevolutionary messages!"

Father was pulled away at once.

"Long Qiru," As I was still emotional, I heard the leader say. "We are very dissatisfied with your performance. You were born and raised in New China, nurtured and brought up by the party, but you have proven that you have not been reformed. You have not drawn a line from your family. Instead, you have shown you do not possess a proper revolutionary attitude toward your father's crimes. There are two roads in front of you. One is to alienate yourself from the proletariat and choose to be the enemy of the people; the other is to thoroughly cut off your connections from your father and join the revolutionary camp. If you intend to have a way out, you must draw this line from your father and disclose his counterrevolutionary crimes thoroughly. Otherwise, we will not be soft-handed with class enemies!" Taking out his notepad, he demanded, "Now disclose your father's crimes to us."

Anxious to prove that I was willing to join the revolutionaries, I searched my memory hard for Father's crimes, but I was unable to identify any. I felt the perspiration all over my body.

"Long Qiru," at my silence, the leader said. "It's impossible that your father never exposed his counterrevolutionary thoughts and deeds to try to poison you in your daily life. If you resist confessing, you will meet with an ignominious fate like your father!"

Waiting for my disclosure in vain, the rebels altered their stance, trying to coax me. But other than my meaningless stammers, there was nothing unusual that I could reveal. At the futile outcome, the rebels whispered to one another. Then the leader said, "All right, Long Qiru. We'll give you some time to submit written material to disclose your father and prove your proper attitude toward the Cultural Revolution."

Finally, I was released.

At the national turmoil created by this revolution and the deaths and sufferings of so many good people, my own family included, my mind was full of questions and skepticisms. My doubts about Mao and his party persistently cropped up in my mind and lingered there. Frightened by my own derailed secret thoughts, I tried frantically to suppress it. How I wished to have someone to guide me out of all this confusion!

THE RAPE

One afternoon in late August, in the narrow passageway in our compound, I bumped into Shuying, a tall, slim, fair-skinned, good-looking girl of working class origin. Since the plunder, I had avoided everyone. But, with her never turning up her nose at our misfortune and no way to circumvent, I nodded my acknowledgment. At this, she smiled and asked me if I would go with her to a 100,000-attendee struggle session in Beijing Workers' Stadium against Lu Ping and Peng Peiyun, the administrators of Beijing University who were brought down by the big-character poster posted by some party functionary.

It was the first time since the raid that anyone spoke to or smiled at me. Having not much to do anyway and grateful for her friendly gesture, I agreed to go with her. I had no idea that this would change me and my fate forever.

When we arrived at the stadium, we found thousands of people already waiting outside. We were lucky to be given two tickets. Those who didn't get a ticket attempted to break through. In the tightly packed crowd, we stood very close to each other to make sure we wouldn't lose each other in a likely stampede.

Suddenly, I felt a tight grip on my wrist. I was shocked at this crude, abominable behavior. My heart pounded wildly. Growing up in a society where physical intimacy was refrained, I was never exposed to such flagrant prurient behavior. Ever since approaching my teenage years, my parents had stopped touching me. Revolted and scared stiff, I didn't know what to do. I wished desperately that Shuying would notice it and come to my rescue. But, distracted by the situation, she was totally oblivious to it.

Timorously, I stole a glimpse in that direction only to find myself leered at by a Red Guard half a head shorter than I, with an unusually swarthy face and lewd stares under a thick animalistic unibrow. I had never met anyone that could cause so much repulsion and loathing in my life. At once feeling soiled, I turned back in repugnance, and never wanted to be caught by his eyesight again. I was sick to my stomach. At his coarse, nauseating nasal mumbles joining the crowds in hollering, I was even more revolted.

I was desperate at Shuying's obliviousness. It seemed that it had taken eons for me to finally get her attention. Her reaction only exasperated me and made me feel even more desperately helpless. Other than frantically and stealthily asking me what we could do, she was totally useless.

Tightly packed by the huge pushing crowd, like a tidal wave, we were shoved into the stadium by the breakthrough attempt from behind and settled on a bench. Settling by my side, he finally loosened his grip.

When the stadium was fully packed and settled, the struggle session was set in motion. Slogan shouting coming from the loudspeakers ushered in four rebels escorting the two targets with their heads and bodies pressed down and arms wrenched backward and upward called "jet position", a standard position invented at the time to torture the accused. With the targets' bodies bent at a 90-degree angle and heads pulled up by the hair to strike a pose and remaining in this position, the denunciation began. The targets were accused of "exercising bourgeois dictatorship and executing the counterrevolutionary revisionist line to suppress revolutionary masses". This was followed by more slogan shouting and speeches of accusation.

It was my first time witnessing a struggle session. At the targets' contorted postures, I was pained by their sufferings and repelled by the unnecessary means of torture. With the boy shamelessly gluing himself to my side, I was unable to concentrate on what was going on—My mind was busily thinking of ways to extricate ourselves. Just then, I heard him ask about our names. At this impudent intrusion of our privacy, I was even more sickened. Brought up in a polite world and never before exposed to anyone so crude and intrusive like this, we didn't know how to handle this situation, but to give our names away involuntarily. Without prompting, he gave us his name and told us that his father was the "ambassador to East Germany".

My school was full of ranking Communists' offspring. But this boy carried the revolting look of a low life. Since I had no interest in getting to know him, I remained silent, hoping this would send him the signal. But he kept babbling.

Suddenly hitting upon a way out of this predicament, I winked at Shuying and we excused ourselves to go to the ladies' room. The moment we stood up, he was on his heels. He followed us to the ladies' room and parked himself outside.

Having exhausted our devices at this nuisance who refused to go away, we panicked and despaired. With our experience and perimeter being home and school almost exclusively, we had never met anyone like this, let alone deal with him.

The rally ended very late. He offered to accompany us home for the sake of our "safety". Again caught unprepared, again we found ourselves unequipped to handle this imposition. Despite feeling crudely trespassed, not knowing how to effectively refuse him, at his insistence, we were reluctantly walked home.

The next day and every day afterward, he called me at school with the publicly listed phone number. Besides phone calls, he wrote me letters. All of his phone calls were intercepted and his letters were opened up and read by the Red Guards guarding the lobby. Whenever I was informed by the Red Guard of the rejected phone calls and passed along the opened-up letters, I was dealt loathing glares, invective and spit.

All the while, my chest and stomach were tightened up by this relentless stalking. Despised and distraught, I felt helplessly vulnerable, alone and forsaken, wishing desperately to have someone to come to my aid to protect and rescue me.

One night before September, when I was home, a messenger from the neighborhood phone service arrived. It was a call for me. Our own phone was disconnected years ago as a precaution to avoid being viewed as "wealthy". Now we were like everyone else relying on public phone service. With no one ever calling me, I instinctively sensed the call was from him. Apparently, he found out the phone number for my neighborhood from the phone book.

Back then, resorting to phone call was rare unless there was something urgent. In a strict society, everyone was supposed to behave in accordance with his status in the family and society. For a teenager to call another teenager, it was simply unthinkable, especially at night when parents and family members were almost for sure home. If any family member was home, at this alarming suspicious call, he or she would interfere with it and scold him for his brazen act and usually effectively kill off any further attempts for such contact. But, with my parents in custody and my siblings away from home, I was left to handle this by myself.

I was very ashamed and distressed at not only being widely noticed in my school but in my neighborhood as someone of my age already having someone from the opposite sex. To avoid more attention, I immediately went with the messenger to answer the call.

Over the phone came his mumbling, stomach-churning whine. I beseeched him never to call or write to me again. However, he ignored my request and kept begging to meet with me at Longtanhu Park.

I had never been to that park. I was only remotely aware that it was located in a ghetto area. Believing telling him face-to-face directly never to call or write to me again was the only way to end this stalking once and for all, I decided to go. At the thought of having to subject myself to his animal leer and hearing his nauseating voice again, I shuddered. But, unable to see beyond this and having no one to handle this situation for me or to turn to for advice, I thought I had no choice but to go there myself.

As he requested, I met him in front of the park late the following afternoon.

Avoiding his eyesight, I handed him the letters he wrote to me and said, "These are the letters you wrote. Please take them back and don't call or write to me again."

I was about to turn and walk away when he stopped me. "Don't go," in a sticky, mumbling voice that sounded like a beaten dog, he begged me. "I need to talk to you. That's all. I beg you. It won't take long. Please!"

Trusting, soft-hearted, having no concept of iniquity and ashamed to be seen with a boy in public at this age, I followed him into the park without any inkling of what was likely to happen.

The park turned out to have few visitors. Before I realized it, the sun already set. Soon I found myself in a deep, quiet, dusky, heavily wooded area with huge ancient trees and no one around.

I was pinned to a tree at once. Sensing something bad was about to befall me, I implored in panic, "Let me go."

Without responding, he thrust his hands into my blouse and grabbed my budding breasts. The moment he clutched me, I froze up and moaned in fright. He ripped my bra open and roughed me up. At the same time, he lifted up his heels and rubbed against me violently with something protruding in his groin area and forced his foul tongue into my mouth. I instantly retched.

Totally petrified, I was unable to think or move. All my faculties froze at the moment and ceased functioning. But when he thrust his hands down, attempting to unbutton my pants, instinct kicked in, directing my hands to prevent him from doing so. Nevertheless, having no concept of self-defense and paralyzed by this bestiality, I was easily overpowered. In no time, I found myself down on the ground. He was on top of me.

My world was savagely torn apart. Like a lamb under a lion's claw, without kicking, I greeted in my own inglorious death, the death of my innocence and of all the things I had placed my faith in. Completely breaking down and in searing pain, I sat on the ground, whimpering uncontrollably.

A sickening roll of satisfying chortles came from the ground level followed by his filthy words, "Fucking cunts is lots of fun. You been fucked, a worn shoe now. No men will want you. You better stay with me. You don't want this to be known to other people, do you?"

At the menace and the filthy, demeaning terms I had never heard of in my entire life, my heart was gouged. I buried myself in sobs of mortification, anger, repulsion, pain and fear.

"What you crying endless for?" He rolled up from the ground and said, "No one's dead. You been fucked. That's all."

The repeated debasing term he used only made me sob harder.

"Enough already," he pulled at me and said. "Let's go."

I have no recollection how I got home. My only memory is that I answered Lu Ma's inquiry by telling her that I had eaten since I had no stomach for food. Instead, I went straight to a bottle of potassium permanganate and soaked myself in the solution for hours as if this could cleanse me of the shame and the slimy stench, heal the sores and protect the tears from being infected.

Since then, life became a void for me. With the things I had held onto dearly so violently taken away from me at the tender age of 16, I had nothing to hold onto anymore. I was in a trance, unable to think or feel, except for a sick knot in my heart and the pit of my stomach and the very real fear and shame. No longer owning myself, I followed him to a factory to "*geming chuanlian* (establish revolutionary ties and exchange revolutionary experience)". In my hazy consciousness, I was in a free fall into a dark, bottomless well, crying for a catching hand to deliver me out of this abyss, but found nothing to grab at and only echoes as my company along the way of my fall.

Since the party's call on September 5 for students to come to Beijing to *geming chuanlian*, with transportation, lodging and food provided by the government for free, the already existing small-scale one-way *chuanlian* from schools into large enterprises and institutions and from Beijing to other major cities had turned into a two-way nationwide *chuanlian*, from inciting revolution to simply sightseeing. Before long, this wave was spread throughout the entire nation. Even backwater youngsters whose feet never left their villages joined in the pilgrimage to Beijing to pay tribute to the place where Mao lived and worked. In a month, millions poured into Beijing. It was a national fever. Anyone born into a "good" family, meaning,

Communist's, worker's, poor-peasant's or army-man's, was entitled to this free trip.

With the right equipment he obtained—Red Guard's uniform and brassard, the beast was lured into this frolicking right away. I was left alone.

❧

In late September, I missed my period and sensed something was going on in my body. I consulted a medical book and was shocked and unnerved to find the symptoms to be signs of a pregnancy.

Ashamed of myself, I delayed seeing the doctor, desperately hoping it would turn out to be a false alarm. But, as the symptoms became more pronounced, I couldn't deny it to myself anymore. In the hospital, my fear was confirmed: I was indeed pregnant.

This confirmation hit me like the end of my world. With this pregnancy, my shame would be exposed to the public. How can I go on living among respectable human beings with this shame? I thought to myself. Perhaps only death can obliterate all my ignominy. Death can't be so horrible. So many people have killed themselves. In just one moment, I could be delivered out of my shame and misery forever. Perhaps I should just die and end my tainted, weightless existence. But, at the thought of what suicide would engender, I was chilled, knowing even in my death, I would still be spit upon and that I would have my family implicated as well.

At the time, all suicides were categorized as a "counterrevolutionary act". Once one killed himself, slogans and big-character posters would appear all over the streets near where he once worked and lived, with words like such and such a person "chose to end his life against the party and the people in his attempt to conceal his crime and evade just punishment. Nevertheless, his death will not expiate his crime. Even in his death, we will pursue to the end the hidden cause of his counterrevolutionary act". Not only this, his survivors had to pay for his "crime" and become the despised "relatives of a counterrevolutionary", at the high stake of becoming a "counterrevolutionary" themselves.

The thought of having a sullied name even after my death was unsettling. I thought to myself, if I live, I may have a chance to speak for myself. With a strong instinct to live on and the hope for a chance to right the wrong myself, I resolved to hold on.

Again, I delayed going to the doctor. But, constantly reminded by my growing belly that I was running out of time, at the last minute, I overcame my nerves and underwent an abortion.

However, this solution didn't restore my self-respect. Instead, I was even more mortified. In the eyes of nurses, doctors and patients, I was just a contemptible, stigmatized vile low-life. I began to question myself: Is my character flawed to the degree that I'm just a low-life that brought this upon myself? Is my resignation to my fate the result of it? Is this the life that I deserve? Drowned in my misery, I was unable to find the answer or regain my strength. The deeper I sank, the more miserable I became.

In my despondent state, I accidently discovered a ripped-into-pieces large classical musical album at the bottom of a suitcase. They were lieders and songs in staff, with Chinese and English translations. They were works of Beethoven, Mozart, Schubert, Brahms, Schumann, Mendelssohn, Chopin and Liszt. I quivered with excitement at this unexpected discovery. I spent the entire day piecing and pasting the thousands of pieces together. It became my comfort and company. Whenever I felt down, I took it out and sang until I felt better. I was unknowingly healing myself.

As time went on, a thought began to take shape in my mind gradually: I cannot live like this any longer. However, the thought filled me with apprehension about the likelihood of having my shame divulged by the rapist as he had hinted he would do. What will happen once he's back from his frolicking and threatens me with this? Where can I get the desperately needed help to stand this? With everyone struggling to survive, no one will pay any attention to my struggle and my cries for help and come to my rescue. Without anyone to stand up for me and protect me, how will I be able to escape from his clutches? The thought of having to stand on my feet and face this situation alone simply terrified me.

Grappling alone, I found myself shaky and my determination to take my life back into my own hands oscillating from time to time. But, as time went by and with him still reveling somewhere, I gradually became steadier and calmer and the fear of standing the test on my own lessened.

THE AWAKENING

In January 1967, the Headquarters of the Revolutionary Revolt of Shanghai Workers, led by Wang Hongwen[12], Jiang Qing's groomed pet, seized power of Shanghai Municipality and established the Shanghai Commune modeled on the Paris Commune of 1871. Mao's immediate endorsement prompted nationwide power seizures. In no time, all levels of administration in every walk of life, from top government branches to grassroots organizations, fell into the hands of rebels from within and outside.

Having his enemies within the party removed through the use of the masses, Mao wasted no time. Army functionaries were dispatched to every institution to take power away from the rebels. With new leadership in place and the purposefully loosened control tightened up, the once feeling powerful, liberated rebels called by Mao to "liberate themselves and rebel against the old apparatus" found their self-ruling euphoria short-lived and themselves again back to being powerless, voiceless masses with the old state apparatus again rolling along its old track, again under the suffocating control of the authorities.

At the time, except for rival Red Guards busy fighting amongst themselves, other students had long fled out of school in the fever of *geming chuanlian* in September 1966. I was able to shield myself in my own world to lick my wounds. Beginning in January 1967, we were urged to "resume school and make revolution simultaneously". But, with fights among rival groups carrying on, it afforded us the luxury to disregard the call and remain in our own world.

Wounds still too fresh, I wanted desperately to be left alone and stay away from new harm. I would rather avoid school at all costs. However, in March, when army functionaries that took over the school had every student tracked down and notified of the mandatory return, my haven ended. At the scenario of putting myself in harm's way, I was apprehensive.

Once back, I found myself in a forbidding environment where no one made eye contact or was on speaking terms with anyone else anymore. The class divide deepened by the Cultural Revolution had alienated us from one another. To my great relief, we didn't have to board at school.

The so-called "school" was nothing but studying Mao's works for the whole day, led by an army squad leader, Mr. Liu, a humble man. Our day began with a standard daily national ritual—saluting and chanting to Mao's picture, wishing "the reddest, reddest red sun in our hearts" and the "great leader, great commander, great helmsman and great teacher Chairman Mao a ten-thousand-year boundless life", and the "beloved Vice-Chairman Lin Biao and the beloved Standard-Bearer Comrade Jiang Qing forever healthy" in the so-called "*zao qingshi*"—seeking instructions from Chairman Mao at the beginning of the day. Then, we would proceed to study Mao's works and go through self-criticism accordingly, one by one. At the end of the day we would again salute and chant to Mao's picture, called "*wan huibao*"—reporting back to Chairman Mao at the close of the day what was accomplished with his teachings.

By then, the cult of personality had reached its apex. It couldn't go any further. The moment the work day began, Mao was there waiting for you. Once you stepped out of your home, your ears would be assaulted by the loud, ceaseless Mao's quotations and songs of his quotations blaring out of the loudspeakers installed in the streets one after another like a broken record; your eyes would be flooded by Mao's pictures, images and statues, and bloody redness everywhere—red flags, red images, red slogans, red, red everything, the so-called "Red Ocean" meant to overwhelm the enemies. You would encounter the masses' propaganda groups here and there proselytizing Mao's instructions or dancing "*Zhongzi Wu* (loyalty dance)". You would see Mao's badge pinned on every chest, big and small, sometimes scores of them. Even in your own home, you still could not avoid Mao. He was there, on the wall, and over the radio. Even the newspapers and books you read, and the money, stamps and stationery you used had his images and quotations printed on them. They just wouldn't leave you alone anywhere, any moment.

I hated meetings and hated to be demanded to say things against my own judgment. Now having to sit in the classroom for the entire day, partaking in those lunatic rituals, and listening to endless twaddle and lies that could literally drive one clinically insane day in and day out every day, I felt like screaming out, pining for an escape. Thanks to my status, feelings of unworthiness, and insecurity caused by sitting among "virtuous" people, my irritation and agony were made less acute. Luckily for me, with the fanatics vying to prove themselves and babbling at length, the day would be over before it was my turn. I was spared this way.

To my great relief, we didn't have to bear this torment for too long. Factional fights amongst rival groups soon got out of hand. Incited by Jiang Qing to take power away from the army she had no control of, rebels nationwide seized weapons. Armed clashes between rebels, and between rebels and army men resulted in 300,000-500,000 deaths nationwide. The armed clashes in July, Wuhan alone caused some 42,000 deaths. Although no weapons were involved in secondary schools, with Red Guards busy fighting among themselves, before long, we were on the loose again.

Once on my own, I resolved to live out of the shadow of my stigma and live like a normal human being again. Having plenty of time on hand, I decided to learn something. But, with Father still in custody, I couldn't afford to take up anything that involved money. At the time, when even parks and decent restaurants were shut down for "catering to bourgeois leisure" and "bourgeois taste", all libraries were closed for being "inundated with counterrevolutionary and poisonous feudalistic, bourgeois and revisionist material". In the bookstores, except a small section for books and manuals of general knowledge about medicine, science and technology of a specific field, there was nothing but Mao's, Marx's, Engels', Lenin's and Stalin's works jamming every shelf, unwanted by anyone—We all had some of Mao's works, repeatedly distributed for free. The only other things available were the banned books and musical records luckily surviving the early stage of the Cultural Revolution. They were secretly passed along among curious, knowledge-thirsty youths.

In the summer, the Beijing Library was allowed to reopen to the public as the only library for "discriminatory application and critiquing". Originally called "Huangshicheng", the library was built in 1534 to house imperial archives. They were palace-like buildings with vermillion walls and yellow glazed tiles, built to prevent fire, to withstand moisture and insects, and to stabilize the humidity and temperature. Carved white-marble flights of stairs lead all the way down to the gate. At the availability of knowledge and resources, many people seized the opportunity. Every day, there was a long line along the flights of stairs waiting to get in.

With a bun I brought from home for lunch, I spent my entire day there reading, dabbling in literature, history, philosophy, music, art or whatever interested me at the moment.

Since very young, books had been my companion. I read or leafed through everything I could put my hands on: the first multilingual dictionary in China on railroad construction my maternal grandfather contributed to as the editor-in-chief of the French version, Uncle Six's medical books, Father's books of all kinds, and personages' memoirs my grandfather lent to Father—As a member of the Central Research Institute of Culture and History, my grandfather had access to those internal publications restricted to a small circle. The Western literature I read throughout the years had opened up my mind and planted noble ideas in me. The readings in the library now as a young adult further expanded my horizons and enlightened me. I became aware that there were relative and absolute truths and that relative truth must yield to the higher and the absolute truth—humanism and altruism, as in the choice the two main characters

Lantenac and Gauvain made in Victor Hugo's *Ninety-Three*. I also learned that my experience was not unique and that all humans had to deal with misfortune and sufferings at some time in their lives, and reached the conclusion that we each had our own unique path, that each search for understanding was individual and never easy, and that the more tests one was subject to, the closer to truth he might become. Once I achieved this understanding, I was no longer trapped in my own misery, but on my way to searching for truth.

Exposed to profound, sophisticated views, I never found Mao's words didactic or inspirational. On the contrary, they sounded crude, overbearing and logically simplistic and faulty. As an idealistic child, I was bothered by his quote "We should support whatever the enemies oppose and oppose whatever the enemies support", wondering why this simplistic quote logically faulty and Machiavellian in nature obvious even to a child like me was lauded. His quote "When it's busy harvest season, consume solid food; when it's slack season, get by on soup" caused me to question whether he had any spirit or sense of progression. I was also troubled why Mao's coarse poems filled with profanity and lines lifted directly from ancient Chinese poems were given lavish accolades. Although I was never a fervent believer of Mao, I had never allowed myself to pursue my skepticism about him. Like most people who didn't have high regard for Mao, I exercised self-censorship, letting my fleeting thoughts flash past. Although I didn't think much of Mao's intellect, bewitched by and besotted with perpetual propaganda, I had accepted the idea that he was a great leader and that it was necessary to build up the nation's future at the expense of individuals and individualism. But the national chaos produced by the Cultural Revolution simply crushed my illusions. My self-censorship could no longer confine my thinking. I was no longer puzzled by the things that were going on in the nation. Something that had been in my subconscious but suppressed by my consciousness now became apparent. My doubts about Mao and his party were progressively settling into shape.

As youths, we should be going through our golden age, the so-called "trial and error" phase, on our own, allowed to rebel, to err, and to learn and mature at our natural paces along our own paths.

Nevertheless, to satisfy one man's dark desire, we were robbed of our youth, our innocence, our quests, our dreams and our rights, thrown into adulthood to jeopardize our lives.

At this understanding, I seethed in indignation and became disillusioned. A man who threw the entire nation into such turmoil and brought upon its people such sufferings in the name of "revolution" and "building communism" just to hunt down his political rivals could not be as good as they purported him to be. A party that allowed such lunacy to take place could not be as good as they declared it to be. Once out of the bounds of the ideological forbidden zone, my understanding accelerated. Like jigsaw pieces falling into their places, all my questions had their answers. The splendid picture of communism I had in my mind crumbled.

One afternoon on my way out, a familiar sickening mumbling voice called out my name from across the street. I was shocked to see my worst enemy, the rapist, there, so close to my new home that we were relocated to months ago. I had thought the haunting nightmare was behind me. Now a year later I found myself still a haunted object, followed and tracked down. I immediately ran inside and hid myself there for the rest of the day.

From behind the curtain, I could see him striding back and forth, shaking his fists like a wild beast. Hours later, he disappeared. But ever since then, he had become a fixture in my neighborhood, hanging around day and night like a ghost. At the haunting daily sight, I panicked, worried about having to go out on my own and being suddenly caught by him. In my desperation, Jingming, a reading friend several years older from my old neighborhood who was recuperating at home after a kidney operation, came to mind.

One day, making sure that the beast was nowhere around, I rushed out to visit Jingming. On my way, I was highly alert. When I finally reached Jingming's home safely, I felt relieved.

Jingming and I hadn't seen each other since my family was relocated. At my appearance, Jingming's eyes popped wide. "Xiaomei," she exclaimed. "What happened? You lost so much weight and look so changed!"

At her concern, I instantly broke down. Weeping like water breaking through a dike, I cried out my pain. I had borne too much by myself for too long. Though I was emaciated and felt like a weightless zombie, crying for attention, no one had noticed anything amiss. They were all too busy with their own problems. I cried for a long time. Shaken by my intense outburst, Jingming constantly dabbed off her tears.

Having cried out all of my pain, I gradually calmed down and resolved to unburden myself by spilling out all of my thoughts that had been bottled up inside me and troubling me for so long.

"Jingming," I began, still sniveling. "I'm not defending myself. I'm indefensible. I cannot forgive myself. I will carry the stigma all my life and live the rest of my life in shame. But, had the Communists not created this chaos that turned the world upside down and sanctioned dregs of society to surface and run amok, I would still be studying at school and would not have fallen victim! If this were a just cause, I would accept the fate that was imposed on me. But, if the cause of the Cultural Revolution were just as they claim, why are the singled-outs mostly the best of the nation, of people with knowledge, skills, conscience and integrity, suffering at the hands of the worst of the population?

"My class was decadent. We deserve our fate. But the Communists are no better. They overthrew one class on the pretext of achieving egalitarianism only to find them replacing that class and become new oppressors a hundred times as brutal and depraved. At least, my class didn't put on a pretense, claiming to represent the interests of the working classes and fight for equality for them like those hypocrites who liberally reward themselves with hefty incomes in contrast to the vast, barely-surviving masses, and segregate themselves in exclusive residences far away from the masses they claim kinship with. Neither did my class have a system solely retained for themselves for supplies, resorts, entertainment, and medical treatment. In addition, we didn't inherit power like the Communist offspring. Instead, we were left to make or break on our own.

"Under the Nationalists, there was democracy. Although imperfect, citizens had real rights to freedom of assembly, of association, of speech and press, unlike the Communists' paper claims. This was how the Communists were formed and took advantage of the democratic system to wage a propaganda war against the Nationalists. Under the Nationalists, even chief Communist offenders were offered a second chance as long as they renounced violence. There were no mass campaigns or mass murders aimed at eliminating certain classes. But nowadays, human life means nothing. An absurd charge can not only lead to a person's imprisonment, but the end of his life. One can be convicted and even killed for his thoughts, his face and even his dream! It is by far worse than the notorious Ming Dynasty (1368-1644), when one could be convicted for his writings. Mao banned this and that in the name of revolution, but he himself says and does whatever he pleases, and leads a corrupt and licentious life as if he is above the rules and laws.

"By trampling on democracy, the Communists have dragged China back for thousands of years! Even in our feudal stage, people had more freedom and dignity than we do now. Nowadays, the nobler one is, the less likely he'll survive. The Communists do everything to squeeze out the last ounce of our decency, self-awareness and independent thinking. They not only brought out the ugliest side of humanity, but purposely corrupted our souls, extracted the essence of our national character out of us and turned the entire nation into cowards, cynics, robots and animals, prowling and devouring their own.

"Unlike the European counterparts in the Eastern Bloc, where trials are open to the public, here, everything is done in the dark. With no media or opposition to supervise them, they can do whatever they want. With no trail left, China's holocaust will never leave its borders! Crimes against humanity are committed every day, yet we are compelled to repeat their lies that declare Mao and his party are 'great, glorious and correct all along' and that Mao is the 'greatest genius throughout human history' whose 'one single line is worth more than anyone's ten thousand lines' while in fact Mao is the foremost mass murderer in human history that should be condemned!"

In one breath, I let out my thoughts.

Jingming grit her teeth and responded, "The Communists are Goebbels' faithful disciples, telling lies as truths. Look how many people they have deceived—hundreds of millions! I'm from an ordinary family. We are not directly affected, but anyone who is not stupid or determinedly blind sees the same thing. My parents have experienced both regimes. They've seen the contrasts. Under the Nationalists, life was much more peaceful and living standard was much higher. People were left alone to run their own lives with their own means. But, ever since the communist takeover, things have fundamentally changed. We are no longer running our own lives, free to pursue our dreams. The party controls every aspect of our lives and decides our future. They intimidates us into submission with their policy 'Those who submit will prosper; those who resist shall perish'. Our lives are never Mao's concern; maintaining his power at all costs is his only obsession. Now, except for the Communists themselves, we are all in the same state of poverty, earning comparable wages, no matter what we do or whether we perform.

"Before the communist takeover, there were old conventions and norms that governed people's conduct that allowed people to live in harmony. The authority in the family clan also helped regulate one's behavior with delineated rules for family members, the so-called '*Jia you jiafa, zu you zugui* (rules for the family and clan)'. By abolishing the old value system and installing the new protocols, the Communists have changed the nature of our personal conduct and the way we relate to one another, upsetting social harmony. What was worse, by taking away the old authority and negating the old protocols, they were able to establish themselves as the new, absolute authority. At the Communists' perpetual daily brainwash, the masses' loyalty to Mao and the party even surpasses their loyalty to their own family. Nowadays, if you dare say anything remotely critical of Mao, they'll tear you to pieces. Not even exhuming the tomb of their own ancestor would generate such fierce reactions. At their perpetual fanning of hatred, the Chinese have become the most hateful, most malevolent people in the world. With nowhere to vent the anger accumulated inside them, they jump at each other and even at people whom they do not know and who have done them no harm.

"To accomplish their ultimate goal of total control of the population, they exercise totalitarianism and obscurantism. They not only indoctrinate, but revise history, block out all references to the past and things foreign, and tell lies. At their perpetual daily brainwash, the nation is becoming hopelessly stupid beyond salvation, with people screaming 'Long lives', dancing loyalty dance, and even pinning Mao's badge into their own flesh!

"But do not despair, Xiaomei. Mao will die one day. There will come a day for him what happened to Stalin, denounced and had his corpse burned and ashes scattered ('*fenshi yanghui*', what we were told). In an era when a stag is identified as a horse and one even has to worry about being betrayed by his words in his dream, it's hard to imagine this. It took almost 40 years for this to take place in the Soviet Union. It might take place sooner in China. Who knows? Have faith. If we are lucky, we may live to see this day!"

Catching her breath, Jingming continued, "Xiaomei, don't torment yourself. You've suffered enough. What happened to you is not unique. Nowadays, humans and devils are changing places. Cases like yours are prevalent in a world where rogues and thugs hold sway."

I had heard of plenty of similar stories like mine: A tall, fragile, sylph-like Polish-Chinese girl my age from my neighborhood was repeatedly raped and became insane. In my school, three pretty girls were repeatedly raped by the same Communist descendant from the same class.

"Xiaomei," Jingming pulled my attention back. "Don't be afraid of that beast. The more you fear him, the more he'll coerce you. I'm recuperating at home now. I have the time. I'll stay with you as much as possible to protect you."

Although I still feared being caught by the rapist, with Jingming's support, I was no longer that shaky and fearful. To protect me and see me through my fragile state, Jingming stayed with me as much as possible.

On the day she returned to work, she took me along to her work place.

In her dormitory, I met her roommate and friend, Shen Ying.

True to the image of Jingming's descriptions, Shen Ying was indeed a spirit, shown through her swift, energetic movement and her infectious, silver bell-like crescendo-to-diminuendo coloratura laughter. At 5'11", slim and agile, she had been an excellent basketball player, representing Qinghua University. At the time, she was dating her college mate, Zhang Yuanzhi, who was involved in the top-secret undertaking of guided missiles. On account of the nature of his job, Zhang Yuanzhi was warned that if he didn't cut off his relationship with Shen Ying, who had a landlord family background, he would be kicked out. But Zhang Yuanzhi would rather leave his prestigious job than lose Shen Ying. With him refusing to bend, they began working on Shen Ying. A handy target, Shen Ying was accused of "seduction", denounced as a "bad element" in the campaign to cleanse the class ranks. But she didn't allow herself to be affected by this. She kept her spirit high and was as cheerful as one could be.

Knowing Shen Ying had likewise learned something about me through Jingming, the moment of eye contact with her, I subconsciously lowered my head. At my reaction, Shen Ying immediately approached me and held me in her arms. This gesture at once brought tears to my eyes. Lifting up my chin, Shen Ying cooed, "Little sister, what happened to you is not your fault at all. Your misfortune is not unique. Look around you: The entire nation is suffering! It should be counted toward the crimes Mao and his Communist regime committed. Look, it's not just you who were raped. The entire nation was raped! See your own worth, lift up your head and live just to show them that we cannot be subjugated and that we will not yield to them!"

Enlightened by her metaphor and grateful for her total trust and understanding, I dissolved in tears.

From then on, I often visited Jingming at work. With Jingming and Shen Ying's support, my fragile sense of self-worth was fortified.

The coward was still prowling around in my neighborhood almost every day. From behind the curtain, I could spot his constant ghostly presence.

One weekend afternoon, upon making sure he was out of sight, I went out to meet Jingming at her home.

When I was halfway between my home and the bus stop, the dastard suddenly shouted out my name from across the street and dashed toward me, emerging like a phantom out of nowhere.

Shocked, I at once bolted with all my might.

The bus stop was not far away. At the sight of an express bus pulling in, I dashed toward the front door and caught the bus as it was leaving. He shouted and grabbed the handle of the moving vehicle at the last second and squeezed himself in through the closing back door.

Once on the bus, he shouted and pushed his way through, and kept moving toward the front car. As he was coming within sight, the bus halted at the next stop. I got off and ran as fast as I could. But he pushed his way through the crowd and got off too.

He caught up with me in a quiet alley corner and took out his knife. Shaking like a leaf in the wind, in my moment of desperation, for the first time in my life, I broke away from the decorum I was brought up with and managed to raise my voice in public, "You devil! Creep! Leave me alone!" I at once began to run.

When I reached my destination and turned around, to my disbelief, he was not behind me. At this moment, I suddenly realized I needed to adopt some tough demeanors against my upbringing in order to survive.

Since then, the rogue had disappeared altogether.

❧

In response to the party's call on Aug. 17th to "thoroughly destroy the bourgeois headquarters", on August 18th, college rebels formed a front line outside Zhongnanhai, the government headquarters, to demand Liu Shaoqi out of Zhongnanhai. The action was joined by rebels from all the universities and Red Guards from prominent secondary schools in Beijing. Traffic was blocked; loudspeakers were employed day and night for slogan-shouting to produce a psychological effect on Liu Shaoqi and his wife in concert with the group of college rebels working on Liu Shaoqi inside Zhongnanhai.

Tormenting Liu Shaoqi and his wife as much as possible was Mao and Jiang's insidious goal as Jiang Qing publicly ranted that Liu Shaoqi and his wife "deserve to be cut into thousands of pieces". No longer under the protection of the security forces, Liu Shaoqi and his wife were denounced, beat up, and deprived of food, sleep and medical treatment daily. They soon fell into the hands of college rebels and then into the hands of professional tormentors of the Mao cult.

THE CAMPAIGN TO CLEANSE
THE CLASS RANKS

With "enemies" within the party gone and the targeted "enemies" singled out, Mao's spearhead now turned to other enemies. A campaign to "Cleanse the Class Ranks" was therein launched to ferret out every single one of the "enemies" Mao specified—traitors; hidden Nationalist agents and spies; unrepentant capitalist roaders; newly-identified counterrevolutionaries; unreformed landlords, rich peasants, bad elements, rightists, and beyond.

The all-inclusive campaign provided a good opportunity for revengeful people to go after their own presumed "enemies" who had provoked their ire or jealousy for even the pettiest reasons, such as bickering and feeling envious of another person's better looks. With the floodgates opened up for revenge, people who were either the best in their field or special or different in any way all found themselves in trouble. Virtually anyone slightly deviating from the norm in any way could be singled out with trumped-up charges. Once a person was cast out, his family members, including his sons and daughters, would be automatically condemned as a "counterrevolutionary".

A family of 14 in Shanghai whose elderly had served as the comprador for Vidal Sassoon already had some members killed in the

"Destruction of the Four Olds". Now in despair of the never-ending persecution, more members ended their lives in this campaign by jumping off the building, gas-poisoning or hanging themselves, totaling 11 deaths. Shi Chuanxiang, a mere night-soil man interviewed and commended by Liu Shaoqi, was denounced as "Liu Shaoqi's loyal running-dog" and a "*Fen Ba* (feces despot)". Doused with human wastes and beaten into a paraplegic, he was deported out of Beijing and died shortly. A similar case was Wang Jinxi, an oilfield worker interviewed and commended by Liu Shaoqi. Thrashed daily and forced to eat feces, he succumbed to cancer and multiple diseases in his prime too. Guo Xingfu, a military instructor commended for his training method, was kicked out of the army and tortured daily. After three years, he was allowed to return home one day, determined to end his life. At the sight of his badly bruised body, his wife cried and decided to die with him. He first killed their three young children with ropes and a knife. Then he slit the veins of his wife. When her blood spurted out, he cut his own veins. His wife woke up from temporary loss of consciousness and thought all were dead, she jumped out of the window of their apartment building. When Guo Xingfu himself woke up and found himself still alive, he broke the light bulb with his hands and was violently jolted by the strong current, but found himself still alive. He then grabbed the scissors and cut off his testicle, but still he didn't die. Desperate, he put his feet on the electric stove, but his trousers caused fire. To spare the neighbors, he pulled off the line and stabbed himself with the knife a dozen times. Blood gushed out and stained the floors. But still something or someone stopped him from dying. As if fate had not played enough cruel jokes on him, years later after he was rehabilitated and resumed teaching, he was run over by a slow-moving truck driven by a16-year accident-free driver and thus ended his life.

"Hidden agents", "spies", "bad elements", "alien-class elements", "counterrevolutionaries", and "enemies" of all sorts singled out and persecuted in this campaign amounted to 30 million, with over 500,000 of them tortured to death. Countless top-tier people in every field, experts, authorities, champions, top performers, award winners and even exemplary workers, perished. Scores died in the hands of Mao's wife, Jiang Qing, a fifth grader and a peasant-turned-lousy actress. In addition to the pact she made with Lin Biao's wife to "help hunt down each other's foes", she frantically hunted down every single one of her "enemies" on her own, from the top-tier officials who had voted to forbid her involvement in party affairs when Mao resolved to marry her in the 1930s down to actors and actresses whom she had worked, lived, slept with, or bickered with when she was in the entertainment business in Shanghai before she went to Yan'an, the Communist base. Not a single one of her enemies or potential enemies escaped. Few survived her insane vengeance and her attempt to do away with anyone she hated or anyone who knew her notorious history.

As more and more people were singled out as "class enemies" with various charges on a daily basis, the days were long for anyone who had not been touched. Released from solitary confinement, Mother found herself back to being a "bad element" and denounced again. As one who had a secret disgrace, I was simply jumpy. Every day, I waited in ominous presentiment.

One day after lunch when we were reposing, there came a succession of rapid, foreboding banging on our door.

Highly alarmed, Mother opened the door only to find two policemen standing there. Both of them bore the surname Li.

"Is Long Qiru home?" the short Li stated tersely. "We are here to investigate her criminal offenses!"

My bedroom window was wide open facing the corridor. I could hear and see everything. In a police state, the sight of police at the door could cause anyone to shudder. Hearing that I was the wanted offender with the definite term "criminal offenses", I shook uncontrollably, unable to believe my ears.

With Mother and my sister swiftly and deferentially retreating to the living room and vanishing behind the shut door, I found myself alone in my bedroom behind the closed door with two policemen, feeling like a petrified cornered and hunted-down animal unable to escape.

Hardly had I had the time to collect myself when the eagle-eyed, diabolic-looking short Li addressed me in a severe tone, "Long Qiru,

I think you already know why we are here. We have obtained all the evidence of your criminal offenses. We are here to offer you a chance to give up vices and return to the right track. You know our party's policy: clemency for those who confess and severity for those who resist. Trying to withhold any evidence will only lead to more severe punishments. Now make a clean confession to your criminal offenses!"

"Criminal offenses", "vices", "evidence", "punishment", "confession"…, each and every single one of his words unfamiliar to my world hit me in the head like a big stick and made my head spin and my body shake. Inured to being categorized as one "born with ill traits", I knew I could be found guilty of something. But, potentially guilty of so many things, I was bewildered, unable to pinpoint my offenses.

"Confess to the crimes you committed together with Xu Zhaoyong! Confess from the beginning to the end!"

Upon hearing that repulsive name, my heart sank.

Unable even to bear the thought of having my disgrace exposed to anyone, let alone men, now I found myself in the position of a "criminal" compelled to reveal my deepest shame to two male law enforcers. Ashamed and feeling terribly wronged at already being decided guilty even before I was given a chance to open my mouth, I wept. They represented law. How could one argue with law? Independent attorneys limping into 1958 had entirely disappeared at the advent of 1959. Trials were now decided by "the people's court" that consisted of no real defender or jury but a court assigned defender and organized audiences—the uneducated proletarian masses that would go along with whatever the authority decided. Once one was indicted of some crime, he would be automatically sentenced, with no recourse to having his case overturned. At the scenario of being taken to jail as a "criminal" and rot there with the filthiest criminals, tears rolled down my cheeks.

At this, the short Li switched his position menacingly. "Long Qiru," he said. "Don't waste our time. Confess! Confess now! Start from the very beginning!"

Very scared, I attempted to comply, but I was just unable to control my tears. At my irrepressible weeping, Li shifted his position again and raised his voice, "Long Qiru, you are testing our patience, aren't you? You refuse to confess, right? All right then. We will turn you over to the masses' dictatorship!"

The term "masses' dictatorship" immediately conjured up in my mind a vivid terrifying picture of being torn alive. At this ghastly scenario, I found myself already beginning to account for what had happened amid my tears.

At my words of having no knowledge about sex or sex organs prior to the rape—taboo subjects not taught at school or read anywhere, the short Li jerked his body again and scoffed, "Bogus alibi! Stop deceiving us! Yeah, right, you didn't know what sex was. Then how did you do it? After you satiated your itch, you are telling us you didn't know what sex was? Who would believe you? Yeah, right, you were a virgin, weren't you? Whom are you kidding? We already have the other criminal's confession. He has testified that you were not a virgin when you did this with him. Listen up: We know how filthy and corrupt you bourgeoisie are. You were born sinful and deceitful! If you dare to mislead us and play tricks on us, we will show you what proletarian dictatorship is like. Is that clear? Now, start all over!"

At his filthy words and the claim that I was not a virgin, I was beside myself. A defiant feeling rose within me.

At the time, despite the absence of information about sex, children born into a poor family could be exposed to sex through sharing the same room and some even the same bed with their parents. Having no exposure to the life lived outside his social stratum, and biased against my "evil, deceitful and immoral" class, Li decided what I said about having no knowledge about sex prior to the rape was a lie.

Although I was demoralized, my mind was still clear. There was something fundamentally untrue about this picture of me. To get things right, I defiantly gave my account in sequence and provided background information about myself whenever I saw the need.

Li stopped me from going any further with his disparagement. "Long Qiru," he said. "You are testing our patience, aren't you? Listen up: If you dare to continue to mislead us and waste our time, just you wait and see what proletarian dictatorship can do to you. Our time is precious; our patience is limited. Stop playing tricks on us. We will not be deceived. Now just answer our questions and stop beating about the bush!"

With his terse debasing questions—where, when and how I did it the first time, the second time..., I was turned into a worthless base creature dictated only by animal instinct. At the untrue mortifying picture of me, I was angry and humiliated, feeling mercilessly reduced and terribly wronged. I tried to clarify the situation. But each of my attempts was stopped and denigrated outright. I was not allowed to say anything more than just answering his humiliating questions. He kept poking and grilling me for more graphic, sordid details accompanied with his lewd remarks until I was completely destroyed, not contesting anymore.

At the dirty picture of myself, I cried and cried, devastated by the humiliation and agonizing over the indignity I brought upon myself, feeling violated for the second time. With my dignity so mercilessly stripped of me, the last vestige of my self-respect was shredded. I felt like ending my life right there. How could I live on with such ignominy? Without self-respect, what was I to live for? I succumbed to copious tears.

After the merciless and seemingly endless grilling and humiliation, I was asked to sign the transcript with the following words: Everything transcribed is unfalsified and undistorted.

Putting away the records of my confession, the short Li concluded, "Long Qiru, the nature of this case is criminal. You have stepped onto the criminal route. Your behavior and life style are corrupt, degenerated and licentious. It proves that you have inherited your class traits—depraved, immoral and deceptive. You must thoroughly reform yourself. If you slip along this track, it will be a dead end for you. You will be put in jail sooner or later!"

At the word "jail" and such low opinion of me, I cried and cried. Reminded daily that people born into my class were "born sinful" and "innately no good", at his repeated disdainful scorn, I was not sure of myself anymore. Serious doubts about my own worth crept into my mind: Am I really that abominable and different from the proletariat, having no sense of right and wrong? Am I really an evil creature born with all the vile traits and destined en route to a criminal path? With the conclusion clearly written in Li's contemptuous expressions, my self-esteem crumbled.

They left me to have Mother briefed. The moment they were gone, Mother and my sister ended their dormancy.

"Well done!" My sister exclaimed as she stepped into my bedroom, "First we were ransacked; now we have this ignominy. To have a political problem is already bad enough. Now we have to bear this infamy. This is much worse than a political problem. With a political problem, you can still maintain your dignity as a human being. But with this, you no longer command any respect. With your conduct, you have not only shamed yourself, you have shamed the entire family! The whole family will be smeared and implicated by you! You will make us all unable to lift up our heads!"

Scourged by my sister's words, I whimpered achingly.

"It's bad enough," Mother stopped her. "Don't add fuel to the fire. Wait till Xiaomei explains everything." Turning to me, Mother demanded, "Long Qiru, tell us everything from the beginning to the end."

A sinner, I had no right to beg for mercy to be spared the anguish and humiliation again, but to obey and go through the unbearable pain and indignity all over again.

When I finished, Mother bemoaned weakly, "This family is indeed accursed. Adverse fate has befallen us. We are haunted by misfortunes one after another!"

Ever since the communist takeover, our family had been hit with tribulations: First, Father was expelled from the prestigious Customs; then my elder brother Tiemin was sent to a reform-through-labor farm for being an "idle bourgeois descendant". Another brother Ciqing was deprived of a high school education for "consecutive thefts of state properties".

"What does it have to do with misfortunes?" Sharply, my sister contradicted Mother, "One chooses his own path and is responsible for his own acts. No one put a gun to her head and forced her to do what she did. It was her own moral defects that led to this. She has no shame, giving herself up to her desire like a low life. And she did this in the wide open like a shameless hussy! Ugh! Even talking about it makes me feel soiled…"

Pierced by my sister's remarks and abashed and despised to this extent, had the ground cracked open at the moment, I would have at once leapt in to terminate my wretched, shameful existence. Overwhelmed by grief and compunction, I cried harrowingly, unable to understand how my own sister could be so cruel to someone sharing the same flesh and blood. Toward a stranger, she would feel the need to spare her tongue and be more discriminating. Why is she so relentless with her own sister who desperately needs tenderness, understanding, consolation and protection? I asked myself. Am I really that dirty and disgusting? Was it really my fault? Did I really bring this upon myself? Was I really born with moral defects? The answers are clear. If I'm a sinner in my own sister's eyes, there must be something fundamentally wrong with me. I must be professing some fatal ill character and moral defects.

The police visit was widely noticed in the neighborhood. Words about me and my "criminal offenses" went around fast. There were all kinds of rumors about me.

Crushed and miserable, I wished I could vanish from the earth forever, but there was nowhere for me to hide in this world, not even in my own home. With the shame I brought upon them and at the fact that their lives were made more difficult because of me, I was simply unable to face them. I dreaded even stepping out of my own bedroom. However, as a free boarder, I had no choice but to go out to run errands for the family and run into the tongue-wagging housewives who had nothing to do but sit outside minding other people's business. Whenever they espied me, they never failed to nudge each other and stare and hurl insults at me and guffaw. Even without anyone to remind me of my ignominy, the sense of being a sinner already made me unable to lift up my head. Disdained and despised even by uneducated lowly housewives, I was simply turned into wreckage.

One afternoon, just as I was trying hard to recover from the police visit, several Red Guards from my class appeared at our door.

"What's the matter, Red Guards?" Mother asked them.

"We need to speak to Long Qiru," the leader answered sternly.

Before Mother was able to say more, my sister pulled her into the living room.

With them retreating to the living room behind the closed door, I found myself left to deal with the situation on my own. It was a group of Red Peripheries-turned Red Guards formed after Mao's review of Red Guards on August 18, 1966, led by a pale boy of Muslim descent whom no one paid much attention to before the Cultural Revolution. Among them were a few non-Red Guards, including my friends Wang Qian and Kong Xiuhua. From the serious, hostile and disdainful looks they carried on their faces, I sensed the visit would be ominous.

Once they were seated in my bedroom behind the closed door, the leader began to harangue, with an air of authority on his face, "Long Qiru, you must be clear what we are here for. We have learned about all of your criminal activities. We are here to offer you a chance to give up vices. The party's policy is clear: clemency to those who confess to their crimes and severity to those who refuse to. To avoid further prosecution, the only way out for you is to disclose your crimes thoroughly. Don't lie. Don't try to play tricks on us. Any attempt to resist the masses' movement is like a mantis trying to stop a chariot!"

I was stunned at my secret being found out and stung by the menacing statement, unable to understand how they could be so heartless to do this to someone already down in the dirt, pursuing her relentlessly and gnashing on her pain. I asked myself, why are they doing this to me? Am I really their enemy? Have I ever done anything wrong to any of them? What are they anyway? Are they law-enforcers? Why do I have to subject myself to this mortification again to those people who are no moral authority over me, a bunch of mediocre students and cowards who have nothing better to do but to live on other people's blood and have no courage or brain to examine themselves and think others are below them? To evade the truth, that is the last trait I would pick up in my life. At the sight of my friends in this group, tears welled up in my eyes. How could they join this group to come to my home to pursue me and witness my humiliation? I thought to myself. It is my shame. It is my secret. They have no right to feast on my pain and disgrace. A feeling of fierce defiance rose inside me.

At my defiance, the leader said, "Long Qiru, you refuse to confess, right? All right then, we will give you up to the masses and let them exercise the masses' dictatorship over you!"

At this bullying and injustice, I was unable to control my tears anymore.

"Stop crying!" The leader bawled. "Don't try to cover up your crime with your tears. We will not be deceived! Chairman Mao teaches us, 'We must flog the cur even when it has fallen into the water.' We will not be softhearted and soft-handed toward class enemies! Stop crying and playing tricks on us. Confess! Otherwise, we will turn you over to the masses. We mean it!"

At this cruelty and threat, I heaved out more tears. For the first time in my life, I experienced the emotion of real rage. However, horrified at having my shame exposed to the public to be humiliated and eaten alive, I complied with my account amid my tears.

When I started at how I got to know the scoundrel and that I thought he was a Red Guard and dared not offend him, the leader went berserk. With a banging on the desk, he roared, "Watch your tongue! That low life does not belong to our rank. If you insult the Red Guards, you insult the proletariat. If you insult the proletariat, you insult Chairman Mao. We will not tolerate this! If you play tricks by dwelling on trivialities and shifting your crime onto the proletariat, you will be severely punished and turned over to the masses to be dealt with. Now, start all over!"

As I was giving my account, a pretty girl who had led a group to raid a lingerie store interjected her insults, "You asked for it!" "It's in your blood, you dirty, shameless bourgeois element!" "We disdain you from the bottom of our hearts!"...

I trembled and heaved in streaming tears uncontrollably at these unwarranted insults and contempt. They were not my friends. I did not want them to see my tears. I tried to swallow them back, but they were simply irrepressible.

Kong Xiuhua, a coarse-looking girl and my friend before the Cultural Revolution, opened her mouth. "Why did it only happen to you but not anyone else?" She remarked slowly, "It has proven that you are no good and that your class is no good. You think you were richly endowed and know everything. Now there's a chance for you to see the real you in the mirror."

I was shocked by Kong Xiuhua's unexpected remarks, unable to understand how this girl who never declined to devour the full knapsack of choicest food, such as foie gras and caviar that Lu Ma packed for me from each of my home visits week after week could join them to denigrate me. Even more hurt and indignant, I heaved in more tears.

Although they had found out that the villain had raped more girls, they didn't see me as a victim or sympathize with me because my "decadent class traits" and my "looks" caused this to happen.

In the end, the leader said, "Long Qiru, we are going to hold a public denunciation the day after tomorrow. Write a self-criticism. We'll see what your attitude toward your crime is. Right now we are going through the campaign to cleanse the class ranks. It is up to you whether you want to join the class enemies' rank!"

A chill shot through me at the mentioning of the campaign.

After they left, my family emerged from behind the closed door.

"Geez," exasperated by the new trouble I brought about, my sister spoke sulkily. "We cannot reside in this place any longer. Not even one day are we allowed to live without feeling the shame. This family is completely sinful! The whole lot is rotten through and through! No one is clean. It's unfit for decent human beings. We'll move out!"

Humbled by misfortunes, Mother, who provided lodging and financial benefit for my sister's entire family of four, failed to respond.

In spite of Qijuan's brave declaration, she and her family stayed on with us for years. They had been living with us ever since my brother-in-law was expelled from the Navy and started working as a factory worker earning 40 yuan a month. He was implicated by the case of his father, who was faulted for having risen from a poor peasant boy on American sponsorship to a doctor of Nationalist lieutenant-general rank. But, despite the trouble brought upon her by her husband's expulsion from the Navy, Qijuan, a person with a great deal of feats and resiliency, had swiftly recovered from this disgrace. She was appointed to a group that was established in every institution to look into everyone's *dang'an* and determine whether the person was "problematic". With all her loyalty to the party, my sister saw no ideological contradiction by remaining in her "sinful" family for financial benefit.

The following day, my teacher, Mr. Zhang Lanxin, summoned me to his school dormitory at lunchtime to help me with my self-criticism.

Upon reading the self-criticism I wrote, Mr. Zhang pointed at the sentence "I was afraid of Red Guards" and the event account, and said, "Cross out these. It could provoke them. Their power knows no bounds. Your case can be treated leniently or blown up to a serious problem. Why give them the chance? Rework it along the line of 'bourgeois family influence' and of 'neglecting ideological remolding'. Otherwise, they won't be satisfied."

With Mr. Zhang's guidance, I rewrote my self-criticism to his satisfaction and returned home.

At night, the thought of having to have my deepest shame exposed to my classmates kept me wide awake. I wept from time to time. To steady myself, I repeatedly sang Susanin's aria before his anticipated death from Glinka's *Ivan Susanin* until I calmed down. Although emotionally spent, at the fast-approaching unavoidable moment, I was unable to close my eyes.

The following morning, the moment I stepped into the class, I was unnerved: the whole class was sitting there. Apparently, they were summoned back to witness my humiliation. Even before my secret was known, the compunction inside me had already made me unable to face my classmates. Now appearing as a public censure was more than I could endure. I was unable to stop weeping, feeling like a helpless sheep being taken to a slaughterhouse.

The meeting began when Mr. Zhang took the center stage.

"Classmates, comrades and Red Guards," said Mr. Zhang. "As you have already known, an unfortunate circumstance has befallen your classmate Long Qiru. She's going to have a self-criticism. Although the nature of her wrongdoing is serious, we should give her a chance to reform and become a new person in accordance with the party's policy. Chairman Mao says, 'To help a comrade who erred, we should adopt the approach of treating the illness to save the patient'. I'm confident that our Red Guards and revolutionary students can execute the party's policy properly. Now, Long Qiru…"

At Mr. Zhang's carefully chosen words to set the tone for the meeting, I was choked with gratitude. In those days, Mao's words worked wonders. Citing them could deter danger.

At the inevitable moment, in unbearable shame and gushing tears, I arose and read my self-criticism, ascribing my disgrace to the "roots of my bourgeois family" and my "innate evil class instinct and tendency that made me lose sense of class struggle and became a bourgeois captive on my way to degeneration and crime".

When the last words of mine were finished, I suddenly noticed the entire class was deadly quiet as if the drop of a pin could be heard. Evidently, they were all disturbed by the depth of my grief.

An inimical-looking Red Guard who never liked me broke the long silence first. "What happened to Long Qiru is not accidental," she began with an assertion. "A fly does not touch an egg that is not cracked; her appearance carries the message. Even before the Cultural Revolution, she had shown traces of her problems. She was frivolous. Not only this, she exhibited her resistance to reforming herself. Given her bourgeois family influence and her innate evil class instinct and tendency, if she does not learn some serious lessons from this offense, she is sure to slide along this path to further degeneration and become a criminal and a class enemy sooner or later!"

Another girl from the core group who had denigrated me at my home continued, "Long Qiru, you should be alarmed by your crime. It is a dangerous road. You must cast off the old self, go through the proletarian reform and strive to become a new person. Otherwise, you will be drowned by the mighty torrent of the great proletarian revolution or be swept into the garbage dump!"

Waiting and seeing no one else intend to say anything, Mr. Zhang seized the moment and concluded, "Comrades, classmates and Red Guards! It was a successful meeting, a live class education. It educated Classmate Long Qiru as well as everyone else in the class. It also proved that the Red Guards executed the party's policy brilliantly by offering the wrongdoer a way out. Now the meeting is dismissed."

The moment the meeting was announced to be over, Li Huiying, a spare-time sharp pistol-shooter and a kind, upright girl sitting by my side who usually was well-composed, furiously scrawled something down on a piece of paper and slipped it into my hand.

I unfolded it and saw the following words: Classmate Long Qiru, we welcome you to rejoin our revolutionary rank to reform yourself. A warm current coursed through my body. But I didn't belong in their world. In my deep compunction of my ignominy, I felt unworthy of anyone's company.

Although I escaped from being singled out as a "class enemy" or a "bad element", my life was not made any easier after my self-criticism. On the contrary, with wild tales about me spread throughout the campus, I became even more of a noticed person, a known "slut", abhorred, disdained or eschewed. At my sight, some felt entitled to hurling curses, spitting, or displaying their righteous superiority to me while others simply avoided me as if I were contagious that even a glance of me would pollute their eyes, and even breathing the same air would make them feel contaminated. The vast contempt sent tremors down my spine. I was devastated, wishing I could vanish from their world forever.

Occasionally, I would meet a quick, hedging, pitiful look from a few kind ones. But even this hurt. My gym teacher, Mr. Hong Jinlong, a warm-hearted upright man of tremendous conscience and feelings, was simply unable to contain his emotions. I had been his favorite. Whenever he ran into me, his eyes would betray his feelings. His pained, sorrowful and concerned eyes made me feel the pain all the more stingingly. No matter how kind people are, one bears his anguish alone. With my heart aching and bleeding, I yearned to have a corner for myself to cry my heart out and die quietly without being noticed.

It had been almost a year, but the wound was still too fresh. Not for a moment could I forget my shame.

DEPARTING FROM BEIJING

At a time when productivity was halted for years to make revolution ("*tingchan naogeming*"), tens of millions of urban youths reaching employment age remained idle, causing social unrest. In August 1968, the *Shangshan Xiaxiang* movement was launched to send urban youths to the countryside for settlement to be "reeducated".

It began with 1966 secondary-school graduates of undesirable family backgrounds. There was no pressure on us 1968 graduates yet. Wang Yu, my friend from my previous secondary girls' school, and Meng Xiaozheng, my friend from my current school, were under tremendous pressure to leave Beijing. Functionaries had visited their homes to mobilize them many times. Without much success, the authorities came up with a clever means by creating a grotesque scene in the targets' neighborhoods. With drums, gongs and cymbals beating loudly, functionaries would post a "good news" poster outside the targets' homes that claimed that the targets' "application for settling in the countryside" had been "approved" and that the targets had been "gloriously selected to carry out this honorable task". Impossible to repudiate the claim and no longer able to resist the pressure, Wang Yu and Meng Xiaozheng relented and registered to settle together in Beidahuang (the Great Northern Wilderness) in the northeastern tip of China.

This news triggered my long desire to escape. I decided to join them. To procure my success, I had to take quick action and not give anyone time to stop me. At the chance to extricate myself from the inescapable shame and pain of living in Beijing as a target, I quivered with excitement. For the entire night, I was wide-awake.

Early the next morning, the moment Mother was gone for work, I was on my way to my school to register for settling in the country-side. It chilled me just to think about going back there. But it had to be done.

Once on campus, I went straight to the registration office and registered there. Told that I needed to have my resident status revoked at the police precinct, I returned home.

There were rigid controls over the population's movement then. If one was transferred from one place to another, he must first have his "*hukou*" (registered resident status) revoked at his current police precinct. With this proof, he would then be able to obtain a grain ration as a registered resident in the new place to live on.

Lu Ma just came back from grocery shopping. Shocked by the unexpected news, she immediately dissolved in tears. At my request for our household-registration booklet so that I could have my resident status revoked, she burst out crying, "No! I won't give it to you! I won't let you go! You will never be able to come back!"

At the time, once one relinquished his resident status in a big city, the chance for him to return from a smaller city would be next to zero. Returning to a city from the countryside was simply unheard of. But I couldn't care less.

"Lu Ma," holding her callused hands, I stamped my foot and implored her in tears. "It's been done already. I cannot rescind. I have to go. I must go. Please give me the booklet! I need it!"

"No!" Lu Ma wailed, face drenched in tears, "I won't give it to you! I won't allow you to hurt yourself anymore!"

In her simple, loving heart, Lu Ma knew I was suffering and struggling mightily. She cried and begged me not to go. I cried too. But I was determined. We were locked in this position. Neither of us was willing to budge. Finally, unable to bear my desperate pleas and tears, Lu Ma gave in. Wailing uncontrollably, she unlocked the chest where family documents were kept and relinquished the booklet to me.

Wasting no time, I rushed to the police precinct to make it official and irreversible. Then I returned to school to have my action sealed.

On my way out of the school, at the corner of a narrow path, I ran into Xu Huping, a kind, pedantic classmate.

With his eyes blinking uneasily behind his glasses, Xu Huping addressed me anxiously, "Long Qiru, the classmates are all talking about your leaving. We're all astounded. Do you know what you are doing? You are giving up a privilege, a security. You will never be able to return to Beijing again!"

The privilege of living in Beijing meant nothing to me. What Beijing brought to me was nothing but painful and shameful memories, a constant reminder of my disgrace. Besides, with my background, I would likely be a live target for the rest of my life. I would rather settle anywhere far away from the Communists' reach to live free and die with my identity concealed than live here with what George Orwell called "thought police" and a label that I would never be able to escape.

At Xu Huping's words, I managed a faint smile and replied, "I know that."

At my certitude, Xu Huping was speechless, staring at me and shaking his head as if he couldn't understand why I wanted to leave at such a huge price.

In the afternoon, at the sight of Mother, Lu Ma at once burst out crying, "*Taitai*, Xiaomei is leaving Beijing! She's going to settle in Beidahuang!"

"What?" Stunned by the news, Mother however immediately grasped the reality and came up with a pointed question, "Has she had her Beijing resident status revoked?"

"Yes…"

"God, she's going to live as a peasant for the rest of her life!" Sweat streaming down her face, she yelled at Lu Ma in a fluster, "Why did you let her go? Why didn't you hold her back?"

For the entire day, Lu Ma had been grieving by herself. Now she cried out, "*Taitai*! How could I stop her? Try it yourself!"

"Alas!" Mother cried, completely overwhelmed by guilt and grief. "How did I raise such a foolish and stubborn child? It is the retribution for inbreeding between first cousins. It brought out all the adverse genes in the children. Except Qijuan, who always confers with us and deliberates her every major move, carefully weighing up advantages and disadvantages, and patiently biding her time, none of the other children are smart enough to do so. And this child is the worst! She makes up her own mind in an instant, never consulting anyone about anything! Other people's children are all smart enough to resist the pressure by inventing excuses and biding their time, but this child jumps into her death as if driven by adverse fate!"

As Mother was overwhelmed by the news, my sister returned. While she was absorbing the shock, Mother urged her, "Qijuan, we have no time to waste. Go to Xiaomei's school with me, right away!"

They rushed to my school and made a strong emotional appeal that my "abrupt decision" was made out of my mental state resulting from the rape, which brought out the sympathy of the personnel officer, who assured them that they "didn't put anything detrimental" in my *dang'an*. But it was too late. My right to live in Beijing as a legal resident had already been irreversibly terminated.

Mother was badly stricken. After dinner, she came to my bedroom with my sister. The moment Mother sat by my side, she put her arm around me and wept. "Xiaomei," she cried. "I beg your forgiveness. I didn't know you were hurt to this extent until now. Please forgive me!"

This was one of the few times that Mother ever embraced me and showed her concern for me. After all, I was her daughter, her own flesh and blood.

However, after what I had been through, anything less severe than the rape and its aftermath would not affect me. To be able to live on, I had locked up my heart and numbed my feelings. At Mother's guilty emotion, I felt a suppressed pain in my chest. I said to myself, it's too late. The wrongs have already been done. The original "I" has already died. No one can give back my virginity, my innocence and my beliefs. History cannot be rewritten. My shame cannot be erased. It is I who has to carry the ignominy throughout the rest of my life. When I cried for help, no one was there. I have borne it all by myself and gone through my journey alone, groping in the dark searching my way out. Now when I have walked out on the world that I once embraced with all my heart, ready to set out for another world and determined to bear all the consequences of my decision, they show up.

My sister, who was never willing to admit her mistakes, murmured a little remorse, "Xiaomei, perhaps you wouldn't leave if we hadn't cornered you…"

Her words only made me feel sadder and even lonelier. I said to myself, when I was fragile, desperately needing understanding, comfort and protection, I was deserted and mercilessly ridiculed. When I needed a corner to lick my wounds, I was shown no mercy, but dragged out and dealt more cruelty and contempt. Now when I'm determined to depart from this world that has inflicted so much pain on me, they finally realized the impact their acts produced on me.

In all her spare time day and night in a week, Mother knit a thick brown wool scarf for me long enough to wrap it around my head and neck twice to resist Beidahuang's bitter cold. My brother Ciqing, who seldom returned home, also chipped in by devoting his weekends to shopping for my departure.

While I was basking in this unfamiliar warmth and attention, I felt a bit comical. Overnight, I was turned from a burden and shame to becoming the center of attention.

Only Lu Ma remained true to herself. Unable to express her feelings and thoughts with words, she wept quietly day and night by herself. The grief and indignation that she was experiencing but unable to understand or express were so strong that she was seen visibly shaking as if she were angry at the entire world for the wrongs done to me. Ever since my birth, she had been devoting her entire love and care to me as if I were her own child. Though she was unable to help me in any way or even say a few words of comfort to me at my distressful moments, she was the only one who loved me unconditionally.

Just as I felt somewhat relieved as the date of departure was drawing near, one afternoon, the Red Guards who had come to my home the first time to denounce me reappeared at our door. It was led by the same classmate, the originally low-key boy who now was shown consumed with his newly acquired power and exhibiting it to anyone who didn't submit to him.

At the sight, my newly acquired angry emotion resurfaced. What do they want this time? I said to myself, I'm already prepared to leave their world permanently. Isn't this enough for them? What else do they want? The last beat of my heart? If they expect the same effects they produced on me the first time, it won't be that easy this time. My senses have become duller. A less sharpened knife will not be able to cause my heart to bleed. Too bad they are too slow to catch up with my changes.

Hardly had they sat down when the leader blustered out, "Long Qiru, your crime has not been fully squared yet, and you already want to slink off? Are you scared of the campaign to cleanse the class ranks and the yearly August Tempest, the suppression of you hoodlums and bad elements? You want to sneak away before the proletarian dictatorship is imposed on you, don't you?" With a loud banging on the desk, he roared, "I'll tell you clearly: there is no way for you to escape!"

"Red Terror will haunt you anywhere you go!" Screamed the same vacuous pretty girl who had denounced me the first time, "No matter where you dive for cover, you can't dodge the campaign to cleanse the class ranks. No matter where you escape to, you'll be yanked out sooner or later!"

"It's the proletariat's world!" Through his gapped teeth, the leader hissed out. "Anywhere you go, the proletarian dictatorship will deliver just, severe suppression to your kind. You have nowhere to hide. You will be denounced anywhere you go!"

At their cruelty and pettiness, I was incandescent with rage, recognizing the true purpose of this visit. They thought they had me as their living target forever and could get their satisfaction through me any time they wanted. With this unexpected move, I foiled their plan. They felt that they were forestalled by me, and hence came here to exert their soon-to-expire power over me and deal me one last blow. I stared ahead, without responding or even looking at them. I pitied them, the small-minded, small-hearted petty souls. They built their confidence upon inflicting pain and sufferings on others, but they had very little to hold onto in their narrow world. To control other people was one; to hold onto the Beijing residence right was another. They meant everything to them. They just couldn't figure out how a spoiled "bourgeois brat" like me could relinquish the price-less Beijing resident status and volunteer to settle in a remote corner of the earth with absolutely no chance to come back. They thought that with my upbringing, I would rather swallow my dignity just to cling to the comfort and the security of the city as they did. How little imagination these timid souls have, I said to myself. Our worlds are too far apart. No language will ever be able to bridge them.

At my wordless response, the leader threatened, "Long Qiru, I'll make this clear: Without our permission, you won't be able to move one step. You want to flee? It won't be that easy. We can detain you if we want to. You want to resist? We can finish you off like squashing an ant. We will not let you slip away this easily. You will see who the winner is!"

Having no perspective about their true position in this world due to their limited exposure and altered ego disproportionately inflated by Mao's class warfare, they indeed tried. But it was beyond the school's jurisdiction. To reverse the result, they would have to obtain some key figure's approval at the municipal level. I thus escaped the inextricable fate.

The departure date finally was here. Lu Ma was all tears. It was too much for her. Early in the morning, her eyes already turned into two slits, red and swollen beyond recognition. Out of "humanitarianism", Father was permitted to see me off at the train station with Mother. My brother Ciqing took a day's leave to help me with the luggage. My friend Jingming came too. Yang Yuhe and Lao Yang, the two girls who had gone through the reform with Meng Xiaozheng and me in the countryside at the beginning of the Cultural Revolution, also arrived to say good-bye to us. Yang Ju came too. Having been deported to the countryside and become peasants, both Yang Ju and Lao Yang depended solely for survival on the *"gongfen"* ("work points", rural supply system based on the accumulation of every day's work). But they sacrificed their day's earnings and came to bid us farewell.

Unexpectedly, two of my classmates, Weng Rulian and Kong Xiangqi, pushed through the crowds and appeared in front of me.

"Long Qiru," in a voice that betrayed her emotions, Weng Rulian addressed me uneasily. "Thank God we found you. We came to say good-bye to you. We may never see each other again!"

I thanked them, ill at ease. We fell into an awkward silence.

I had tried very hard to put everything behind me by steering clear of anyone who knew my history. Their sight and words only reminded me of my ignominy again.

"Long Qiru," Weng Rulian let out a remark contemptuously. "I can't believe how vicious those people are that they exercised their power one last time over a victim who has already decided to remove herself from this world!"

With a kind, incredible look on her face, Kong Xiangqi shook her head and gently chimed in, "It's unbelievable what they did to you, Long Qiru."

Having long withdrawn from their world and feeling alienated, mentally, I had already drifted away from their world. I was unable to appreciate their kindness at the time when all I wanted was to run away from the hurt and from the people who knew me and who could remind me of my shame.

At the last call for boarding, we got onto the train. When the horn honked and the train started chugging, the crowds wailed out loudly. It felt like the plaintive cries over a lifetime separation imposed by conscription. After all, it was not a common occurrence. We were the first large-number of students being sent away. Who could tell what was awaiting us? Would we ever be able to come back and see our family again? No one knew. Our fate was decided by the Communists. We didn't have any say in our own lives. This could be the last time in our lives that we ever saw each other. Just then, a triumphant song burst out of the loudspeakers installed in the train station: "*Navigation depends on helmsman... Making revolution depends on Mao-Zedong-Thought...*" The exalting, celebratory music discordant to the scene was only met with and drowned out by the crowds' louder resentful cries.

A number of mothers were unable to bear it and collapsed.

All of a sudden, Father raised his fist among the heart-broken crowds, shouting with all his might, "Long live Chairman Mao!" At this shout and comical act incongruous to the scene, everyone nearby broke into hooting.

My poor tragicomic father. Who knows what was raging in his heart? He must have been stirred up by the grieving scene at the lifetime separation and our impotence at controlling our own fate in the face of insanity. But unable to express his anger and grief in a normal way, all of his complicated feelings were turned into a fashionable slogan.

LIFE IN THE COUNTRYSIDE

Our destination was Nehe, county seat of Molidawa Qi in Inner Mongolia by the Nenjiang River, where the Tahur, descendants of the Khitan, inhabit. It is about 180 miles (300 kilometers) away from the Soviet Union. At the time, Inner Mongolia was being substantially carved up to devastate the power base of Ulanfu, a Mongol and the party head there. To remove him, Kang Sheng, China's Beria, lodged a "separatist" crime against him. We arrived at the juncture of having this Qi (county, originally a Manchu caste division) put under the jurisdiction of Heilongjiang Province.

While we were waiting at the county seat in the courtyard of the vacated county secondary school to be assigned to some commune, we decided to stroll around.

In this tiny, sleepy rural town, there was hardly anything worth seeing, except layers of slogans and big-character posters posted all over the county office building and along the intersection of the two main streets to ferret out "separatists". They formed an incongruous sight in this slumberous place and confirmed the vast extent of this witch hunt we had learned about in Beijing that implicated millions and caused some 22,000 deaths. At the sight of the small county co-op, we went in. There was only a bored, indifferent-looking female shop assistant there. The shelves were mostly empty. All the store had were some locally made poor-quality household necessities, such as soap, toothbrushes and toothpastes, light bulbs, flash lights, batteries, candles, matches and kitchen utensils. A few bolts of earthy, coarse cotton cloth lay on the counter. A small stock of expired canned goods nobody wanted and a minuscule left-over stock of powdery, stale cookies were the only food items there. There was nothing worth purchasing or even worth seeing, but we bought some cookies anyway. In about half an hour, we found we had exhausted our little exploration.

After lunch, Wang Yu and Meng Xiaozheng decided to look into the possibility of a better arrangement for our future life there. For my pride, I didn't want to tag along again. Instead, I offered to keep an eye on our luggage. Having experienced so many adversities in my life, I was glad to be away from Beijing, the political center. It didn't matter to me whether we were assigned to the east village or the west. Anywhere we were relocated to could not be as bad as Beijing. Apparently, Wang Yu and Meng Xiaozheng had a different perspective and were trying to take things into their own hands as much as possible. Half an hour later, they returned to inform me that we were going to be allied with a group of boys from Boys' School No. 5, a prominent secondary school in Beijing. Then they departed again.

A while after they were gone, I saw a chiseled-faced, broad-shouldered compact young man looking to be in his 20s striding toward me. Turned off by his rude piercing stares and commanding mien, I looked away.

"Hi," he addressed me tersely. With his sharp gaze and jaw pointing to a direction ahead, he continued, "You see the two carts over there? Move your things to the cart behind."

Although I knew he must be one of the boys that we were going to live with from now on, at his peremptory demeanor and abruptness with me, I didn't move or respond. I said to myself, do I know you? Who are you to give me orders?

With Wang Yu and Meng Xiaozheng arriving and beginning to move the luggage, I joined them in carrying the luggage to the cart where three boys and a graceful pretty girl were sitting.

At the sight of equal numbers of four boys and four girls, I said to myself, our future lives are already planned out for us. Am I enjoined to form a family with one of the boys?

In a while, a tall, lanky, mirthless country man with droopy eyes and a crane-neck approached us. Drily addressing himself as "Carter Wang", he told us he was here to pick us up.

We were finally on our way. It was a long ride southward. As we left civilization farther and farther behind, we found ourselves driven across a vast wilderness.

While some were chattering and others were lounging in the toasty sun, the young man seated next to Carter Wang who had come to speak to me was the only one fully alert and in charge. He exchanged a few words with Carter Wang from time to time. Ensconcing at the end of the cart, I occupied myself with the scenery: The sky was azure blue. The ripe crops were basking in the sun's golden rays. The earthy scenes reminded me of Millet's paintings—same earthy colors, same vast expanse, and same rural solitude and serenity.

Out of boredom, Carter Wang began to hum a ditty:

> *"Beidahuang, the 'Great Northern Wilderness',*
> *Indeed is a place of desolation and barrenness,*
> *Where rabbits and wolves run rampant,*
> *The sight of young maidens is absent..."*

We were instantly drawn to his humming, all sitting up and tuning in.

Carter Wang turned out to be a temperamental, talkative man. Without much prodding, he readily pattered out things about Beidahuang that came to his mind at the moment—that the ancestors of the villagers were from Shandong, fleeing from the famine three generations ago, that we arrived in the midst of a harvest season, and that summer, which was here now, lasted about two months while the winter here would linger for about half of a year, with the average low temperature from December to February at -22 Fahrenheit (-30 Celsius) that "can freeze off your cock if you take a crap outdoors for too long". As city folks, we were entertained by his raw terms and his tale about his close encounter with a bear. At our inquiries, Carter Wang said, "Bears usually don't stray into this area. But, if you do run into one, don't run like a chicken. Walk away slowly. If he's right behind you, don't turn your neck. He'd lick your face off…"

In a couple of more hours, we arrived at a vast open expanse. A cluster of mud houses gradually emerged from the horizon. With his whip, Carter Wang made a sweeping motion and said, "Look! This is it. This is where you are going to settle for life and where we have settled for generations. We were born here, live here and will die here. We've got no choice. We live the earth and eat the earth. Too bad you students from Beijing with so much ink in your bellies have to spend your lives digging the earth with us."

Before long, we were already breathing in the smell of the fresh hay and fermented manure heaped in the open lot, knowing we were already within the vicinity of the village where we were to settle down.

Into the village, at the sight of a mud courtyard, Carter Wang told us that we had arrived at the headquarters of the branch production brigade. Upon entering, a row of mud rooms, and a sheep pen, a pigsty and stables surrounding the other three sides came into view.

We got off the cart and began unloading. While we were taking things out of the cart, we found ourselves surrounded by excited chirping little children and grinning village elders, addressed as the "students from Beijing" with admiration and reverence as if we were some distinguished guests who deigned to set foot among them. Apparently, our arrival was a big event in their quiet, uneventful life. At our inquiries, they told us that all able bodies were still working in the fields and that they would return soon.

Not long after we unloaded and washed the dust off ourselves, the peasants were back from their work. At the sight of us city folks, the villagers were overjoyed to have us there as if it were their honor to have people from Beijing to settle among them.

Since junior high school, we all had experienced country life being sent down annually to the countryside during harvest season for "labor education" and "thought reform". Settling in the country was not much of an adjustment for us except the toilet, which was a hole dug in the ground surrounded by mud walls or corn and sorghum stalks with flies buzzing around and maggots wriggling in the mixture of feces, blood and urine. The sight and stench were unbearable. You had to hold your nose and come out as soon as possible. After you came out, you still carried the stink with you for a long time.

Sent here as unwanted people, we thought we would encounter some form of discrimination and hostility. At what we received, we were simply thrilled. Evidently, the villagers in this remote area were largely unaffected by the Cultural Revolution. Locked in their own simple life, mindset and judgment, they were indifferent to the party's agenda, displaying no class hatred or even class consciousness. To them, we were simply human beings like them.

At night, almost the entire village turned out to welcome us at the branch production brigade's meeting room. Li Dayin, the boy who had spoken to me, was delegated to take charge of our group. While the boys were assigned to lodge in the brigade's meeting room, we four girls were sent to stay with an aged widower, Lao Yin (Old Yin), and his three children, about 15 minutes walking distance from the branch brigade center. Like his countrymen, the brigade leader Wang was generous and congenial. He gave us three days off to get ready for our new life there.

The first day after we had breakfast at the branch brigade center, Li Dayin gathered us together and dispensed cooking duty, assigning a girl and a boy as a cooking unit. I wasn't happy to learn that I was to cook with Li Dayin, the boy who had left me with a bad first impression.

Afterward, Wang Yu, Meng Xiaozheng and I decided to stroll around to get ourselves familiarized with the environment. Since the post office was what mattered most to us, we went there first.

When we arrived there, we noticed layers of still fresh public execution notices posted all over outside the mud building, which indicated that every once in a while, there were people executed for being a "counterrevolutionary" or for having committed some major crime such as killing or raping a minor. The so-called "counterrevolutionaries" executed were merely locals attempting to sneak over the borders to a neighboring country—the Soviet Union, North Korea or Mongolia where life seemed more livable, seen from afar.

"Heck!" Riled by the sight, Wang Yu grouched, "Even in this wretched place, they won't leave you alone!"

Originally, the secret reason behind our decision to settle in this remote place was the chance to flee the country as our last resort when the situation worsened. The sight of execution notices for simply attempting to flee the borders dashed our hope.

"Thank God," Meng Xiaozheng commented. "We're not desperate, forced to take the drastic step like those unfortunate souls. Well, as the saying goes, 'The sky is high and the emperor is far away'. Since this place is far out of the reach of Emperor Mao, I guess we can settle down for now."

The next day, not long after we finished our breakfast at the brigade center, our door was pushed open. A big, tall, authority-looking minatory figure stepped in as if he owned this place. At the sight, we all tensed up, wondering who he was and what he came here for. The peace and ease we felt were instantly gone.

Menacingly addressing himself as "Party Secretary Liu of the *entire* production brigade", he demanded us to disclose our personal background while pacing, eyeing and gauging each of us with a threatening look.

We had barely felt relieved at escaping the situation where we had been treated as sub-humans. At this command, we instantly cringed and felt we were back in Beijing again.

Just as we were feeling edgy, to our surprise, Li Dayin walked up to Liu with a nod of acknowledgement. Ignoring the tense moment and Liu's intimidating posture, Li Dayin took out a packet of cigarettes he brought from Beijing. Offering Liu one and stuffing the remaining packet into Liu's eager hand, Li Dayin took one out of another packet. Lighting the cigarettes for Liu and himself with a cigarette lighter, with a puff, Li Dayin deftly chatted Liu up like an old acquaintance.

Thus having the hostile Liu disarmed, Li Dayin turned to us and gesticulated, "OK, folks. Report your family backgrounds to Secretary Liu."

Already a captive of a packet of cigarettes brought from Beijing, at our answers, Liu hemmed and hawed, and swiftly excused himself.

At his abrupt exit, we all burst into laughter, amused by the comical scene, feeling fortunate to have Li Dayin as our leader.

"Dayin," said Li Weilin, a bespectacled handsome, scholarly-looking boy. "I didn't know you could smoke. I've never seen you smoke before."

"I don't smoke although I can," Li Dayin explained. "The cigarettes were brought for situations like this."

We nodded in awe of his maturity to be able to anticipate situations like this and be prepared, and handle it deftly and resourcefully.

Looking pensive, Li Dayin broke the silence and said, "Folks, there are things we need to talk about."

In our eyes, Li Dayin had earned our respect by the way he handled things. At his words, we were all ears.

"Since we are going to spend the rest of our life here together," Li Dayin began. "There are things that need to be straightened out beforehand." Pausing, he then resumed, "As non-proletarian descendants, we all have experienced discrimination, being treated as sub-humans. Here, we don't have to live like that. We don't need to perpetuate the Communist agenda of class struggle, class label and class hatred, and straitjacket ourselves with it. Here, we are all equal human beings. No one is superior to anyone else. Everyone here should feel free and be allowed to be him- or herself. We will not tolerate any form of bullying. For our own well-being, we need to set this tone for our life here. We should learn to get along with one another and make the most of our life here."

Having lived as a subhuman for so long, at his words, I was very relieved and felt fortunate to be spending our life here with someone who spoke the same language and spoke the truth so daringly and unambiguously, glad to have him take charge of our life here. Like a wind that cleared up the clouds, Li Dayin's unexpected words swept away my bad first impression of him.

The first day of our work there, we were taken to a field 18 miles away to harvest soybeans.

The crops were about a foot high. We had to bend almost 135 degrees to cut them. At 5'8", with a slim, stiff build and particularly long legs, I had to bend my knees to do the job. After a while, my knees started to stagger. However, seeing everyone ahead of me, including Jin Ping, the girl two years younger than I right at the heels of the men, I was anxious to catch up. But, no matter how hard I tried, I was unable to keep up, being left farther and farther behind.

When I stretched up again, I found them already out of sight of the undulating field and myself left behind alone in the quiet field. Irritated and dejected, I cast aside the sickle and threw myself onto the field.

While I was simmering in anger, I heard some rustling. I sat up and found someone helping me cut the soybeans. It was Li Dayin. He was on his second row back already, even ahead of the peasants. A large area ahead of me had been cut.

We had never talked to each other before. This time, he didn't say anything to me either, not even glancing at me. A warm feeling rose within me. In shame, I picked up my sickle and resumed my left-behind work.

Ashamed of what I did in the soy field, when we returned to the branch brigade center, I was very alert of signs of disrespect from my teammates. But what I overheard from the boys' talk relaxed me. They were joking benevolently to allude to what had happened in the soy field and seemed to be drawing much fun out of my act. At their magnanimity, I was relieved, feeling like a pampered little sister.

After dinner, Wang Yu, Meng Xiaozheng and Jin Ping tarried at the branch brigade center as usual. Ever since the rape, I had been like a wounded doe, hurt and highly alert, watching out for sign of danger and keeping my distance from all. With my history, I felt intensely inferior and insecure around people. I wanted to go back to our own lodging to avoid contact with people. But, with Jin Ping wanting to be with her boyfriend Li Weilin and Wang Yu and Meng Xiaozheng having fun there, I remained.

Although Wang Yu, Meng Xiaozheng and I came together, the distance latent between them and me was presenting itself now. Initially, we were bonded by our comparable family background, similar outlook and love of classic literature. But the deep mark left by my debasing experience set me apart from all. I was unable to relate to them in reality. Although Wang Yu and Meng Xiaozheng got to know each other through me, they now had bypassed me and become close friends. In their eyes, I was probably just a wretched younger sister that they took pity on and took along with. With them mainly communicating between themselves, I was pretty much alone. At their clear distance, I became even more insecure about myself and about my secret being divulged by them.

Knowing they had no intention to leave any time soon and feeling intensely uncomfortable around people, I decided to go by myself.

Before I left for our own lodging, I cleaned myself at the branch brigade center as usual. When I was going to brush my teeth, Li Dayin came to me. Pointing to my toothbrush, he said, "Long Qiru, your tooth-brush is too big and hard. It's not good for the gums. Besides, you brush your teeth too vigorously. It hurts the gums." It was the first time that any of the boys ever communicated with me. At his words, I became aware that I was being observed. To avoid more attention, I hurriedly finished the cleaning.

I was finally on my way. Once by myself, I felt relaxed.

Walking alone on the boundless stretch of grassland with an unimpeded view of the night sky, I noticed for the first time that the night sky where millions of stars seemed to hang low looked like a dark vault. I was awed at how vast and mighty the universe was and how insignificant we humans were. At the millions of the stars hanging alone revolving along their own orbits that rarely intercept with other constellations, I realized we were all alone like the stars, as Maupassant depicted in his short story *Solitude*. Having thus reconciled to being alone, I decided to bear and embrace loneliness, and appreciate the solitude and serenity that were brought about only by being alone.

Since then, I walked to our lodging by myself almost every night.

We went back to Lao Yin's home only to sleep. It was like an unpleasant dormitory, inhibiting and inconvenient. The Yin family had to squeeze in on one row of "*kang*" so as to vacate the opposite row to accommodate us four. The Yins led a dull and subdued life. In a world devoid of entertainment and a household where exchanges were limited to just a few words, all their comfort was sleeping. They retired to bed very early. By the time we returned, they had fallen fast asleep, which made the situation even more inhibiting and us even more aware of our imposition on them. It was hard to imagine this as a long-term arrangement.

After some days, Wang Yu spoke to the branch brigade leader about relocation. He responded readily, "No problem! City folks have their own way of life. I'll send people to empty the meeting room to accommodate you there."

With the boys occupying the center room next to the kitchen, we moved into the innermost room of this row-structured building at night. The eight of us settled down.

At bedtime, at puppies' whimpering outside our window, I put on my clothes and went out to look for them. Under the flash light, I saw several puppies curl up together, shivering in the cold by the foot of our window. Full of pity for them, I picked them up in a basket and brought them in. They kept whimpering.

"Damn it," Wang Yu snapped. "Can we get some sleep?" She turned on the light, put on her clothes and went out to dump the puppies somewhere away from our place.

At her rough act that seemed to suggest her slight for me, I sank into my quiet grief at my inferior status and at the puppies pitilessly left to die in the cold that reminded me of the brutal puppies-slaying scene in Turgenev's *Mu Mu*.

In the still night, Wang Yu's words could be heard clearly by everyone. But no one intervened. Nevertheless, ever since then, the boys all had begun treating me gallantly as if I were their little sister that needed their protection and special care. Li Dayin seemed to be paying more attention to me. Although he never said anything to me, I felt his probing eye.

Once after dinner, Li Dayin claimed that he could tell fortunes and proceeded to do so. The girls were all drawn in, eagerly to have their fate predicted.

At Meng Xiaozheng's turn, Li Dayin commented, "Meng Xiaozheng, your forehead is full, and your jaw is broad and round. You are blessed with a lady's fate."

Reluctantly dragged into it, at each of Li Dayin's accurate tales, I shuddered inwardly, worried about my secret being detected.

When it was my turn, Li Dayin looked me in the eyes and said, "Long Qiru, you were born with an aristocratic maiden's body but a maid's fate…"

I was jolted by these unexpected words. It was too late for me to withdraw. Gazing at me, Li Dayin went on calmly and reservedly, "Long Qiru, your pupils are large. It's a sign of honesty. You don't know how to lie. Your eyes will betray you…"

Disarmed, I panicked. My head spun. Pausing and observing me intently, Li Dayin went on, "Long Qiru, I can tell you have a tragic lot. You are fated to have a rough and bumpy life beginning from your mid-teens…"

I almost broke down.

Seeing my eyes brimming full of tears, Hu Xingfu, a kind, cheerful diminutive boy, nudged Li Dayin. "Dayin," he whispered. "Enough. Stop here."

As if talking to no one, Hang Shiren, a comical-looking boy with droopy eyes and a large, hooked bony nose nicknamed "Long Man" for his well above 6-feet height, remarked slowly and casually, "Don't listen to his nonsense. He's a charlatan, selling snake oil."

"OK," waving his arm as if he were a referee, Li Weilin ruled. "Let's change the topic!"

I was rescued.

꧁꧂

For the first time in our life, we were permanently away from our own families and took control of our own lives. We were quite content with our new life here entirely free from the class labels that we had carried with us for so long. We no longer cared about politics, but our own immediate interest. We worked hard, but nothing made us feel that we were less of a human being. Having similar backgrounds and outlooks, we didn't need to be on guard anymore. We got along like a big family. Cut off from the outside world, away from class warfare and pandemonium, we felt as if we were experimenting with utopian ideal, trying to create our own land of happiness. Despite the hardships, this settlement unexpectedly turned out to be a respite in a land that was plagued with hatred and political insanity.

For years, I had not breathed the air freely. Now I felt completely liberated and left alone. It was the happiest times in my life since the Cultural Revolution.

One day, it was Li Dayin's and my turn to cook again. It was the second time we worked together.

Since we had become acquainted with each other, we struck up a conversation this time. It was our first communication. I found that behind his tough looks, he had a sharp mind, pointed views and a high literary appreciation.

The first time we cooked together, it was Li Dayin who took charge. To prove myself not some pampered "aristocratic maiden" incapable of daily household tasks that they perceived, I offered to take charge this time.

We had been dieting daily on coarsely cracked cornmeal, stir-fried potato slices and pickled Napa cabbage soup. The meals were uninspiring. But our situation was much better than that of the majority of the sent-down youths, for the area that we were sent to has rich soil and produces high-yields. At least, we could fill our bellies, unlike those who had to endure constant hunger.

To make my folks happy, I decided to make something different from what we had day in and day out. With the only materials being potatoes and eggs, I made a whole basin of potato-and-egg salad and French Fries.

All the while, Li Dayin just watched me indulgingly without saying anything. Till I finished my work, he remarked casually, "Long Qiru, we have used up our entire month of oil ration."

I felt like a fool. With my act, the image of me being an "aristocratic maiden" not only wasn't changed, but enhanced instead. I said to myself, it's only the beginning of the second week into our settlement here. Without oil, what are we going to do for the rest of the month? Why didn't he tell me about this ration earlier and stop me from making myself a fool?

Li Dayin didn't seem to be concerned. When the branch brigade leader returned from the fields, he spoke to him and had the problem resolved deftly. We were allotted with another bottle of oil.

At the dinner table, at the sight of the salad, an unfamiliar Western dish, my teammates looked subdued. Seeing them silently consuming the alien course I made, I was very embarrassed.

The second time we had something different was a chance occasion.

That day, we stopped working at noontime thanks to the downpour. Since Day One we started working, we had not had any time off. As peasants, we didn't have the luxury of weekends. We worked all the time. We were happy to have this unexpected time off for ourselves to take care of our delayed personal business, writing letters to family and friends and washing our garments.

Li Weilin went out to take a walk in the heavy downpour. Half an hour later, came Li Weilin's spirited shouting at the door, "Folks! Look what I've got from the roadside!"

We all bounced up at his words and saw Li Weilin walk in with several ducks in his hands. At the sight, we burst out in loud hoorays.

"Golly, where did you get these fat babies?" Long Man Hang Shiren asked, displaying unusual zeal.

"They are gifts from heaven," Li Weilin replied. "They were just killed by the torrential cold rain."

With great zest, the girls all chipped in, plucking feathers, cleaning, chopping and cooking. We made a huge stew. Breathing in the luscious meaty cooking aroma, we were never before as thrilled.

The dinner was like a celebration. We stuffed ourselves with plenty of succulent, delicious duck meat until our stomachs were unable to contain anymore.

After our stomachs were overfilled that night, we experienced an inglorious anti-climax. Branch Party Secretary Li arrived, informing us that those ducks belonged to a peasant who had graciously accepted his loss. We felt terrible about what we had done inadvertently to the poor peasant who was more in need of money and nutrition.

With those witty, free-spirited, fun-loving boys around, not one day we spent there was dull.

One late afternoon, while we were back from work washing off sweat and dust in the yard, Li Weilin was chasing a pig, attempting to drive him back to the pigsty. The pig was incredibly fast and smart. He seemed to be teasing Li Weilin. Each time when Li Weilin was about to catch him, he would slip away and wait ahead as if goading Li Weilin to chase on. We all looked on, drawing much fun out of it.

Tired of the chase, Li Weilin was about to stop. Just as he was slowing down, Long Man Hang Shiren began to cite Mao's quotation in an indifferent tone, not looking at Li Weilin, "Hold out a little longer. The victory is within sight in the last, unremitting effort."

At this seemingly unintended deadpan effect and Hang Shiren's comical look with his jutting Adam's apple bobbing under the skin, we all doubled up, bursting into hysterical laughter, entertained by the comical scene and the irreverent, mocking citation. Long Man often entertained us with his witty, sarcastic citation of Mao's words and the party's line at the most unexpected moment.

Around dinnertime, we found Hu Xingfu, the boy who was assigned to herd a flock of sheep, still out of sight. As time went by, we began to worry. The boys went out to look for him, but found him nowhere near.

Sometime around 9 p.m. we heard the sheep's bleating and Hu Xingfu's spirited hollering attempting to drive the sheep into the pen. We all jumped up to greet him. Hu Xingfu turned up with the flock unharmed and in his usual high spirit.

"What happened, chap?" Li Weilin inquired.

Before Hu Xingfu could answer, Long Man Hang Shiren got in, "We thought you were in the belly of a bear already."

"No way!" Hu Xingfu responded with a loud chuckle, "I'm too young to become meal." When he saw the set table, his eyes brightened up. Breaking into a broad grin, he exclaimed, "Are you still waiting for me? Let's sit down and eat first!"

The dinner table was set long ago. We quickly sat down and devoured the food, eager to relish Hu Xingfu's story. After wolfing down some mouthfuls to suppress the hunger, Hu Xingfu's story came out.

"Guess what?" he said, "Bears? I didn't have the luck to run into any. But wolves, there were plenty! On my way back, I lost the direction. Before I could find my way back, the sun had already set. Soon it turned dark. At night, there was no recognizable terrain in the pasture. It all looked the same! As I was trying to find any familiar landmarks in this indistinct dark wilderness, I suddenly found a pack of wolves following us at a distance. Their eyes were like bright red lights glowing in the dark. It was really scary! I said to myself, I've weathered through the big waves of the Cultural Revolution. I won't allow myself to capsize in this small ditch. I will not die here! But the sheep didn't listen to me anymore. They whined and moved about piteously. To calm them down and keep them together, I knew I had to remain calm. I kept walking and calming them. Just as I was worried about how to keep the persistent wolves at bay and thought I would have to wander the entire night away, I saw lights from afar and knew we were safe!"

That night, the dinner tasted especially good, spiced up with Hu Xingfu's delicious story and other tall tales.

In and out of the fields, we had developed a rapport with the peasants. Some often stopped by to check on us and lend us a hand. Among them was Li Shu, the teenage son of a deceased landlord.

It was our first close contact with the rural landlord class, demonized and treated as the "worst" and the "most evil" in the Communist classification. Contrary to the images created by the Communists, Li Shu was the nicest, the most intelligent and the most industrious among the villagers. He was a handsome sunny boy, with a pair of disarmingly gentle, smiling eyes, white teeth and pinkish fair skin. He liked to hang around with us and often did things for us no one else had thought about, unobtrusively dropping off firewood for us and filling our water vat. Although abstractly called "*zhezi* "("warped", a term used by the locals for a landlord's offspring), he was in fact well-liked by the villagers for his fine qualities. In contrast, the least liked were the poorest peasants who were often the dullest and the laziest.

Among the villagers, there were two orphans taken care of by the production team. The older one was a 9-year-old pretty girl with a pair of large, hauntingly beautiful, expectant and melancholy doe eyes while the younger one was a humble, quiet boy of 7. They were often seen holding hands strolling around in quiet contentment. Although they themselves seemed content, their situation broke my heart. I knew it was wishful thinking, but I wished I could adopt the girl and provide a home for her. Though I wanted to do something to help them, all I could do was to talk to them whenever I ran into them, hoping this small gesture could add a little warmth to their lonely life.

Mother and father

Sister (back left), mother, two grandmothers, brother
Ciqing (front), Cousin Xu Jian, and me

My nieces Peining, Peiyi, and me

Wang Yu (front left), Yang Ju, Yang Yuhe, Jingming,
Kong Xiangqi, Wang Yu's mother (back left), Meng
Xiaozheng, me, father, mother and Weng Rulian

Me, Shen Xiaoping and Chen Ting

Weng Rulian, Shen Xiaoping and me

Chen Ting, me, Weng Rulian and Shen Xiaoping

Me (front left), Chen Ting, Shen Xiaoping and Weng
Rulian before Weng Rulian's departure from Beijing

Wang Ying, Chen Ting, Weng Rulian and me seeing
Weng Rulian off at Beijing Railway Station

me

Me (front left), Jennifer and Li Xianglin

Me and Jennifer

Me(left) and Lynn

My son

Me becoming a teacher

Me and my fellow teacher Yin Li

me

Me (left). Peining, mother, sister

Me

Me

Mother and me

Ciqing (back left), Tiemin, Peining, me, mother, sister, Peiyi and son

Me, son and mother the day before I left China

Me, the day before my school began in America

Me and my co-worker Chen Hong

Me and my co-worker Sasha

My landlord Nino Altamura and wife Angela and classmate Eileen

Brian Lee's son, Little Tiger, and me

Son, after he arrived in America

Son and me in the backyard of our first home ever

SANCTURY ENDS

Located inland at about 50 degrees latitude north, some fifteen degrees shy of the Arctic Circle, at the end of September, this place already felt the imminence of winter. With the temperature fast dropping close to the freezing point, we had to race against time, working 18 hours a day to gather in all the crops as well as large quantities of dry plants enough for heating and cooking for the long, cold winter ahead. Now that all the crops were harvested and winter was getting closer by the day, we had to work even harder, threshing grains day and night at the branch brigade center. The original 13-hour workday extended to 18 hours now stretched to 20 hours. We took turns at eating and at stealing a few hours of sleep. Sometimes, we were so exhausted that while we were still working, we would fall asleep on our feet. The intense work brought us urban youths and peasants all together and made us feel that we were a big family and cared about each other like brothers and sisters. Though we were exhausted physically, we felt blessed and blissful.

Before we knew it, it was already December, bitterly cold. We seldom saw a clear sun. When it came out, it was often pale, hazy, accompanied with tiny snow pellets sprinkling down continuously. To resist the cold, we put on almost all the clothes we had. Underneath our thickly padded cotton uniform allocated to us before our departure from Beijing, we layered ourselves with every-thing we had—wool or cotton turtleneck, sweater, sweat pants... Even thus equipped, staying outdoors for some mere minutes, we would feel the sting in our faces and foreheads and the pain in our numbed toes and finger tips. With our nose hair frosted, breathing would be like breathing through a valve. At each blink of the eye, our eyelashes would stick together. The moisture that came out of our nostrils and mouths would freeze stiff whatever we used to cover our mouths and noses with. Wrapping my head and neck twice with the long, thick wool scarf Mother knit for me, I left only my eyes and forehead exposed.

One afternoon, when the weather permitted, Wang Yu, Meng Xiaozheng and I were assigned to turn over the huge heap of manure outside the branch brigade center. The surface of it had frozen to about three feet deep. We had to dig from underneath.

Suddenly, something very heavy hit my left calf from behind. Before I realized what happened, I found myself already kneeling on the ground of the narrow passage between the turned and the untouched heaps. My left lower leg was buried under a large frozen chunk. I shrieked in pain, unable to get up. Wang Yu and Meng Xiaozheng carried me back to our room immediately.

The commune's "*chijiao yisheng*" ("barefoot doctor"—local paramedic with very limited basic medical training) arrived. At the sight of him applying some suspicious-looking, non-alcoholic yellow solution to my leg, I inquired. The man puffed up his chest and answered, "It was sulfur solution". We knew sulfur could do nothing to ease the conditions of my leg that had no open wound but almost unbearable sharp pain. At his reply, we exchanged a sarcastic look at one another and held our tongue out of politeness. After he left, we burst out laughing at the quack's prescription, hoping the injury was not serious.

That night, I could hardly sleep. The next morning, Li Dayin came to me. Upon a moment of observation of me, he said, "Long Qiru, there're dark circles under your eyes. Obviously, you didn't sleep well. If you can't bear the pain, just scream and wake us up."

I smiled and didn't say anything. I knew I was perceived delicate and fragile. But what they didn't see was my self-respect and resolve underneath my looks. Everyone thought it was just a superficial injury.

After three days, my leg didn't show any sign of improvement. On the contrary, it bulged up to the size of a bruised log. At the worsened sight, they realized it was serious. The branch brigade leaders decided to take me to Qiqihar, the nearest big city some scores of miles south, for treatment.

When the moon was still high in the sky, we were already on our way. At each jolt of the cart, Carter Li and Li Dayin would pull and tuck the blankets and fur coats to make sure I was properly covered. Though the temperature was low, I was wrapped in their care and warmth, feeling like a baby under mother's meticulous care. At noon, we arrived at the hospital.

When I was carried into the hospital on a stretcher, the medical worker in the emergency room stopped us. "Wait here," he ordered. "What family is she from?"

Before I could give an answer, Branch Brigade Leader Wang already shouted out, "Poor peasant!"

I was taken in right away.

Amused by the scene, I asked myself, do I look like a peasant? What if I weren't a peasant? Would I be kicked out like those unfortunate people who were denied medical treatment on account of their status and backgrounds? Many sick people were literally pushed out of the hospital because of their status and backgrounds. Wang Yu's father was rejected for his "ex-rightist" status when he needed urgent care. Li Dayin's father was turned away when he had chest pain due to his doubly disadvantaged status of being a Nationalist Youth League member and an "ex-rightist", and left to die. Luckily, a strong character, Li Dayin's father survived with the aspirins they had at home.

When I was transferred to an examination bed, someone accidentally bumped into my broken leg. I shrieked in pain and found myself leaning on the chest of Li Dayin, who happened to stand behind me. It was then that I realized what he meant to me—I was in love with him. Feeling his chest rising and falling strenuously, I knew he was stirred up by my unexpected revealing act and struggling to regain his normal state.

Empathetic with my pain, the doctor started chanting Mao's quotation devoutly and repeatedly, arms hammering in rhythm with his chant, "Toughen up, give all and conquer all to win!"

At this citation, we all burst into uncontrollable laughter. What an amusing scene, I thought to myself. According to the Communists, Mao's teaching can lead to victories in everything, whether it is sports or production. His *Little Red Book* is also used as a weapon to deter enemies and defend territories. Do they truly believe Mao is universally revered and that his words, the so-called "*zhisheng fabao* (all-conquering magic weapon)", could dictate the entire universe as well?

The X-ray showed my broken and dislocated tibia and fibula. At this diagnosis, I said to Li Dayin shyly, "You see? I'm not as fragile as you think. It's been proved…"

"You are fragile," Li Dayin contradicted me. "Had this happened to Wang Yu or Meng Xiaozheng or even Jin Ping, it might not be like this. Their bones might not be broken."

I blushed at these unexpected abrupt remarks, regretting my foolish attempt to change people's perception of me.

Back in our village, all I could do was to rely on my resilience.

My injury made me the center of attention. I became the concern of everyone. My teammates and Carter Li checked on me all the time. My injury also made the good peasants very uneasy as if it were their fault. Every day, some villagers would stop by to find out how I was doing. Like a big sister, without a murmur, Meng Xiaozheng shouldered all the trouble of helping me go through daily life, taking great pains to take care of me every way—bringing me meals and water for drinking and cleaning; and emptying and cleaning the basin I used as a night chamber… Every night, she would vigorously rub my body head to toe with a hot towel to make sure I was in good hygiene.

At their care, especially that of Meng Xiaozheng, I was choked full of emotions and gratitude, ill at ease for burdening them.

Days later, Branch Brigade Leader Wang decided that it was in my best interest to put me in my own family's care. I was on my way home accompanied by Wang Yu and Meng Xiaozheng.

At the train station, I was again stopped and questioned about my family background. After examining the certificate provided by the branch brigade that listed my background as "poor peasant" and reason for traveling, I was admitted to the train. Wang Yu and Meng Xiaozheng, who carried the stretcher escorting me back, were also allowed to board the train.

When I caught sight of Mother and my brother Ciqing at the Beijing Railway Station, I was excited to be reunited with my family again. At my sight, Mother's eyes moistened.

"I don't know whether to believe in fate or not," she uttered as if musing out to herself, tears welling up in her eyes. "But one after another, all the misfortunes seem to befall you alone! When you left, you had a pair of good legs, but now you may become crippled…"

Mother's words drew out my fatalistic feeling too. I was acutely aware of the possibility of becoming handicapped forever. Nevertheless, immunized by the rape and its aftermath, I had learned to live with adversities. I didn't allow myself to think too much. Dwelling on misery doesn't serve any purpose.

Having stayed and lived as peasants for almost four months, back in Beijing, we felt like strangers breaking into others' home. Things here were completely different from what we were used to in the countryside. Alienated and trivialized, we were keenly aware we were no longer part of the scene. We especially felt so when we were at Jishuitan Hospital, where the best orthopedists were concentrated. Refined and distinguished looking, the doctors seemed beyond our reach. Life went on. Now we had become unwelcome outsiders in our own hometown, some refugees seeking shelter and assistance in Beijing.

What made it worse was the thickly-padded midnight-blue uniform we wore—trademark of country settlers. Each time when we were on our way to and from the hospital, it would warrant tons of attention, sympathy or disdain. Some petty city folks felt superior to us, derisively calling us "*Chadui de* (country transplants)", or worse, chiding us and telling us to "go back" to where we "belong".

At the snobbery and disdain, we became defiant. Whenever we went out, we would put on the uniform. Let them laugh, we said to ourselves. Yes, we are the lowly urban exiles. Our social standing is even lower than those who were sent to the production and construction corps and state-run farms since we are not on the state payroll like them. We have none of the benefits that they receive. We have no income, no pension, no rations, no weekend, no vacation time and no uniforms. Other than this purchased uniform and hand-to-mouth food, we have nothing. And worse, our prospect is to become a downright peasant. But we have earned our right to exist, to identify ourselves and demonstrate our right to exist among them. Our uniform is our badge of honor.

In the slack season, Li Dayin was sent back to visit me. I was delighted to see him. Having lived and worked day and night and gone through thick and thin with them for almost four months, I had missed the collective and all. A good story-teller, Li Dayin regaled me with his vivid accounts of their life there. From there, our talk would extend to a wider range of topics: literature, philosophy, history, politics, and arts. Li Dayin was witty and infectious. Every word of his meant so much to me.

He visited me every other day. Each time, I couldn't wait for him to come. What I didn't know was that each time he visited me he would have to extricate himself from the crowd that was gathering in his home almost daily.

Once, Li Dayin arrived with a record player and a few records of classical music. In those years, cultural life was virtually absent, except songs composed of Mao's quotations broadcast daily through the loudspeakers installed in the streets and the eight "revolutionary model plays" broadcast daily over the radio. Since we had lost our records of classical music in the raid, the only source of classical music for me was from Voice of America, which was jammed, barely audible. Living in a spiritual desert for so long, I had missed classical music terribly. I was thrilled at this pleasant surprise.

After closing all the doors and windows, Li Dayin hung a thick blanket on the window of my bedroom to block the sound from leaking out, and turned the volume of the record player to the lowest possible setting.

There weren't many pieces, only Tchaikovsky's *Swan Lake*, and Drdla's *Serenade* and *Reminiscence*. The familiar music brought back my memories of the long-lost world—the largely gentle and civil past when love, innocence, and human dignity were still allowed to exist. My heart melted in the emotion-dredging music.

When the music was over, Li Dayin put away the records and the record player, and left my bedroom. I overheard him speak to Lu Ma.

When he returned, he closed the door behind him. This unusual act at once filled me with apprehension, alerting me that the inevitable moment was finally here.

Sitting on an armchair a desk away from me, Li Dayin however remained silent, seemingly struggling at breaking the silence. His tenseness only made me even more apprehensive. For a long while, he didn't open his mouth, letting the atmosphere simmer. As the silence continued, my heart pounded harder and harder and my feelings surged higher and higher to the point that I felt I would break down at any moment and throw myself into his arms had he sat right next to me.

Though we were attracted to each other, we never expressed our feelings for each other. He knew it was his strength that captured my heart and that if he showed his "weakness", I might look down upon him. Deeply influenced by Stendhal's work *Red and Black*, we were like the two main characters Julien and Mathilde consciously jostling and measuring strength with each other.

Eventually, Li Dayin broke the silence, uttering in a controlled, slightly quavering strange tone, "Long Qiru, I would like to do something to make you happy."

There was something far more than this simple statement. Astonished by his tone, I turned toward him and met his blazing eyes. I was immediately out of breath. I turned back, heaving strenuously in extreme giddiness. There was an unbearable long silence. Finally, Li Dayin stood up and walked out of the room.

When he returned, the unbearable moment was over. We had both regained our composure. But that moment was lost forever. Li Dayin never pursued it again. We resumed our talk, changing the topic to Tolstoy's *Anna Karenina* that we had just read. At my comment on Anna Karenina's bravery in seeking love and an honest life at the risk of being excluded from her hypocritical high society, Li Dayin interrupted me and demanded, "Look me in the eye, Long Qiru."

I immediately panicked and instinctively lowered my head. My heart began pounding.

"Long Qiru," I heard Li Dayin say. "You are a complicated aggregation of paradoxes. You are the most dogged person I have ever met in seeking truth, ideal and happiness. But, when you face your true love, you run away. Talking about bravery, Long Qiru, you're not brave. You're escaping."

Unprepared to be seen through this easily, I blushed and turned my head away from his dogged, pursuing eyes. He's right, I admitted to myself. My past is preventing me from opening my heart. Deep down, I felt unworthy of him.

Two days later, Li Dayin returned to the branch brigade without saying good-bye to me.

Having waited anxiously for about half a month, I eventually received a letter from him. It was a farewell letter. At the end of the letter, clearly speaking for himself, Li Dayin expressed his regret, "Long Qiru, though you have left this collective forever, you will always occupy a corner in our hearts. We will miss you and cherish every moment you spent with us... Farewell, and take good care of yourself."

It was very touching to learn from others that for a long while after I had left them, at every meal, a pair of spare chopsticks would be placed on the table where I used to sit. There was no doubt that Li Dayin was the one who initiated this to mourn the past.

Two months after Li Dayin's departure, Wang Yu and Meng Xiaozheng were to return too.

Before they left, I asked Meng Xiaozheng to buy me the same beautiful violet blue and white floral nylon gauze scarf that she was wearing to be given to the beautiful orphaned girl there. After their return, in a letter Meng Xiaozheng wrote to me, she related the girl's "indescribable, heartbreaking expression" upon receiving the unexpected gift from me.

Half a year later, rumors arrived about Wang Yu and Meng Xiaozheng's fierce jostle with each other for Li Dayin's attention. Li Dayin chose Meng Xiaozheng, the pretty and even-tempered one. Years later, Li Dayin and Meng Xiaozheng married each other.

At the news, I felt betrayed. It was my first love at the tender age of 19. I was hurt. It was evident that I was not as worthy as others. Nevertheless, having built up a wall to protect myself from being hurt, I convinced myself that this kind of man who didn't stick to his original pursuit was not worth seeking.

They remained in Beidahuang till 1973, when the party decided to open the college doors wider from the selected few with trusted backgrounds beginning in 1970 to taking in more people with a worker, peasant and soldier background. Some with an "OK" background who had proved themselves to be obedient and of some use to the party were also picked. Li Dayin's classmate, Feng Zhiqiang, a tall, handsome, sunny boy with a bright smile and honest eyes who was in charge of the Beijing settlers in adjacent branch production brigade, was chosen to represent us 16 settlers of the entire production brigade. This return to a city life caused a huge stir among the sent-down youths everywhere. With some having some connections returning to the city also, it turned into a wave of return nationwide. Those who didn't have the connection had to bribe their way out or sell their bodies as an exchange for permission to return.

My teammates were all able to return to Beijing through a back-door connection: Meng Xiaozheng became an English-speaking clerk working for Beijing International Post Office. Wang Yu returned as a factory worker. Later on in the 1990s, the once fiery, cynical and fiercely irreverent girl and a staunch Anti-Communist who had been drawn to radical ideas such as Robespierre and Jacobin Party, the Russian Decembrists and the Russian Populists, turned into a passionate preacher of Christianity. Upon his return, Li Dayin worked as a factory worker for four years. When college examinations were resumed in 1977, he was able to go to college, and became an engineer.

RETURN TO BEIJING

Back in Beijing, I soon felt the effect of living in the dystopian land again.

The 9th Party Congress was convened in April, 1969. With more than 80% of officials purged, Mao's status as the "absolute authority" and his thought as the guiding ideology reinstated, Lin Biao legislated as Mao's successor, and leftists used by Mao in his game against Liu Shaoqi placed in every instrumental position, order was restored to end the anarchy. In 1968, core members of grassroots organizations were taken into custody. Now anyone who had actively participated in the Cultural Revolution so far having been spared found himself arrested or taken into solitary confinement in each institution euphemistically called "study class" to be investigated and account for his deeds during the early stage of the Cultural Revolution. In Beijing alone, hundreds of thousands of college students were investigated, and tens of thousands were arrested and sentenced, while millions of workers nationwide were investigated and even jailed as "*da-za-qiang fenzi* (elements who had vandalized, destroyed and looted the much-hated *dang'an* and other official records)".

My brother Tiemin's friend, Ma Yonglan, a hot-blooded, frustrated young man of working class background with a lowly temporary-worker status for years, saw the opportunity in 1966, when Mao incited that the "proletariat must liberate themselves" and "rebel against the old system". Together with other youths of the same status, he founded the Headquarters of Beijing Workers' Revolt. It soon saw itself grow into a city-wide organization of hundreds of thousands of members. Now he was taken into a "study class" to go through investigation and interrogation. Thanks to his family background and his non-involvement in destroying personnel dossiers, he was released half a year later. Feeling cheated and used, he lost all his faith in Mao and the party. A crushed, bitter man now, to numb himself, he resorted to heavy drinks and poker playing. The boozing worsened the hypertensive condition he contracted during his detention. He died of arteriosclerosis and cerebral hemorrhage in his late 40s.

As the situation was tightened up, massive arrests of criminals and trials and retrials of criminal cases were underway. At the likelihood of having the rape case reopened and the possibility of even being arrested and tried as a "criminal", I was on tenterhooks. Every day, I waited edgily.

One morning, at alarming voices and footsteps in the corridor, I instantly braced myself, knowing they came for me.

Lu Ma opened the door and let in a tall, low-key army man in his early 30s and an older, shorter, unassuming policeman. Although I was prepared, at the sight of the policeman, I was unable to control my composure.

"Long Qiru," the army man stated, "I'm Functionary He, in charge of this neighborhood. This is Comrade Li from the district bureau of public security. He's here to investigate your case. All right. I'll leave it to Comrade Li to handle." He promptly excused himself.

At these words, all of my hard-fought built-up sense of normalcy was gone. I shivered uncontrollably, immediately seeing myself back to being a lesser human being faced with the possibility of becoming a "criminal".

In a calm manner, Li took his notepad out of his attaché case and asked me to give my account of what had happened.

To recall the buried memories was like going through that life again. It dredged up all of my nightmares and shame. Blood burst out of my nostrils. With the not-yet healed scab reopened, I cried at the fresh pain and the new humiliation.

"Sorry," troubled by my inconsolable grief, Li commiserated with me. "It's my duty to go through this."

Li was very gentle, treating me as a normal human being, allowing me time to compose myself and give my account without interruption.

Having had my recount manually recorded, Li was ready to leave. To my dread, before his departure, he told me that he might return for more information.

And he did. The next time he came, he started the new session with a question right away.

"Long Qiru," he asked. "Did you write him a letter?"

Blood at once pumped into my head, pounding it violently and making it spin. In shame, I nodded my head as a reply. Upon the confirmation of my pregnancy, in my suicidal moment, I had indeed written to him. Evidently, the fiend deliberately kept the letter and cowardly turned it in to prove this was not a rape, but a "consensual act".

Incriminated by my own words written in black and white, with an outburst of nose bleeding, I wept harrowingly, overwhelmed by grief and mortification, knowing that I could never redress the wrong to vindicate myself and cleanse myself of the filth, but instead, I would be permanently branded with an indelible mark and nailed together with that low life.

My nose bled from time to time for days. It worsened whenever Li returned for more information. For days, I waited in agony for the case to go away.

For a long while, Li didn't show up. But one day, he turned up unexpectedly.

At the sight, my quivering emotions were all violently stirred up again. Sensing it was about the verdict of the case, I was unable to calm myself down.

Li was in no hurry. He opened his attaché case and took out the file. In a mild but business-like tone, he announced, "Comrade Long Qiru, the case has been finally wrapped up. I'm here to inform you of our findings." Clearing his throat, he proceeded, "We have concluded what happened to you no doubt bore the mark of the times. During that extreme period, dregs surfaced and acted upon the occasion. A lot of young girls were not careful enough and fell victims. But yours was not a rape case. It was not a one-time situation. The relationship was established. Besides, you didn't resist as hard as you should have resisted. You bore the responsibility of protecting yourself. A lot of girls in the same situation would fight to the death to protect their virginity."

Ouch. Tears instantly welled up in my eyes. Having had my innocence robbed of me and life ruined by that low life, and going through the indignity, torment and humiliation all over again only to be informed of this mortifying verdict, I was devastated, unable to reconcile myself to this conclusion. I felt terribly wronged. But it was a fact that I didn't defend myself as hard as those "good girls". I couldn't understand why I was different then. I didn't know it was because I had lived in a well-insulated environment that I had had no need to defend myself and no role models to learn from like those "good girls" who were exposed to harm and acquired defensive mechanisms from their tough environments. For years, I had lived with the wrong done to me, bearing unjust slight, calumny and disdain. Now not only was justice unaddressed, with my fate officially sealed, my case would never be overturned, my name would be permanently sullied and myself irreversibly connected to that low life. At another outburst of nose bleeding, I sobbed irrepressibly.

Patiently and understandingly awaiting me to compose myself, till I finally got hold of myself, Li said, "Long Qiru, sometimes bad things can turn out well, just as Chairman Mao teaches us. A good result may come out of this lesson. You are a big girl now. You should be able to take better care of yourself now. There's still a long way ahead of you. I sincerely hope you can handle things better in the future."

Usually, the term "girl" in China connoted being virgins. At the kind choice of the word, tears gushed out of my eyes again. For years, I had been called a "slut", or at the best, a woman who couldn't guard her virginity. At this belated merciful inclusion and kindness, years of anguish resurged in me. I was consoled by it.

In the end, Li handed me the file and said, "Long Qiru, I need you to sign these papers."

Once again, I saw myself endorse my ignominy with my own hand.

Li left. He no longer visited me. But I remained in this grieving mood for days, unable to get over it.

Each time I struggled to walk out of the shadows, I was hit right back, reminded of my disgrace and my "inferior" character. Like a drowning person, I cried for help. I wrote a letter to my maternal uncle Ke, who cherished me more than his own children, to seek assurance. I had no knowledge that he himself was going through his own much worse ordeals in the ongoing persecution, haunted by the reopened and reexamined old case suspected of being an "imperialist agent" simply for having worked for the United Nations Relief and Rehabilitation Administration before the communist takeover. Less did I know that at the beginning of the Cultural Revolution, he had been hung upside down on a beam and walloped in an attempt to force him to admit to a crime that he did not commit.

Having waited in anxiety for weeks, I eventually received Uncle Ke's letter in the mail.

"Qiru," he wrote. "I apologize for responding so late. Your letter was like a knife piercing my heart. I was unable to get over the pain and address you in a calm manner.

"I treasure the trust you placed in me with your deepest shame. You can rest assured that I will carry your secret to my tomb.

"Among the next generation, you were the only one who seemed to a limitless future. You were the prize and the light of this declined family. To my great grief and disbelief, it was you who fell victim to this upheaval… The terrible image of your being violated haunted me day and night.

"I'm old. I have lived my life and have little regard for my own life. Had it not been the concerns for the family and the children, I would have been long gone. But you are just beginning your young life. A flower not yet in full bloom thus mercilessly trampled on, I don't know how to comfort you. I myself am inconsolable. My hair is graying in just weeks…"

At the pain I caused him and his unreserved, unconditional acceptance, I wept, greatly solaced by the thought that I still meant the same to him, notwithstanding my fall. Although I had disgraced myself, Uncle Ke didn't reject me but accepted me just the same. His anguish and trembling rage soothed my wounds and provided me the needed strength to hold on and to sustain. In those days, his letters served as the only human connection and the only confirmation that I craved for and missed for so long.

When I was still immobile, Functionary He often came to my home and bid me not to go out to "avoid danger". When I began to limp on crutches, he came again one morning.

"Long Qiru," he said. "Come with me to the neighborhood study group. It's good for you."

I had no choice but to toughen myself and go there with him. At the sight of me, a "despicable person" who didn't belong there, the whole room of housewives immediately stirred, muttering disapprovals and shooting me angry looks.

I was rattled by the reactions. Just then, I heard Functionary He's cheerful voice, "Comrades, let's warmly welcome Comrade Long Qiru to join us in our daily studies!" He started to applaud.

At the sparse, reluctant clapping, I was even more discomfited. I sat down at a corner near the exit away from everybody.

I was asked to read Mao's work and take notes of the housewives' gibberish. From then on, reading Mao's works and the newspapers became my daily role, which saved me from having to open my mouth.

One morning months later, Lu Ma told me she ran into Functionary He, who hurriedly informed her of his immediate recall and anxiously asked about me. At the news, I felt relieved for not having to attend the torturous meetings anymore.

❧

As more and more new "enemies" were singled out day after day in the campaign to cleanse the class ranks, the Communists' hands were full. They began to loosen the control over the "class enemies" who had been under their custody for almost three years since the beginning of the Cultural Revolution. With Father's case considered a dead one, not much to be squeezed out anymore, he was allowed to return home.

On notice of Father's release, I went to his college to pick him up on Saturday morning. When Father emerged with his luggage looking like a blithe, innocent child, I rushed to greet him. Clearly, he was transported by the freedom he was tasting now for the first time in three years. Clean-shaven, he looked gaunt, aged and unwell. It grieved me to see such changes.

"Pa!" I greeted him, heart filled with all sorts of emotions.

At my greeting, Father flashed out a rare broad, hearty grin, exposing his perfect specimen white teeth. I took his luggage and led him to the gate.

Before we stepped through the gate, Father suddenly stopped and uttered, "Wait a minute." Turning around, he went back to his wardens, with me in tow. Bowing to them, Father blabbered unctuously, "Comrades, I apologize for the trouble and the inconvenience I caused you to go through for the past three years."

Being locked up for three years for absolutely no reason, Father now was apologizing for the "trouble" and the "inconvenience" of having him locked up. At his act and words, I was shame-faced, beside myself. I squeezed his arm covertly, but he ignored me and continued with his prattles, "What I received is what I deserved for the crimes I committed. I am guilty. I beg the government's forgiveness. I am grateful to the party and the people for practicing revolutionary humanitarianism and for allowing me a second chance to start a new life. I will not disappoint the party and the people's government in reforming myself…"

Exasperated at his customary self-disparaging act, I pinched him hard, chagrined at their toying castigation of him, "Long Xuan, if you don't leave, we'll take you back to confinement!"

With a succession of nodding and bowing, and hemming and hawing, Father finally excused himself.

Smoldering inside, once onto the quiet country road, I screamed at him, "Shame on you for apologizing for being locked up for no reason!"

"What do you expect me to do?" in a pained tone, Father asked.

"Why don't you go back and apologize for your existence and for breathing the same air as well?"

Still peeved and ashamed of being seen with his stultified and contemptible behavior of bowing to strangers, on our way home, I sped up to keep a distance from him, while he tried to keep up with his agonizing inquiries about family members. I ignored him mostly and only answered his persistent questions with a grunt. Once onto the trolley bus, I swiftly disappeared from his sight.

Approaching our stop, I went back to Father to remind him to get off. Once off, I sped up and walked ahead of him.

When I was near our home, little children's angry chants came from behind, "Counterrevolutionary! Counterrevolutionary!" I looked back. It was a group of children not even school age that were taunting Father.

It was the first time that Father ever set foot in the neighborhood of his new home that he had never seen. I wondered how the children figured out Father's political status, perhaps just by his wretched appearance and sorry demeanor. At the time, even children's antennas were up against class enemies. I rushed back to Father's rescue.

"Little friends," with a nervous obsequious smile on his face, Father said edgily. "Don't say such a horrible thing. It's not true!"

"Who's your friend?" They shouted louder, "You are a Counterrevolutionary, a class enemy!" "Counterrevolutionary!" "Counterrevolutionary!" Some even pelted gravel at him. One piece hit Father's eye ridge, immediately causing a lump.

At the little monsters' brazen act bullying a downed elder, I flared up. "Who did this? Go away and mind your own business!" I hissed under my breath while Father nervously tried to palliate and stop me.

The children were not a bit intimidated by me. They followed us and chanted "counterrevolutionary" all the way.

Concurrent with Father's return, in the late afternoon, my brother Tiemin also returned home from the production and construction corps in Ningxia where he had been transferred. Like everywhere else, people exiled to the corps had also formed rebel contingents to seize the opportunity to settle personal accounts. By virtue of his writing and debating abilities, Tiemin was chosen to present their cases to the Central Cultural Revolution Reception Center to appeal for justice. Ciqing was also called back for this rare reunion.

For the first time in years, the family was reunited and felt whole again. With ten people crowding our three-room apartment, we could hardly move about without bumping into one another. Needless to say, we were all in high spirits. Tiemin and Father were especially so. Having been absent from home for so long, for the first time, they found themselves home again in their new home. Tiemin was exuberant, animatedly regaling us with stories about his life away from home—from the factional fights in his corps to the heroic riots of the local Hui Muslim minority against the tyranny and the Communists' bloody suppression, machine-gunning down every single one of the hundreds of rioters, while Father remained quiet, looking subdued. But, from the detectable dim smile and the absent-mindedness shown on his face, I knew he felt he was home and savored this reunion in his own way. For the first time, I noticed his originally massive dark-shadow now had turned into busy salt-and-pepper stubbles.

Mother and Lu Ma prepared a big meal. We were all crammed around the round table, ready to celebrate this rare occasion.

Ciqing opened a bottle of champagne. At the loud release of air, we all hailed along.

After toasting around, we sat down to enjoy the meal. It was nothing more than just what a working-class family could come up with—a pork stew, a braised bean curd dish, cabbage soup and assorted cold dishes Mother managed to put together, far from what we used to have. But it tasted like a banquet.

With so much to exchange with one another, we could hardly wait for others to finish their words before getting in our own. After a while, the excitement was replaced by the feeling of ease of being home.

We retired very late. Qijuan and her family returned to their own home to make room for Tiemin and Ciqing.

Hardly had I fallen into sound sleep when I was awakened to vociferous voices, trudging footsteps in the corridor and loud poundings on our door. "Open the door!" They demanded.

Awakened by the loud banging and noises, we scrambled up. We were jumpy, not knowing what was going on. At the time, many arrests were made at the most unexpected moment. Our neighbor, Huang Yong's father, a tall, brilliant-looking handsome man in his 30s, was recently lured out of his home by the neighborhood activists at midnight and taken away by the police. He was never seen again.

As usual, Mother answered the door. It was the flying squad formed by neighborhood activists of about seven or eight on nightly duty, patrolling the neighborhood to catch "enemies". At the sight of an old man whom we called "Uncle Hao" dodging in the crowd, Mother immediately gathered that it was him who led this group here—When my brother Tiemin just returned, Mother spotted the old man rubbernecking.

Once they swarmed in, some immediately dispersed to search every room and under the beds with their flashlights while the head of the group, an old woman, demanded to see our *hukou ben* (household-registration booklet).

At the sight of Father, she questioned, "Who's this man? Why didn't we ever see you in the neighborhood?"

"I'm Long Xuan, listed as the man of this household," Humbly and apologetically, Father answered. "I was being investigated. Now my case is cleared. I return home legally."

"Who's that?" she next questioned Tiemin.

Having just returned home from traveling for days on the road, awakened from his sound sleep to the questioning, Tiemin seemed disoriented. He finally grasped that he needed to prove his identity, his legality to be here, and his relatedness to us. At the menacing number of people and their chilling stares, Tiemin was unable to locate the permit for his return. In jitters, he emptied all the contents in his luggage bag and retrieved it from among his folded clothes.

There was an awkward silence at this unexpected turnout. But it didn't take long for the head of the group to lecture righteously again, "Why haven't you reported to the police precinct to apply for a temporary residence permit? This way we both could have saved some trouble."

Looking uncomfortable, Uncle Hao congealed up a smile and placated Tiemin, "Never mind. Just tell us the reason. That's all."

"I'm sorry," Tiemin explained apologetically. "When I arrived home, the office hours were about over. There wasn't much time left for me to do so."

"That's all right," someone in the group mediated. "Just remember to register Monday morning. OK? Let's go."

With some already shuffling to the door, they were ready to depart. But, as if to justify the visit, the head of them stopped at the door, haranguing again, "I'll repeat the party's policy: sheltering a fugitive is a criminal act in itself. If you know of anyone who has sneaked back to Beijing and conceal it, you are equally guilty. Next time when someone returns to Beijing, get a temporary residence permit first!"

After Mother closed the door, we finally breathed a sigh of relief.

Since then, their midnight visit had become a frequent occurrence, even long after Tiemin's departure. So used to home invasion and daily abuse by the authority and the mobilized proletarian masses, we took them as the norm of life. At the communist takeover, our rights were reduced to just paper claims. After the Anti-Rightists campaign, the entire nation was silenced. We effectively lost our paper right to freedom of speech. Before the Cultural Revolution, ahead of each holiday, the police and the activists would knock on your door, warning you to "behave" and "not to make trouble". When the Cultural Revolution began, even a mob could invade your home any time they wanted to, take your properties away from you, beat you up and even kill you. We lost all our rights.

The armed clashes between China and Russia in 1969 in Zhenbaodao (Damansky in Russia) that led to considerable losses prompted a series of frantic war preparations—building underground systems, shelters, evacuation routes for top-tier officials, deploying the population, and relocating institutes and industries from *Yi Xian* (First Line, major cities and coastal regions) and *Er Xian* (Second Line, inner cities and surrounding areas) to *San Xian* (Third Line, remote realms). The relocation of military industries to *San Xian* commenced during the Korean War (1950-1953) in fear of having military industries wiped out but was halted due to its in-supportability and impracticality. It was now picked up again.

Beginning from Mid-1968, some educated, "problematic" government cadres were already sent to the countryside to be "reformed" and "revolutionized" on Mao's May 7, 1966 Directive in the so-called "May 7 Cadres Schools". Now at the decree of relocation and deployment, government branches, research institutes, colleges and industries all joined the rush to be sent or relocated to the countryside and remote areas. The "May 7 Cadres School" wave was then followed by the deployment of medical workers and the remaining handful of entertainment troupes to go lengthy rounds in factories and the countryside to "serve the workers and the poor peasants". In October, Lin Biao's Order No. 1 led to another deployment to extradite political prisoners, people with questionable backgrounds, and the elderly to their origins as a war preparation. It was executed and escorted by the police down to every single family. Liu Shaoqi, the number-one "enemy", already hanging on his last breath, was thence transferred from Beijing to Kaifeng, Henan Province.

At the decrees of deployment and relocation, anyone within the range of being sent away was to be sent away, senile or not, infirm or not. Many were sent away on stretchers. With Beijing's population to be reduced from the current 8 million down to 2 million by

1970, the capital city bore the brunt of all these deployments and relocations.

Father's college was to be relocated to the Red Flag Canal in Linxian County, Henan Province, an area known for its highest endemic stomach and colon cancer rates in the nation, to be "revolutionized" and in line with the college specialties of hydraulic engineering and hydroelectricity. While the "most revolutionary" appointed themselves "rear personnel" that would never experience one day's hardship of the countryside and the main body to be subsequently dispatched could still drag out a few more years of comfort and convenience of living in Beijing with their families, Father and other undesirable personnel, released from three years of confinement not long ago, now found themselves sent there as "advance troops" to build lodging for themselves and for the oncoming main body, and meanwhile, sleep in the wide open. My classmate and friend, Weng Rulian, whose family had been separated into six parts by the deployments, was to join her mother's college in Xinyang County, Henan Province while her father was dispatched to Jiangxi Province. Her boyfriend, Li Keji, was to be sent to Shanxi Province with his Film Academy. Before their departure, they rushed to tie the knot. Shortly after they had the marriage certificate secured, they parted way to their own destination. Another classmate and friend, Shen Xiaoping, saw herself turned into a surrogate mother to her two younger brothers to fend for themselves in Beijing at the departure of her parents to the Army's Political Work Department's May 7 Cadres School.

These looming relocations and deployments put hundreds of millions on tenterhooks, uncertain about their future and worried about leaving on short notice. A multitude of problems arose from Mao's decrees. His god-like chairmanship, the vaunted "great strategist", was too grand to be bothered by trivial details such as building infrastructure and providing transportation, resettlement, housing, supply, jobs, schooling and medical care for the relocated. Little people's problems arisen from these decrees were even less of his concern.

Separated from their own spouse, two of my neighbors from the Foreign Trade Ministry sharing the same two-room apartment, a man and a woman unrelated by marriage left behind by this deployment, found themselves alone in this apartment for years. Quite naturally, a liaison was formed between the two lonely people. Years later, when the couples reunited and the affair was exposed, it turned into a tragedy, with one man, a bespectacled frail man, almost chopping off the other man's hand. Jiang Jin, my future colleague at school, related to us a story about what happened in the Air Force's May 7 Cadres School in Jiangxi Province that she went to with her husband: Sleeping in a single-sex barrack for years on tightly packed straw mattresses on the floors with no personal space at all, one night, army functionary Zhu (a surname homophonous with the word "pig") sneaked out to relieve himself on a sow whose loud, continuous squealing woke everyone up. He was caught and earned the nickname of *"Zhu Siling"* ("Pig Generalissimo"). Without parental care, a lot of youngsters simply turned into hooligans. Luckily for my Uncle Ke, his entire family in Wuhan was able to stay intact as one unit relocated to Jingshan, a mountain area in Hubei Province.

WAITING TO BE ASSIGNED A JOB

Years of unceasing persecution and injustice had created pervasive destitution. With hordes of petitioners from other parts of the country pouring into the capital city camping in the street waiting for their cases to be heeded by the central government, Beijing had turned into a refugee camp. After months of waiting, they found themselves broke or literally pushed out of the government door. Resources and means exhausted, they were unable to return to their homeland and became destitute. Together with the Beijing residents who were expelled from their own homes and became homeless, they formed quite a scene.

One afternoon when I was on my way home, I heard someone call me out by my nickname. I looked to the direction and saw a fair-skinned filthy young man barely covered in tatters approaching me. It was my uncle, Wenli, the youngest son of my grandfather's fifth wife. I hadn't seen Wenli in four years. The last time I saw him was before the Cultural Revolution. Then he was still seen in a sports jacket and khaki slacks, thronged and toadied to by a crowd of parasites who busily set him up with beautiful women and dined with him at the finest restaurants. Now he looked like this.

As I was shocked at the sight, I found ourselves enclosed in a circle by a throng of onlookers, taunted and sworn at. Wenli was used to this, not a bit ruffled by the sight. More and more people were gathering.

Feeling like the center of a monkey show, I urged him, "We're making a scene here. Go to my home with me."

Wenli responded in a tranquil tone, "Let them look and laugh at me. Nowadays fate is unpredictable. They are laughing at me today, but who can say for sure tomorrow he's not going to be the next to be laughed at?"

On our way, Wenli told me since he was kicked out of his home in 1966, he had been driven in and out of a detention center and a mental institution many times. Wenli lived in his own world, paying no attention to the following horde and talking surrealistically about his dreams of buying a Steinway grand and traveling the world once he had the means. All the way home, spectators stopped to stare and jeer at us, with some even following and hooting us all the way home.

Drawn by the commotion, Lu Ma was already in the corridor. At the sight of Wenli, she demanded, "Go away. What are you doing here? We don't know you!"

"I'm here to visit Xiaomei," was Wenli's gentle response.

A trifle vexed at Lu Ma for daring to think she had the right to interfere, I said to her bluntly, "It's none of your business."

Lu Ma ignored me and threatened Wenli, "Go away! We have nothing to do with you. Don't come here anymore, or I'll call the police!"

At Lu Ma's not showing us any respect, in a fit of anger and irritation, I spat out under my breath, "How dare you act this way? He belongs to the Long family. Who are you? Let us in!"

Lu Ma showed no sign of yielding. She continued to make a scene in the corridor. More neighbors drawn by the noise came out to watch.

With Lu Ma obstinately refusing to let Wenli in, there was no way for us to enter. At this, Wenli graciously complied, promising never to come again and left.

At night, Lu Ma informed Mother of Wenli's visit. At this, my sister scolded me, "Are you out of your mind that you connect yourself with that doomed, insane creature?"

"He's my uncle, and yours too, not 'that doomed, insane crea-ture'!" I shot back.

During those difficult years, my personality had changed. To be able to endure constant ruthless abuse, I had toughened myself and learned to fight back. My new personality often clashed with Mother's and my sister's.

"Don't talk back," Mother got in. "Haven't we suffered enough from the disgrace and trouble you brought upon us? From now on, you are forbidden to see him again!"

Mother's castigation effectively shut me up.

With the new address Wenli gave me, I visited him a couple of times subsequently at his new lodging assigned by the police. It was a less than six-feet (two meters) wide room severed from part of a passageway in a yard in Dongsi area. There was nothing in the room except a bare board on the hardened dirt floor used as his bed.

In spite of his utter privation, Wenli never mentioned his hard-ships or resorted to my help. Born a better-off, carefree child, I had no understanding of what poverty meant in reality. It never crossed my mind how he got by and that he might be in dire need of the most basic—food.

Once I dropped by, but Wenli was not home. A big padlock on his door indicated something ominous. I peeped into the gap, but I could see nothing. There was no way for me to find out what had happened to him except asking his neighbors. But I wouldn't do that.

As I was on my way out, a door creaked open and a head popped out. A middle-aged, worker-looking man stepped out of his door, approaching me gingerly.

"Is he your uncle?" with his chin pointing to the padlocked door, he asked me.

He seemed to have something to say to me. I nodded. Obviously, he had found out from Wenli about the relationship.

At my acknowledgement, he said, "I see the resemblance, the exact same cut." With qualms in his voice, he continued, "Your uncle has been taken back to Fangshan Mental Hospital." Looking around furtively, he proceeded in an undertone, "Since you're his relative, I'll tell you the truth: He's not insane! His words are always measured. He never opposed Chairman Mao and the party, not even once!"

Grateful for his good will, his sympathy and sense of justice, I thanked him sincerely and left promptly to avoid getting him into trouble.

Months later, I received a creased, blood-smudged letter with no return address on it. It was from Wenli. There were only a few lines in it. He begged me to take him out of that unnamed place where he was dealt constant beatings, food and sleep deprivation, and other forms of inhuman treatments. From what he wrote and no address left and from his postscript asking for a tin of coffee at a time when survival should be his sole concern, I could tell he was already in a state of intermittently losing his mind.

In a world where nothing was left but a life hanging on the verge, with even daily essentials in shortage, where can I get him a tin of coffee? I said to myself, how can I get him out? Where could I possibly accommodate him? I myself am at the mercy of my family. With no listed address and no access to transportation, I'm unable even to visit him.

Ever since then, Wenli was never heard from again and was said to have died there shortly.

To my regret, I never made any attempt to visit him in Fangshan Mental Hospital, located somewhere in a mountain area scores of miles southwest of Beijing. With his own sister turning him away, I was the only one he counted on. But I failed him. Benumbed by prevalent injustice and misery, I had become oblivious to them. In a world that utterly disregarded humanity, Wenli was betrayed and deserted by everyone. This world was too small to contain a most gentle, harmless and innocent soul.

Back in the wave to "establish revolutionary ties", my friend, Yang Yuhe, who had worked in Anding Hospital, another mental institution, told me of similar situations Wenli briefly mentioned in his letter. It was a situation many times as bad as was portrayed in *One Flew over the Cuckoo's Nest*. She also informed me that many oversensitive, idealistic youths deemed "insane" were also confined there for their unrealistic dreams, including one who wanted to become Chopin and another who wanted to be a poet like Pushkin.

What was shocking was that no one had ever questioned the treatment of the inmates or the cause of so many questionable deaths occurring during their hospitalization in those mental institutions during the Cultural Revolution.

A well-known case was Chen Lining, who was locked up in a mental institution for his letters against Liu Shaoqi before the Cultural Revolution. At the beginning stage of the Cultural Revolution, he was released and hailed as a "hero" against Liu Shaoqi. In less than a year, he was re-hospitalized for daring to question Mao's wife Jiang Qing, his other minions and even Mao himself. Since then, he was never heard of again.

An insignificant man, Wenli's ordeals died with him. No one will ever find out what he had been through. What we do know is that he died in his healthy prime in his late twenties, not of natural causes.

In late spring, 1970, the movement of sending urban youths to the countryside came to a halt. With 18 million youths ranging from 13 to 20 years old sent to the countryside, it had increased the burdens on the already impoverished peasants. Meanwhile, it had caused a significant number of illnesses and injuries among the sent-down youths. With officials besieged and traffic blocked by hundreds of daily sit-down petitioners for months, a modified policy was made, allowing the return of the ill and the injured and the restoration of their Beijing residency.

My legal resident status in Beijing was restored. By rejoining the family, I was back to being their burden again. I couldn't wait to extricate myself again.

At the time, there were tens of millions of frustrated idle youths like me. With a great many of them having nothing to do but loafing and loitering on the street looking for fun or trouble depending on their mood, it had become a threat to social stability. It was made worse by the extreme shortage of supplies caused by years of interruption of productivity to make the Cultural Revolution and by prevalent "backdoor" practices.

With Communists taking the lead capitalizing on their power to obtain rare supplies, all those who had some capital cashed it in: doctors traded on their power of writing paid sick-day leave for rare goodies; parents with access to commodities used them to gain special treatments for their children at school; shop assistants bartered their merchandise for whatever they needed... Goods were often gone before they reached the shelves. In the markets, the shelves were empty almost all the time. Fruit was rarely seen; meat, fish and eggs were nearly out of sight. Every day, at the opening of the market, irate shoppers would swarm in, rushing for whatever was available. Late arrivals would go home almost empty-handed. For the powerless, even meeting daily basic needs could not be guaranteed. Whenever anything rarely seen became available—usually substandard, rotten or defective dumped to the market to be sold for profit, an irate mob would flock in, fighting for a share.

Furor was felt everywhere; a fight could break out at any given moment. Paucity had driven people to the edge. With the large force of youths remaining idle and continually wreaking havoc, the problem demanded a solution.

Through their connections, many high Communist officials, in position and sidelined, had quietly arranged for their offspring to be enrolled in military academies, armed forces or serve military institutions. Beginning from late spring, urban youths that should have graduated from 1966 to 1970 were gradually assigned jobs. Youths from "good" families were given priority. Sidelined Communists' offspring who couldn't obtain a job on their own were provided with a teaching or an office job while youths from working class families and the ones who never went astray were allotted state-owned factory jobs. With job assignment going on stratum by stratum according to the Communists' priority list, youths with disadvantaged backgrounds had to wait for their turn.

At even junior high school students assigned to teaching high school, I was ill at ease. One day I went to the District Office of Urban Youth Settlement to volunteer my service.

The man in charge there looked me up and down in disdain, and asked, "What family are you from?"

At my answer, he scorned, "A person like you wants to teach? No way! Those jobs are for people from good families only. For your kind, there are only menial jobs. If you can get one, you should thank the government. Get out! We are busy enough. Don't make trouble here! Out!"

Treated like worthless garbage in every interaction we had with the empowered proletarian masses, I stepped out livid. Having a prestigious job in the fields of foreign affairs had seemed to be my destiny. Now even getting a menial job was too beyond me.

While I was anxiously waiting for a job, my brother Ciqing brought his co-worker, Wang Fusheng, to our home. In front of me, Wang looked extremely bashful. Whenever his eyes came in contact with mine, he would blush and his breath would strain, very unlike other young men who were confident of their "capital" that I was so used to seeing. I was flattered by his reactions.

One morning, Wang unexpectedly showed up at an hour when no other family members were likely home except me.

During our chats, he invited me to join him and his friends in their weekend excursion to Xiang Shan (Fragrant Hill), where maple leaves had turned fiery red this time of the year. His bold invitation took me by surprise. But, since I had nothing to do, I agreed to go.

When Sunday arrived, I went to Xiang Shan.

I was a little late. When I spotted him alone in front of the park, I was taken aback, realizing I was tricked. I said to myself, he's not some shy man that you perceived. But, if you turn around, you'd make yourself look like an inexperienced girl. Although he seems pretty bold and not very honest, he's your brother's friend, unlikely to do you harm. Besides, he doesn't look like someone who can do harm. Since you're already here, why don't you take advantage of this rare occasion and enjoy yourself a little bit instead of returning home feeling superfluous? There's no harm anyway. I hence proceeded with the plan.

When we climbed the hill, Wang sometimes lent me a hand, which I, as he could see, as nimble as a gazelle, obviously didn't need. Later on, he became bolder and found a chance to embrace and kiss me with his tongue prying into my mouth.

I was turned off by this bold act. But I didn't resist. I needed to feel wanted. At my psychological stage—defiant outwardly but inferior deep down, I was destined to be self-destructive. I said to myself, with other rational men, you'll be a "mercy" case. Your past will be microscopically examined and then grudgingly accepted or rejected outright. But he wants you without any condition. I acquiesced in his act. Emboldened, he kissed me again.

In a rash and self-destructive moment, a relationship was perfunctorily established.

Wang was ecstatic, giving no heed to my past. That relieved me. In his eyes, I was a "godsend". The lowest in social rank, no matter how tightly he held me, he never seemed to believe that he could have a woman like me. I drank in his worship. What more do I need than a man's complete devotion?

Half a year later, my family intervened. Father, who had developed colon cancer when he was relocated to Linxian, Henan, was allowed to return to Beijing temporarily for his unceasing bloody diarrhea due to failed medical treatments he received in the countryside. Infuriated by my foolish behavior, he battled me day and night. There were severe confrontations in the family. To avoid his grousing and battling, I stayed out late.

Once, I came home late again. As I was slipping into my bedroom about to lock the door, Father pushed it open and forced himself in with Mother in tow.

"Long Qiru," tersely, Father addressed me. "Don't try to dodge us. Sit down. We need to speak to you."

With no way to escape, I complied.

"Long Qiru," Father blustered out. "Do you know how many of my young colleagues and acquaintances begged to become my son-in-law but were rejected by me because I value you and don't think any of them is good enough for you? But you sold yourself cheap and gave yourself away unconditionally to a wretch that no one would spot even with a lit lantern. You somehow managed to find yourself one. Any woman who is not desperate would shun a rogue and an uneducated coolie like him who can barely support himself, let alone have a father executed by the Communists. But you are different. You jumped into the abyss voluntarily. You think you're rescuing him? No, you fool! Right now the rogue's congratulating himself on having you volunteer as his sacrifice. Do you know the consequences of your foolish behavior? You would live as a family member of a 'counterrevolutionary' and an impoverished, abject life forever with no chance to get back to your own people. Why are you doing this? Why are you throwing away the life we are struggling so hard to hold onto? Are you doing this to hurt your mother and me? No, you fool! You are hurting yourself!"

"What's bothering you that you always do things to hurt yourself?" Mother got in. "Although our family fortune has declined, we can still preserve it if you choose to. With your looks, you have plenty of chances. Why do you choose to go down further and chop off the possibility of getting back to a dignified life? It seems that you can't wait to break up with this world…"

"Listen, Wretch," Father interrupted Mother and reviled. "'*Tian zuonie, you keshe; Zi zuonie, bu kehuo.*' If you fall by some uncontrollable exterior force, you are absolvable; but if you bring doom upon yourself, you rightly deserve it. I hope you won't live to regret your foolish behavior!"

"Leave me alone!" Turned off by my parents' superciliousness and their attempt to use me to preserve the family, I sassed back, totally closing myself off to reason, "You object to him because he's poor, you snobs! I'm not your plan. I'm my own person and have my own life!"

The more they interfered, the more defiant I became. In rebellion against my parents and driven to get rid of the psychological stain left by the rape, I offered Wang sex to make it a fait accompli. Although I still felt numb from the rape, it satisfied me seeing him humbly submit to me.

Despite the knowledge of my parents' strong objection to him, Wang continued to sneak in and dine here when no one was home.

At wit's end, my family resorted to speaking to Wang one Sunday night.

"Wang Fusheng," Mother began politely. "You and Qiru have little in common. You don't have a comparable background or education. The differences between you will show in real life, causing big problems. It is wise for you two to break up now before the rice is cooked. It will be too late then…"

"It's Qiru who wants me," shamelessly, Wang claimed. "Ask Qiru whether she wants to break up with me."

I was shocked and horrified at what I saw and heard. It was the first time that I ever saw the other side of Wang that was hidden from me. He was no longer a shy, gentle man, but someone cunningly and impudently holding his ground, a trait that was so alien to the gentlemanly world I was familiar with. Nevertheless, mercilessly put in this position, I was unable to budge. To leave no room for my parents to intervene, I screamed, "It's our own business. Leave us alone!"

At the presence of Li Songshan, my brother Tiemin's friend and a martial arts master, I insisted on seeing Wang off.

Shortly after we came out, we found Tiemin and Li Songshan out looking for us.

When I was led by Wang to dodge the chase adroitly, I was sickened to catch sight of Wang's sly nature.

With Wang's world gradually unfolding in front of me, it opened me up to a world of unfamiliarity and made me wary of the depth of it.

I became hesitant. Once when I visited my friends Jennifer and Lynn while Wang was waiting outside, I deliberately stayed past the promised time. At the sight of my emergence, Wang banged his forehead against the brick wall violently. "Long Qiru, Long Qiru," he swore, blood streaming down his forehead. "You're trying to get rid of me, aren't you? Go ahead and do it!"

Appalled by such a violent reaction to my coming out some 20 minutes late, I immediately perceived the outcomes of a breakup with him and began to fathom the consequences of my reckless behavior, knowing it was too late for me to retreat.

⁋

In spring, 1971, as a war preparation, another national movement *La Lian* was on the way to have city populations field-trained in the countryside for the presumed forthcoming "Armageddon" with the US, Russia or the Nationalists. Wang was sent to the outskirts of Beijing, together with thousands of others, about one third in his factory, to be field-trained.

Three months later, Wang returned one night from his regimental training. Still having his luggage with him, he came straight to see me. When I came out from my home and appeared in front of him, he held me tightly in his arms as if he were holding onto something so dear to him that he was afraid that someone might snatch it away from him.

I was irritated by still depending on my parents at that age, angry at the world and my family. Powerless against the world, I directed my anger at Mother, who I felt exercised too much control over me. I contended with her fiercely. However, with me still depending on her, my contention was futile. Marrying Wang would make me independent from her and provide a perfect opportunity to deal her a hard blow and get even with her.

At my self-destructive psychological stage, I couldn't wait to walk out on the world that I had no part in. As a matter of fact, I wanted to sink further to the lowest rank. Up or down, I didn't care, since my future was already ruined. Wang's love and passion for me made me overlook his defects and deficiencies and believe that his love and passion alone could make up for his shortcomings and inadequacies enough to sustain me in my standoff against the world. This was a move I must make. I thought both Wang and I were social rejects and that we matched each other in this regard and that by marrying Wang, I would send out some form of protest against Communists' class label and my haughty family. What was more, marriage would make my past invisible. In a rash moment, I suggested marriage to Wang.

Lu Ma was no longer in our home. Domestic services were no longer permitted, condemned as "bourgeois practice" and "class exploitation and oppression". Worried about her future, Mother had matched her up with a widower next door. It was my maternal grandmother in charge of important belongings now. Romantic at heart and sympathetic with Wang, she was more than eager to conspire with us and provide us with the convenience. I obtained my resident card from her without any trouble.

With this card, I was able to register at the local Civil Affairs Bureau, officially married.

I returned home with Wang and his uncle to get my luggage. When we stepped out, Lu Ma was in the corridor. At their sight, she shouted at them, calling them "robbers" and "kidnappers" while I told her to mind her own business.

To show Mother she no longer had any power over me, I moved out without notifying her.

MY FIRST JOB

With youths of "good" and "OK" backgrounds from 1966 to 1970 all allotted a job, in the summer of 1971, youths with disadvantaged backgrounds finally got their turn. However, what we received were but collective-owned jobs.

The so-called collective-owned businesses assumed sole responsibility for their profits and losses. The workers there were not on the state payroll. Therefore, they had no right to transfer to a state-owned business. Once one was allocated this kind of job, he or she would be stuck there for life, working among the urban poor with the illiterate, semi-illiterate, urban paupers, former rural emigrants, ex-tramps, ex-prostitutes, dregs and petty ex-convicts, and people with various disadvantaged backgrounds, in primitive working conditions, and earning the lowest urban wages.

Among the last to be placed, I was assigned to a small photoelectric lathe factory in Chaoyang District. I knew clearly what situation I would be getting into, but I had no other options.

On the appointed day, I arrived at the factory. It looked like a junk yard, with steel plates, rusty angle steel and oxidized cast-iron cabinets stacked here and there.

The moment I stepped in, I noticed all the women working in the yard stopped what they were doing to stretch their necks to gawk at me and whisper to one another unconcealed, as if I were an alien from outer space. I was pissed off by this manifest ignorance and crudity. At the sight of a bunch of below-par youngsters standing at a corner of the yard, evidently new employees like me, I was even more disappointed, knowing from now on I'd be stuck with them. To mollify myself, I said to myself, it's just a job that you have to do to make a living. You don't have to have anything to do with them anyway.

Not long after I joined them, a short, scrawny man probably in his 40s' with a cunning, inscrutable face, a stooping posture and a leopard's gait approached us, a stack of gloves, uniforms and sandpapers in his hands. With the list in his hand, he called out four names. I found myself taken aside together with a tall, loquacious girl; a loafing boy with large vacant eyes; and a quiet, subdued-looking teenage girl wearing thick-lensed glasses.

The man dryly introduced himself as Chief Xue of the Fitter Workshop we were assigned to. After a brief speech to inform us that we were in a three-month try-out period and that there were certain rules for us to follow, he led us to the open field where three-feet-high rust-crusted cast-iron cabinets were sitting and said, "See the cabinets here? Sand down the rust on them with the sandpapers."

With the gloves and the uniform distributed to me put on, I began tackling the task and soon became engrossed in my work.

Near the end of the day, when I was still busy working on the rust, Chief Xue, accompanied by a master-worker, arrived. Pointing to the sanded-down cabinets in front of me, the master-worker inquired, "Are these all done by you?"

I nodded. In my total immersion of work, I had sanded down several of them.

At an earshot distance, I heard the master-worker comment to Chief Xue, "Look, this girl alone did almost the equal amount of work of everyone else put together. And look at the quality of her work—There's not a bit of rust on any of them. See the difference between what she did and what the others did? It's worlds apart!"

Brought up with strict standards and getting used to praise, at this compliment, I said to myself, what's the fuss about sanding down rust? It's the simplest task that even an idiot can handle adequately.

Does this warrant any comments? I don't think so. But, drawn by his remarks about others' work, I couldn't help darting a glance at their direction and espied a pathetic, sloppy sight.

Chief Xue didn't respond to the comments. He went on to giving us instructions on what to do the following day, and had us dismissed for the day.

The following day, after taking us new hires on a tour of the workshop, showing us different tools and machines and demonstrating how to use or operate each of them, Chief Xue led us into a room within the workshop. Handing out some blueprints to each of us, he said, "Finish them according to the requirements. If you have any problems, go see Master-Worker Wang that you met yesterday afternoon."

It was the first time that I ever put my hands on a blueprint. I figured the diagrams must be for the miscellaneous parts to be assembled onto the photoelectric lathes. The work required some basic mathematical and geometric knowledge, involved calculating, measuring, cutting, sawing, milling, drilling and filing the steel plate and angle steel into the required shapes such as triangle, trapezoid, or pentagon to fit onto the lathe. I was glad that the job turned out not to be boring and that there was a chance for me to get my long-dormant brain stimulated a little bit and apply what I had learned in my math and geometry classes.

It didn't take long for me to finish my assignments.

As I was walking briskly passing by the alley, I bumped into Xiao Lu, the shy girl, and found her weeping quietly at a corner, assignments in hand.

Xiao Lu was only 16 years old. When the Cultural Revolution began, she was only a fifth grader, not even out of primary school.

Surmising she must have had trouble with the blueprints, I stopped and asked, "Are you all right, Xiao Lu? Having trouble with your assignments?"

She nodded, large drops of tears rolling down her cheeks.

I cooed, "Don't worry, Xiao Lu. We'll finish them together."

Squatting on the ground, with a blue print unfolded on the ground and a pebble securing each corner, I found it to be an easy task that required only a few steps. I began by teaching Xiao Lu how to read scale and then explained to her what was needed to be done. For the mathematical and geometric parts of the work, I demonstrated to her with my work, embellished with my clarifications. One by one, we finished all her assignments together.

Seeing the smile of relief on Xiao Lu's face, I was glad I was able to help.

Xiao Lu might be a little slow, but she was conscientious and capable of learning something simple. With my help day in and day out, gradually, she acquired some ability.

Since then, Xiao Lu and I became friends. She opened herself up to me: Her working class background initially placed her in a state-owned factory. But she was dismissed shortly due to her severe near-sightedness. As one with a humble background and a timid, submissive nature, Xiao Lu never challenged authority and never strove for or even expected anything out of life but simply took whatever was doled out to her. Nevertheless, she possessed some simple sound values. She was humble and proper. The idea of lying to get ahead never crossed her mind. I appreciated her as a good person and for her companionship. This friendship made life in this alien environment much easier and fun for both of us. We enjoyed each other's company. Left alone to do our work, we felt happy and content. Days went by fast.

One day, when we were busy with our tasks, Chief Xue and Master-Worker Wang came to check our work again. At an earshot distance, Master-Worker Wang commented to Mr. Xue, "I've been observing the apprentices for a while." With his chin pointing to my direction, he went on, "This girl's really smart. All the work she did was clean and precise. Beautiful!" Turning to Xiao Lu, he continued, "Even this Xiao Lu isn't bad. She's slow, but she can get something simple done." Directing his eyes diagonally to the vacant-looking boy, he remarked again, "Look at that boy with the same high school diploma. He can't figure out anything!"

All the while noncommittal, at Wang's comments, Chief Xue said, "Send that boy and the gossipy girl to night-watching."

Since then, Xiao Lu and I were the only two remaining in the workshop.

One morning, while I was working, I was called into the office of Mr. Xiao, the factory director, wondering what it was about.

At my sight, Mr. Xiao, a handsome, prudent middle-aged man, smiled and stood up. Pulling out a chair, with clear satisfaction shown on his face, he gesticulated to me and said, "Sit down, please."

After we both were seated, he said, "Long Qiru, I hear that you've been working very hard and working very well too. I intend to switch you to a more suitable environment, the technological office, to work with technical personnel. From tomorrow on, you'll formally begin to work there. Report to the office this afternoon and become familiarized with the work and the environment first."

This was a pleasant surprise I hadn't had in years. I thanked him and left with a light heart, grateful at the respect and trust I had not had for years and glad to have a chance to learn something and exert myself.

Returning to the workshop, I informed Xiao Lu about the change. Xiao Lu looked disappointed, but took it in without any fuss. I assured her that we would still be friends.

In the afternoon, I reported to the technological office. There, I met the head engineer, Mr. Wu, a swarthy terse man; Ms. Shen, his assistant and a draftsman, a middle-aged, doll-like pretty woman with a pair of large, melancholy, narcissistic eyes; and Chen Mei, a placid, seemly female engineer and my assigned mentor.

Serenely, Chen Mei taught me basic knowledge about drawing and the use of related tools. With the orders given by the engineers, I began my work right away. It was auxiliary work. Though the work so far had seemed monotonous and uninteresting, I felt more at home working among better educated people.

The following day, I arrived at the office and was about to resume the work left from the day before when Mr. Wu came to me and said curtly, "Sorry. There's nothing for you to do here. Go back to the workshop."

I was taken aback, wondering what was going on. But, accustomed to harsh treatments and unexplained changes and having learned never to expect anything, I wasn't that upset. After all, I was returning to my buddy and familiarity, the comforting, accommo-dating Xiao Lu.

At the sight of me, Xiao Lu broke into a broad smile, palavering excitedly as if she hadn't seen me in ages.

At noon, when Xiao Lu and I were sitting on the ground against the wall outside the workshop eating our lunch, a woman's raised angry voice came from the open window.

"Why is this bourgeois young diehard getting all the attention? She's just beginning her work here but was already promoted while we've been working our butts off for more than 10 years without even receiving any acknowledgement. Are we carrying out the party's class policy by promoting a bourgeois young diehard? Did anyone notice her attitude? Other people with a bad background have all become meek and humble, but this girl's showing her contempt and defiance!"

I at once sensed I was the one she was talking about. She wasn't wrong about my attitude. Just by the clothes I wore and the way I looked, I already stuck out like a square peg in a round hole where everyone else blended in perfectly. While everyone else seemed to have effaced himself in this environment, I alone stood out with my nonconformity.

While I was digesting her rant, I heard Chief Xue say, "I agree with you. She should remain here."

In no time, Chief Xue and the woman filed out of the workshop and headed for Mr. Xiao's office.

Upon their return, I was officially informed to remain in the workshop.

At the end of the day, I came across Chen Mei at the trol-ley-bus stop.

"Sorry about what happened to you, Long Qiru." Chen Mei said regretfully, "This morning before you arrived, there was an ugly out-burst in the technological office. Ms. Shen, the 'surreptitious' mis-tress of Old Wu who probably perceived you to be her potential 'amorous rival', got into a shouting match with him, threatening him with leaving if you remain. Wu was compelled to go to Mr. Xiao to request your recall. At the strong opposition coming from both sides, Mr. Xiao had to drop the idea."

I chuckled at being perceived as someone's "amorous rival", no longer puzzled over the reason for this inexplicable change.

As a result of Mao's preaching of "More men, more power" in the 1950s against Ma Yinchu, a Yale-trained economist who was branded a "Malthusian disciple" and banished for his advocacy of population control, there was an exponential population growth. This and the years of interruption of productivity to make the Cultural Revolution led to an extreme housing shortage. Married couples in need of their own lodgings had to wait for years for their turns of allotment. Some had waited for more than a decade. Many were stuck in whatever arrangement they could make while others had to get by in a single-sex dormitory with a chance of reunion only on holidays and weekends when everyone was away. As for life-long bachelors, there was simply no chance for them ever to obtain their own place but to be stuck in their parents' home or an overcrowded dormitory for life. As a newly-wed couple, we had no choice but to sleep on the floors on a small straw mattress in the same room with my mother-in-law while waiting in line.

One day, we were informed that we were going to be allocated a room of our own as a special treatment for being the relatives of my husband's fifth brother, a mason working for the housing bureau. At the anticipation of our own home, my husband and I were both excited.

We took the following day off from work for this move.

We met the man in charge of housing in his office and followed him to our assigned place.

Three stops away from my mother-in-law's home, we found ourselves standing in front of a dilapidated building by the doorway of a yard with a public toilet and a public water facility adjacent.

At the sight of this shabby place, my heart sank. The moment I stepped on the tacky dirt floor of the 80 square-feet (7.4 square meters) tiny room, I already wanted to get out. The badly erod-ing walls revealed bricks and mortar. A small, prison-like window faced the street. With bus and trolley stops only several yards away, even with the window closed, we could hear clearly the perpetual, nerve-wrecking cacophony produced by shrill brakes, whizzing vehi-cles and ceaseless honking from the irritated drivers. I couldn't imag-ine spending my life here.

At our tepid reactions, the man declared haughtily and indiffer-ently, "If you don't like it, hundreds of couples waiting in line would break their necks to get in."

We had no options but to move in.

It didn't take much to have this tiny room filled. A sunken full-size bed and a worn loveseat we bought from a pawnshop that could only be found at the curb or in a dumpster in a developed country were all it could take, leaving only a few square feet of spare room for us to maneuver.

With only a bed to sleep in and a place to sit, and no books, no newspapers, no radio, no desk or even a table, we began our ple-beian life.

It was a hard transition for me. The tiny room was simply too small for two tall people. Even moving a few steps involved some maneuvering. One had to tilt his body or sit somewhere to make room for the other to pass. Relighting an extinguished stove after a long day's work on a daily basis was dispiriting. By the time we arrived home, the stove would be long dead. The free time left for us was made even less because of the coal's poor quality. It simply refused to burn. Since I was the one who came home earlier, the task of lighting the stove fell on my shoulders. After the stove was lit, it took a long time for the flame to become strong enough to make the water warm enough so that we could clean ourselves and have some hot water to drink. At the time, I was pregnant. Day in and day out left with hardly any time to relax and communicate plus the severe reactions caused by my pregnancy, I was exhausted and disheartened.

However, my husband seemed to have settled for this life. Having a father executed for being a Nationalist colonel and a county mag-istrate, he was used to being treated as a sub-subhuman as a family member of a "counterrevolutionary". With all of their properties confiscated at the communist takeover as the relatives of a "counter-revolutionary" and six growing children to raise, his mother had to get by with making matchboxes and selling popsicles. All six children had to help out. With this family background, three out of five of his siblings were sent to a labor camp in disguised form. One strikingly handsome brother who had wanted to become a movie actor was farming at Nankou Farm in Changping County, Beijing. Another was coal mining in Datong, Shangxi Province while his sister was farming in Inner Mongolia. Like his eldest brother who was lucky to be assigned a teaching job in a rural elementary school in the relatively lenient early 1950s and his fifth brother who became a mason during Liu Shaoqi's lenient reign in the early 1960s, my husband was given a factory job during the same era. Growing up with such a family background at the high risk of becoming an "active coun-terrevolutionary" himself, my husband had learned from an early age to literally keep his mouth shut and endure hardship without any murmur.

By nature, my husband was a gentle soul and a passionate lover. I was his purpose and obsession. However, since moving into our own home, his passion was gone. Sex became just a physical need. Sometimes it occurred while I was sleeping.

At first, I was gratified to be able to provide some comfort and a sense of home for this weary poor soul who could leave all his trouble behind and sleep like a baby. But, day in and day out, I was there alone while he, the one who was supposed to be my most intimate soul companion, existed only physically as a sleeping man. Watching him sleep day in and day out, I couldn't help feeling drained and used.

Accustomed to being around well-versed, communicative people and exposed to vision and sophisticated views, living with my husband, whose scope was limited and whose needs were simple, I felt that I was living in a spiritual vacuum, completely cut off from the world and left utterly alone, going to work having little to do with my coworkers and coming home only to find myself in the same void. I couldn't help admitting to myself that my marriage to him was a mistake.

On October 1 that year, we found the celebration of National Day inexplicably cancelled. We soon noticed Vice Chairman Lin Biao, Mao's "closest comrade-in-arms" and legislated successor, mysteriously disappeared from public. His pictures and Mao's *Little Red Book* with Lin Biao's inscription in it also vanished from all public places and bookstores. Meanwhile, we noticed the beefed-up public security: Policemen were seen even in outlying alleys, in uniform or civilian clothes. They stopped, questioned, harassed and even arbitrarily arrested people for any suspicion or sign of disturbance. Even spitting out some curse words under breath would warrant detention. Proletarian or not, we were all treated as potential enemies and all choked full of silent wrath. At the sudden changes, we all wondered what was going on.

One November morning, I arrived at the workshop and sensed the air tense and secretive. All the veteran workers were gathering around the engineers who were dispatched here from a state-owned enterprise to help us master the newly imported technology. Looking nervous and baffled, they surreptitiously whispered to one another. As I was wondering what was going on, Old Ma, a tall, sinewy lanky man with a weather-beaten face sidled up toward me.

"Little Long," in an undertone, Old Ma spoke to me furtively. "Have you heard of… something unusual… lately?"

Since the marriage, I had not been well informed. At his words, I couldn't make head or tail of it. Knowing he didn't say this out of nowhere, I pressed him to reveal the information he had heard.

"Nothing," he hedged. "You'll find out later."

At the time, if information about the party was to be released to public, it was filtered down with details reduced at every level according to social strata, first within the party hierarchy, then the public by occupation. By the time the stripped-to-bone information reached us collective workers, it would be known to almost everyone except the classified "class enemies" and the peasants who were instrumental in Mao's armed revolt against the legally elected Nationalist government but were treated in reality as if they didn't exist.

Old Ma was the only one who occasionally exchanged a few words with me beyond just work related. He must have heard of something from those engineers. If he refused to share the information with me, there would be no way for me to find out what he hesitated about. My husband, a state-payroll worker, happened to have a night shift that day. He wouldn't return until the following day. But, even if he weren't on a night shift, with him, an apolitical man, I wouldn't find out much.

The following day at the emergency meeting, I was shocked to learn that Lin Biao was alleged to have conspired to assassinate Mao with his son's plan "Project 571" ("571"—homophone of "armed uprising") and died in a plane crash in Mongolia in his failed escape attempt dubbed "9/13 Incident".

The story was simply incredible. Lin Biao had been designated as the "beloved Vice-Chairman", the "closest comrade-in-arms" and "legal successor" of Mao. How could this take place all of sudden out of nowhere? I asked myself. There must be some horrendous inside stories behind it. Besides, there were just too many unbelievable scenarios and holes in their narrative, too bizarre to be credible.

Fed up with the forever duplicitous and untrustworthy Communists, I had no interest in figuring out or conjecturing what had happened behind the scene but simply dismissed it as a "dog-eat-dog" power struggle. However, in the eyes of the masses who had revered Mao like god that "knows all and sees all" ("*dongcha yiqie*", official definition of Mao's supreme perceptive power at spotting potential enemies and conspiracies), Mao and the party now lost their credibility.

The next day, after work, we were told to stay late for another emergency meeting. Recently, our three-time per-week one-hour meetings had been extended to two hours. By the time it ended, it would be 8 p.m. Angry and exhausted, by the time we finally got home, all we wanted was to sleep. It left us no time or energy for anything else. Upon learning on top of the extra meeting we just had yesterday there'd be yet another emergency meeting on a Saturday when there was supposedly no meeting, I was seething inside at being left with no life.

After the roll call of the attendees in our workshop and the people from other workshops assigned to attend the meeting in our group, Chief Xue, who presided over the meeting, gave an opening speech, "Comrades, tonight we are holding another emergency meeting, in which everyone is mandated by the party to display his political stance at this Lin Biao Incident. Lin Biao attempted to assassinate our great leader Chairman Mao. He is not alone. Class enemies are ubiquitous, waiting every minute of their lives for the right moment to strike us down and sabotage our red regime, just as Chairman Mao has pointed out." Sweeping his eyes menacingly over the entire assemblage, in a cryptic undertone, he continued, "Even in this room, there are class enemies sitting right next to us. We must raise our vigilance and class awareness to a new height and watch them closely, making sure we are able to see through their disguises and conspiracies and crush them timely."

At his calm, threatening tone and specification, I raised my head in alarm and found all those who had some weakness scared stiff with their heads lowered.

Just then, I heard Chief Xue proceed, "Comrades and revolutionary workers! Our party and our nation have arrived at a critical, life-and-death moment. Every revolutionary worker is obliged to defend Chairman Mao and our party. It is a crucial trial for all of us. Now the moment for you to demonstrate where you stand is here."

At his words, the workers, including the illiterate and the ones that looked uncomfortable, all vied to prove their loyalty to Mao and the party to avoid being singled out as a "class enemy". One after another, each put on a spectacular show, parroting the official tune to condemn the conspiracy and pledging his or her allegiance to Mao and the party.

Sitting there earful of interminable babbling of lies, clichés and sometimes illogical nonsense, I felt as if I were sitting on a needled mat. From the window, I could see it was already completely dark outside. By the time I got home, it would be 10 p.m. I stole a look at my watch. It was about 15 minutes to eight o'clock when the meeting was supposed to be over. I felt relieved to be able to escape the torment another time, getting ready to leave.

Just then, I heard Chief Xue ask, "Anyone else wishes to speak?"

Among the whole room of people, Xiao Lu and I were the only two who hadn't said anything. We felt the pressure and glares. I said to myself, it's almost eight o'clock and it's Saturday. Give us a break already. Determined not to join the lying chorus against my own judgment, I stared into the space, ignoring the demand.

When I was anxiously waiting for the bell to ring, I heard Chief Xue's calm voice again, "I need to point this out: In this workshop, there is some alien-class element who has never opened her mouth, not even once, not even at the party's mandate that demands everyone to demonstrate his political stance. Is she trying to resist the proletarian dictatorship with passive obstruction? I'll make this clear: Anyone who attempts to resist the proletarian dictatorship is courting destruction. Anyone who opposes Chairman Mao, the party and socialism, whether actively or passively, will be flushed out, no matter how well he or she conceals him- or herself."

At this not too veiled accusation, the workers all cast their eyes on me, eagerly and collectively identifying me as the sole offender, feeling relieved to have someone else as the target and the sacrifice. Although Xiao Lu was the other one who never once opened her mouth like me, with her working class background and her own humble, harmless demeanors, she was obviously not the meant "alien-class element".

At this tense moment, I said to myself, it is no life, just a physical existence anyway. There's not much more to lose anyway. The whole nation is like a huge prison without walls. What's the difference whether you are in the big prison or a small one? Any way you look at it, you are in prison. One way or another, you don't have freedom or prospect anyway. In addition, living with an unseen label causes even more anguish than a definite prison term in some sense. The leash around your neck is constantly tugged, making you nervous and insecure all the time. Having weighed the situation, I decided to abide by my principle and not to be intimidated into submission to join in this monkey show to tell lies against my own principle.

Time ticked away slowly in my unabashed adamant silence. Finally, the bell rang, announcing the end of the meeting. A breast-feeding woman asked to be excused and scurried off. At the sight, the crowd became restless. After an exhausting week, all were anxious to rush home for the one-day weekend getaway. I was spared.

I didn't know someone was protecting me at his own expense until I came across Chen Mei at the trolleybus one day. She related to me that Chief Xue had brought my "case" to an administrative meeting to request a formal punishment for an "alien-class element". At this, Mr. Xiao, the factory director, responded, "She didn't commit any concrete crime, did she? There isn't enough ground that warrants a formal punishment. She's a good worker and she's still very young. We should give her another chance." But, at a subsequent meeting for party members in the factory, Mr. Xiao took the heat for his decision of sparing me and for "giving priority to productivity over politics".

At seven months into my pregnancy, I went to Mr. Xiao to request a lighter job. Given my serious medical conditions, Mr. Xiao granted my request right away. I was dispatched to another workshop to produce monocrystalline silicon.

As I was walking into the workshop to report to my new assignment, I noticed everyone there was female. As I was trying to pinpoint the one in charge of the workshop, a peasant's earthy accent drew my attention to a rustic, middle-aged woman with a pair of Mongolian bow-legs swaying toward me. "I hear you're a 'special' person," she spoke acerbically. "From one good job to another good job, you are like walking with a free pass to anywhere you want to go. There were so many people who vied for this job, but they couldn't get it. And you got it like this." Snapping her two fingers, she came to me.

I was struck by this unwarranted hostility, knowing she must be the one in charge of this workshop. I said to myself, big deal. To you, it's a good job. To me, I'm down on my luck. Leave me alone.

She assigned me to sit next to a girl who told me that the hostile woman was the head of the workshop, Ms. Ma.

Working there, I found myself unable to relate to anyone. As the labor was approaching, I became dissociated more and more.

With anemia, high blood pressure and partial separation of my pubic bones, traveling to and from work became even more of a struggle for me. The severe snowy winter made it even worse. I struggled with every step, in pain and dizziness. Nixon's visit added more to the hardship. We were locked down and only released at the end of the day after Nixon's entourage was long gone. Staying beyond work day every day, everyone was full of rage, rushing to get home. When the much delayed vehicles finally showed up, everyone would relentlessly jostle his way through to get on, with no regard for anyone else, young or old. I was sometimes pushed to the ground, bleeding and weeping bitterly. I cursed to myself, to hell with Nixon and his entourage who legitimize an illegitimate government.

This ordeal was finally brought to an end with the baby's early arrival. One morning, I woke up seeing stars in my eyes. My lips trembled too. My husband took me to the hospital. I was diagnosed with pre-eclampsia, a life-threatening condition, and hospitalized right away. In two days, I gave birth to my son prematurely.

On the third day, I was discharged from the hospital. That night, I developed postpartum hemorrhage and a high fever, shivering through the night.

Troubled by the thought of losing me to possible puerperal fever, my husband stayed up for the entire night to take care of me. He constantly changed my perspiration-drenched clothes and blood-soaked sanitary pads and underwear, wiped off my sweat, put cold towels on my forehead, and fed me with hot water, antibiotics and aspirins… In my half sleep, I heard him frequently add coal to the stove and water to the kettle to make sure the room would maintain a constant temperature and humidity.

With his meticulous, selfless care, at dawn, I gradually calmed down and fell into a tight sleep.

The next morning, I awakened to find my fever miraculously gone and my husband leaning on the loveseat with his eyes bloodshot and voice hoarse. I was choked with gratitude.

Near the end of my maternity leave, Fang and Ma, the workshop leaders, unexpectedly arrived at my home.

As they sat down on the uneven broken loveseat, they fell against each other awkwardly and let out a shriek. In embarrassment, I murmured an apology.

With a forced smile on her face, Fang began to exchange amenities with me, "Long Qiru, is everything all right? Is the baby fine too?"

I told them everything was fine and thanked them for their concern.

"When was your child born?" Fang asked.

I told them the date of my son's birth. I didn't tell them he was born half a month earlier than the predicted date. I didn't think it would concern them anyway.

"When were you married?" Ma took over and inquired.

At this intrusion of my privacy, I was uncomfortable. But, not having the slightest suspicion or anything to hide, I told them anyway.

"Will you show us your marriage certificate?" Ma demanded.

I was shocked at this unexpected righteous demand and finally grasped the true purpose of their visit: They traveled all the way across three districts just to find out whether my son was born out of wedlock and that if I was married, whether my pregnancy took place before my marriage by matching the presumed length of pregnancy with the length of my marriage.

I was irked at this naked assault of my integrity and sovereignty. With an effort to have my ire suppressed, I said to them, "I'm not going to satisfy you. This is my home. I'm not going to take the insult in my own home. If you want to, send in the police. Otherwise, you may leave."

Dumbfounded by this unexpected response, after an awkward moment, Fang murmured embarrassedly, "Shall we go?"

Ma snarled as she rose, "This woman is ungrateful. We were doing her a favor, taking half a day off from our busy work and traveling through three districts to visit her, and we got this in return. Let's go!" They left in a huff.

Still indignant, I mulled over the whole thing and recalled the stares and whispers I had received from some workers in the factory during my pregnancy and finally grasped where this whole thing came from.

Shortly after the women's visit, just a few days before my maternity leave ended, I was informed that I was transferred together with the workers from the same shop to another collective-owned factory where components of silicon-controlled rectifiers were produced.

IN THE NEW FACTORY

At the end of my allowed 15-day maternity leave, I was still bleeding heavily, unfit to return to work. In addition, my new-born son was unwell due to the damp condition caused by the water facility right by our home. The day before I was due back to work, I went to the new factory to extend my leave of absence. Generously granted two more weeks, I returned home with a light heart.

Two weeks later, I returned to work. To my surprise, I was assigned to a special experimental group to translate the newly imported technological material. At the time, Premier Zhou Enlai had adroitly convinced Mao to reinstate some sidelined capable hands in order to clean up the huge mess created by ultra-leftists and newly promoted worker-/peasant-turned officials. Deng Xiaoping was one who was reinstated later on to revive the bankrupt economy. Under the new leadership, new technologies were introduced from abroad to catch up with the world. Like my previous factory that had switched to assembling photoelectric lathes, this factory was also engaged in the new venture of producing silicon components. The assumption of the need for English-speaking personnel thus "qualified" me, a one-year English student, for this kind of work in an era of extreme shortages of everything, English-proficient personnel especially.

Trusted to work in this special group, I again felt like a respectable human being, grateful for again not being viewed as a borderline "class enemy".

On my way to the group, I heard rapid footsteps behind me. I looked back. A tall, handsome, polished man with grizzled hair respectably combed back over his broad, receding forehead was loping toward me. At the moment of eye contact, we both felt the connection between us. I was thrilled at the unexpected pleasant addition to my new job.

The man approached me and extended his hand. "Long Qiru," with a twinkle in his eyes, in a refined voice and a suave way, he addressed me warmly as he shook my hand. "Welcome to our experimental group. I'm Tan Qingqi, in charge of this group. I'm glad to see you finally show up."

I immediately apologized and began to explain my situation.

"I know, I know," grinning, Tan Qingqi stopped me. "I was just kidding. I saw you when you first came here two weeks ago. Since then, I have been expecting you. I'm glad to see you here finally."

I was overjoyed at the prospect of working for someone I could relate and talk to. Briskly, I followed him into the office.

"Folks," Tan Qingqi said excitedly. "Here comes our long-awaited colleague, Long Qiru."

At his introduction, all the three teenage girls there—Weiping, Xiao Fan and Xiao Li—greeted me warmly.

"There," chin pointing to the woman in her late-twenties at the far corner, Tan Qingqi said again. "That's our boss Wang Shumin."

In a positive mood, I approached and greeted her.

Sizing me up with a shifty, suspicious look, Wang Shumin returned my greeting with an affected smile that looked more like a smirk and swiftly disappeared for the entire day.

For the whole day, there wasn't much to do, except following Tan Qingqi and the three teenage girls to the workshop to cleanse the silicon chips and check the sintering silicon from time to time.

It didn't take me any time to feel entirely at home in this new environment. The factory was located near Yong'anli, where loads of leftover past personages, old fogies and known scholars were concentrated. The workers there were used to seeing unique, distinct-looking people like the odd characters jumping out of Balzac's novels. There were the Nationalist Mayor of Beijing, He Siyuan, a handsome, brilliant man in his youth but now an unkempt, eccentric, shriveled old man, and his quizzical-looking, mumbling, disheveled French wife, a great beauty in her prime. With the majority being upbeat local youngsters whose education was interrupted by the Cultural Revolution and better-exposed decent locals, the workers there were way more sophisticated than those in my previous factory. In their eyes, I was not that much different from them. I was very pleased with this unexpected easy, pleasant environment.

Three days later on Sunday, when my son reached a month old, I returned home to visit Mother, as I had promised Lu Ma and an old neighbor, Elder Aunt, who unexpectedly visited me a week ago to plead with me to go back home and make amends with Mother. Their teary reactions to my deplorable living conditions and teary pleas had made me see the follies of my action and reckon the responsibility for taking the first step in my reconciliation with Mother.

I didn't expect Mother to answer the door, but here she was, stiff and unsmiling. Unnerved, I uttered an awkward greeting. Mother responded with a frigid acknowledgement.

Mother and my maternal grandmother were the only ones home. My sister and her family had returned to their own home for the weekend.

At the sight of my son, Mother's face softened a little and let an affectionate remark escape her, "The mite has fine facial features."

"Yes, Mother," I murmured.

With our memories still fresh and emotions still raw, we fell into awkward silence instantly. After some uncomfortable moments, Mother broke the silence and inquired, "How's everything?"

"Everything's fine," I responded.

This was followed by more brief superficial exchanges between Mother and me and awkward silences.

My husband and I felt like unwelcome strangers, some low lives taken in by charity. To avoid further embarrassment, I decided to leave. But Mother stopped me and insisted that we stay for dinner. Unable to refuse, we stayed on.

At the dinner table, no one spoke except Mother, who occasionally broke the silence by telling me to help myself. As if seeing through my malnourishment, Mother kept heaping food in my bowl and ignored my husband for the most part as if he didn't exist. I could see my husband's face red like a steamed crab. Other than swallowing the rice in his bowl, he seldom touched the courses. During the silent meal, Mother suddenly became emotional. "Qiru," she said. "Originally, you were the most promising child in the family. But now your situation is the worst..." A drop of tear rolled off her eye.

Mother was not a woman of tears. My situation must have filled her with regret and disappointment. At her words, I burned with shame. I was expected to be in the foreign service and help revive the family line, but instead, I wound up as a disgrace to the family.

The more attention I received, the more painfully aware I became of my pathetic state. I was stung by the scrutiny, especially that of my maternal grandmother, who had disapproved of my rebellious behavior and warned me that I would "not end up well". Now her prophecy about me had unfortunately turned true. By obeying authorities, one is guaranteed to end up OK and get his or her share of the dole-outs. By rebelling and daring to take a different path, he or she would be ostracized, receiving no dole-outs but hits in the head, and ridiculed by the herd.

Mother asked me about my job. I told her that the new factory I was transferred to was within walking distance from her home. At this, Mother extended an offer, "If it's too inconvenient for you, Qiru, you can move back with your son."

Mother's proposal triggered pangs of ache in my heart. It was indeed inconvenient. I had experienced this for three days. It was not fun carrying my infant son traveling two and a half hours each way transferring several times, struggling to get onto the always delayed overcrowded vehicles. Every morning I had to wake him up from his sound sleep and leave home with him at 5:30 to allow enough time to get to work on time. By the time I picked him up at the daycare center, it would be nearly 12 hours later. At the bus stop, we would be at the mercy of irate passengers to get onto the vehicle. Once onto the vehicle packed far beyond its capacity like a can of sardines, unable to move or even breathe freely, I would be worried sick about my son's little life. Heart problems, passing out and sexual harassment on the vehicle were not uncommon. Once we got home, I would have to leave my son to sleep in the damp, frigid room to light the dead stove. We had experienced all of this. It had proved very hard. If I remained in my own home, it would mean my son would have to live like this every day. It broke my heart to see my new-born son have to endure this. However, prideful and not happy that Mother excluded my husband but allowed my brother-in-law to lodge there, I decided to turn it down.

As if having read my mind, before I could say anything, Mother said, "Don't tell me you're fine. I take public transportation myself every day. I know what it's like. Mine is only one express stop. I can imagine what it's like to travel in all weather conditions across three districts with an infant stuck in overcrowded vehicles. Besides, I can imagine what kind of life you have with your meager 16-yuan apprentice's monthly pay plus Wang Fusheng's 38-yuan second-grade worker's wage. I can see it with my eyes: The baby doesn't have much baby fat. I'm afraid the child is suffering because of this. Don't be too prideful. Think about the baby."

I was guilt-ridden at Mother's words. Indeed, with our combined below-urban-average income, we couldn't afford to provide my son with the needed better nutrition, but to rely on my nutrition-deficient milk produced by a diet of mainly carbohydrates on a few kinds of vegetables and rationed flour or rice, plus a combined monthly ration of half a pound of pork for the entire household. Our living standard was further cut down by Wang's monthly 10-yuan chip-in support of his mother, which reduced us to living from paycheck to paycheck. When the baby needed medical attention, we had to borrow money from Wang's mother. Overwhelmed by my sense of guilt, for my son's sake, I swallowed my pride, and gave in and murmured words of humble gratitude.

That night, I didn't return home. From then on, I shared Mother's apartment with my sister's entire family of four and returned to my own home only on weekends.

⁂

As days went on, I found out that there wasn't any translation work and that it was just a pretext that Tan Qingqi used to get me into this group. Every day, I trailed behind him into the workshop, mechanically following the examples of his three assistants ultrasonically cleansing silicon chips. This and checking the sintering chips only took a few hours. The rest of the day we would retire to our office to relax, chat or read. What we did was robotic and monotonous. It had been almost a month, but I still didn't have the slightest idea of the nature of our daily work, except dutifully observing the seemingly meaningless procedures. Day in and day out, wearing a doctor-like white garment, following the three teenage girls—Weiping, Xiao Fan and Xiao Li, I felt pretentious, useless and superfluous like a fool.

Noticing my boredom and uneasiness, Tan Qingqi assuaged me, "Long Qiru, I know your heart is not here. Obviously, this isn't your calling. It's OK not to like this job. Don't give too much thought to this non-essential position. You are not alone. We are all more or less in the same situation of what is called 'shiwei sucan (occupying a position but doing virtually nothing)', or 'messing from the big socialist wok (meaning, having no accountability)'. Just relax and enjoy the pleasant environment. It's good to have you here."

Though I was not thrilled at the new job itself, I was more than happy to have Tan Qingqi's company and to be among civil, affable and receptive people. The advantage of the job was that we had plenty of time to talk about things and exchange our thoughts and viewpoints.

Tan Qingqi was indeed well versed and well informed. He had a sharp mind, full of pointed insight about things. His vision and abilities could put him among top-tier achievers. I wondered how he wound up in this collective-owned factory among the uneducated with his degree in electrical engineering.

With him around, not one day was passed without brain stimulation. Between Tan Qingqi and me, and sometimes joined by Li Weiping, the bright scholarly girl, we had plenty of thought-provoking discussions, with topics ranging from politics to history, philosophy and classic literature, from ancient times to the present, from domestic matters to foreign affairs.

Having someone that I could share thoughts and views with had taken the mundaneness and staleness out of my life. In a stifling, thought-controlling police state, this connection was all the more precious. It allowed us to live above the reality. It was something to look forward to and to live for.

One September morning during the Japanese Prime Minister Kakuei Tanaka's visit to China, Tan Qingqi arrived with the news about Mao's talk with him.

"Guess what happened when Kakuei Tanaka apologized for the Japanese invasion of China?" he asked.

Tan Qingqi often feasted us with fresh news and juicy inside stories about the Maoists and the power struggles within the party. His question immediately aroused my interest.

"Mao stopped him," Tan Qingqi answered his own question. "Instead, he thanked the Japanese for their invasion because it provided the 8,000 communist remnants the needed relief from being pursued and annihilated by Chiang Kai-shek and led to the eventual Communist victory."

Exasperated, I muttered, "Shame on him. The rogue does not have an ounce of decency."

"The real shame is that such an unabashed low life who incited the peasants to attack landlords and told them to 'roll over' to desecrate landlords' wives' and daughters' beds and flagrantly declared the acts 'ruffians' revolts' is cast as a saint, a god to be worshipped by the millions."

"Mao's nothing but a rogue," I said. "He believes in no creed and is bound by no rules. He's law unto himself. This so-called 'Communist' never read *The Communist Manifesto*, a pamphlet of some scores of pages. All that he is interested in is how to usurp power and lay hold of it. His bibles are books about lawless bandits and power-play intrigues such as *The Water Margin* and *The Romance of the Three Kingdoms*. With the lessons he learned from these books, he procured an assemblage of bandits, gangsters, half-witted naïve, disaffected or devious intellectuals and people with severe character defects. With such an assemblage, he was able to ride the coattails of Communism and fulfill his emperor dream through artifice and violence. Now they dress themselves up as 'saviors' and 'heroes' with 'noble ideas' for the common good."

"It doesn't take much to fool the uneducated, ignorant masses," Tan Qingqi commented. "Unable to make it to the top, they are innately drawn to egalitarian ideas that promise equality to all. But in reality, there's no such thing."

With the train of thoughts on my mind, when Tan Qingqi finished his words, I went on, "The Communists are shameless people. They have no conscience and will do whatever to achieve their goals—lying, deceiving betraying, assassinating, stopping at nothing. Their only creed is 'End justifies means'. Take Zhou Enlai for an example. He successfully concealed the Communist guile and real intent, deceiving the public into believing that their only objective was to form a 'united front' against the Japanese threat. He prodded Zhang Xueliang (young Nationalist Marshal) to hold Chiang Kai-shek captive in the Xi'an Incident (December 12, 1936), which obliged Chiang to cease his pursuit of the Communists and form a 'united front' against the Japanese aggression. It not only upset Chiang's plan to be fully prepared for the war against the Japanese invasion and his plan to annihilate the armed Communists, but allowed the nearly annihilated Communist remnants to regrow that eventually brought him down."

"The Xi'an Incident was a turning point," concurred Tan Qingqi. "Zhang Xueliang, the Communist puppet being used and played in their scheme, was a historic culprit whose act forever changed the course of China. It turned the tide to the Communists' favor, allowing them to pose themselves as the ones who were genuinely devoted to the task of fighting the Japanese and providing them the needed time to recuperate and recruit troops that eventually brought doom to Chiang Kai-shek."

"It was the Nationalists that were fighting the Japanese," I couldn't wait to add more. "While the Nationalists were engaged in major battles against the Japanese and encumbered with 3 million fatalities, the Communists hardly lifted a finger. After eight years of war, the exhausted Nationalists found themselves in another war in the final showdown against the well-rested, geared-up Communists poised to take over China. Chiang Kai-shek may be a controversial figure, but Mao is simply a rogue. Chiang had no chance against someone in the position of do or die. In addition, the Communists are a mafia-like organization that exercises tight control over its members while the Nationalists are but a loose democratic alliance, free to join and leave."

"America's wrongful China policy also played a hand," Tan Qingqi added. "Based on biased information about Chiang and the Nationalists provided by Communist and pro-communist journalists, liaisons and cabinet members, Truman came up with a plan of 'unity government' to be formed by the Nationalists and the Communists only to have Chiang handcuffed, compelled to play the Communist game and give way to their demands: funding them and ending his pursuit of them—what the Communists termed the 'civil war'. It weakened Chiang Kai-shek's position and aided the Communists' growth with the funds."

Having summarized the causes of the Nationalists' defeat to our best, we fell into silence, mourning the fate of China. After a while, I broke the silence and said, "Too bad Dr. Sun Yat-sen's bourgeois democratic revolution was not successful."

"Bourgeois revolution is inevitably cursory and merciful, unlike the violent, relentless proletarian revolution," Tan Qingqi responded. "One of Sun Yat-sen's critical mistakes was to ally with the Russian Communists."

"Sun Yat-sen had no choice," I said. "The Western powers all turned their backs on the nascent republic, leaving him no choice but to ally with the Russians, who opportunistically exploited and looted China and exported Communism, which forever changed the course of China."

"Communism is a disaster for the world," Tan Qingqi stated. "It is ruthless. Before the Cultural Revolution, there were still some corners not yet touched by the Communists. For the moment, those people were allowed to run their courses. But the Cultural Revolution took the last corner away from them, making them totally uprooted." Pausing, he then proceeded, "There's a saying: 'It takes generations to make a class.' Wealth does not make a person; education and edification do. These people are the products of generations of refinement. Many of them are naturally endowed and talented. There are many brilliant and ambitious individuals in that class, but they are doomed and victimized by the communist revolution."

At his words, my two friends, Jennifer and Lynn, came to my mind. Reared in a family that nurtured many highly-accomplished figures and PhDs from Harvard, Caltech and MIT, the two talented, aspiring sisters would no doubt be able to accomplish something like their predecessors in a normal society. However, under the Communists, they never had a chance. Jennifer was lucky to be able to go to Beijing University in a more lenient era. But, when the Cultural Revolution started, their paths were permanently changed. Their parents were taken into Qincheng Prison, where high-profiled prisoners were concentrated to exact information against Liu Shaoqi's wife, Wang Guangmei[13], only because their father had been a professor and past neighbor of hers. To put Liu Shaoqi in a deadly position, the Mao cult put over 10,000 in prison to pursue any useful lead against him. Wang Guangmei's interpreting service during General George Marshall's failed attempt (1945-1947) to form a "unity government" between the Nationalists and the Communists was used to accuse her of being an "American agent". With their parents arrested and home ransacked, the two sisters were kicked out of their own cozy residence into a tiny, crude room. Shortly, Jennifer was taken into a reform-through-labor team to exact information against her father. She was beaten to permanent disability, walking on crutches. She was put in a dusty, airless storage room under the stairs that was hot in summer and cold in winter. She developed asthma. With Jack London's *"Love of Life"* and an English-Chinese pocket dictionary she found there, she tackled the book word by word and was able to delve into the story. Inspired by the character in the book, she was determined to survive and outlive Mao. With this goal in mind, no matter what they did to her, beatings, hard labor, struggle sessions and denunciations, she never yielded. Lynn, a 16-year-old girl then, was left alone to survive on her own to deal with hunger and constant harassments of the police and army functionaries. When cold season arrived, all she had were the summer clothes on her back. Resourceful, tenacious with an optimistic outlook and a fire burning in her belly like her sister, she somehow survived. No matter what ordeals the two sisters faced, they stood by each other and never lost their sight of or faith in the future. For this goal, they defied the subhuman status imposed on them, consciously made their life more livable with outings, eat-outs, photographing, and making colorful, fitting clothes for themselves with their old clothes as the templates at a time when the entire nation was draped in ill-fitting drab Mao uniforms of gray, blue and yellowish-green.

At their stories, Tan Qingqi commented, "It's a pity that so many quality people who wanted to accomplish something are wasted. Revolution brings about violence and destruction. There's nothing new about it. We've learned about it from the French Revolution and the Russian October Revolution, which even devoured their staunch advocates. But never before has any social change in Chinese history been like this, eliminating certain classes and obliterating every single member of those classes. There is no place left for them in this proletariat-ruled country. Softened by leisurely life, many of them are unable to adjust themselves to the new situation, since they never had to struggle to make a living. When the Cultural Revolution began, they bore the brunt and collapsed at the fatal blow. The only thing for many of them to do is to die with their class, consciously submitting to their doomed fate without struggle."

With a heave, Tan Qingqi ended his elegy.

Since very young, I had become painfully aware of my class's fatal shortcomings: our indulgence in the ease of life, our deep-rooted distaste for merchants and physical labor, our naivety and inability to deal with worldly matters and people outside our own circle that were amply displayed in my family, myself included. At Tan

Qingqi's words, I was full of shame, lamenting over the doomed fate of my class, my dying family and my own nothingness. Deprived of any opportunity and training, we would never achieve anything. Gnawed by sense of failure, I said to myself, should there be a day to meet my ancestors, I would have no nerve to face them. Not only do I have nothing to claim under my own name, I sullied their good names with my disgrace.

"Long Qiru," while I was billowing inwardly, I heard Tan Qingqi say in jest. "You don't have to deny it. The moment I saw you from afar the first time, I said to the guy by my side, 'This is a highbrow.' The other guy also recognized it."

Roused from my own disquieting thoughts, I had trouble finding words to respond. Before I could think of anything to say, Tan Qingqi already turned to the three joining girls, saying half-seriously and half-jokingly, "Folks, don't look down upon collective-owned factories. They are the places that harbor dragons and tigers. Many interesting people down on their luck sojourn here. When time is right, they will rise again. You have a lot to learn."

FAULTED FOR AIDING TAN

My escape was at work. It was there that I lived in my element. Once, after our routine morning round at the workshop, Tan Qingqi, Li Weiping and I returned to our office to relax. Tan Qingqi started the conversation with the news that the Russians had presented Tolstoy's epic *War and Peace* on screen.

Before the Cultural Revolution, I had seen pictures of the cast members Director Bondarchuk chose for the characters in the novel. They all seemed to fit the exact descriptions of each character. At the news, I regretted that we wouldn't be able to see this epic due to the present political situation in China.

When we were talking about the plot, characters and themes of the book, Wang Shumin stepped in, examining everyone and inquiring suspiciously, "What are you talking so excitedly about?"

"Nothing," Tan Qingqi replied with a smile. "Just a book. Sit down, Minzi, and join us."

Awkwardly, Wang Shumin sank her bottom down right on my knapsack where I kept my sunglasses in a soft slip.

Gesturing toward my knapsack, I said to Wang Shumin hesitantly, "Excuse me, Shumin. My bag. My glasses are in it."

She lifted her bottom. I pulled out my knapsack. The 18-karat gold-rimmed crystal glasses I kept in it had been crushed into pieces.

"Oh, my glasses," I let out a soft lamentation.

Looking at the fragments, Tan Qingqi picked up a few pieces from my hand and asked, "What are they made of? They feel weighty. They don't look or feel like the usual chemical stuff."

"Crystal," I answered.

"Let me see," Wang Shumin said, full of suspicion. Picking up some fragments, she weighed and examined them in her palm, and said, "Such a wretched thing? Are you sure it's crystal?"

At her derision, I heaved and said softly, "Positive. And the frame is made with 18-karat gold."

Again examining the pieces and the mangled frame, she said, "To me, it looks like a piece of junk!" This said, she cast them into the trash can in contempt.

I had no intention to ask her for compensation, but her reaction simply astonished me.

At Wang Shumin's unconcealed rancor and contempt, Tan Qingqi palliated in a conciliatory tone, "Take it easy, Minzi. It's all right. Qiru didn't ask you for compensation. The crystal glasses are old-fashioned. They are not produced anymore. Anyway, the loss of a possession is nothing compared with human lives. Nowadays, nothing much is valued anymore anyway. The only thing that matters is that the person stays out of harm's way." Clearly in an attempt to pacify Wang Shumin, he switched the topic, asking her warmly, "Minzi, how's everything with your fiancé?"

"It's coming along," nonchalantly, Wang Shumin answered, and sauntered off.

Though Wang Shumin's appearance always spoiled the atmosphere, she was not around most of the time.

❦

Tan Qingqi was on business in Shanghai. Since Day One of his absence, we had realized what he meant in our daily life here. Without him, the office turned into a lifeless place. Not only was the pleasure of going to work gone, but the daily gathering in our office also ceased to exist. There was no coagulant force to hold us together anymore.

Half a month later, one morning, not long after my arrival at work, Tan Qingqi's loud, vibrant greetings outside the office announced his return. At this, we all jumped up in excitement. With his return, returned the vitality. The quiet office instantly turned lively and dynamic again. Tan Qingqi appeared at the door, looking exuberant. At his sight, everyone greeted him excitedly and enthusiastically.

No sooner had Tan Qingqi settled in his chair than he exclaimed with ardor, "It's so good to be home again. I missed you. Did you miss me?" His moist, feverish eyes swept over all of us and then fell on me and fixed there searchingly.

My face instantly flushed and my heart began pounding at his persistent, revealing blazing gaze. At this instant, I realized I was undeniably in love with him. At my feelings for him suddenly revealed to myself and perhaps to anyone who paid attention, I was very embarrassed. I turned my face away from his gaze, struggling to regain control of myself. After a long, embarrassing silent moment, I was eventually able to restore my composure.

For the rest of the day, I avoided Tan Qingqi for fear of an outburst from either of us. Internally, I was struggling mightily to overcome my ungovernable emotions.

After the experience with Li Dayin, I thought my heart had been sealed off from love and that it would never pound again. At this discovery about myself, I was angry. I said to myself, stupid, you're not a young girl anymore, but your heart still pounds like a young girl. Tan Qingqi is a married man. And you are still married too. Where is this going to lead to? Can you live with yourself in dishonesty? This is foolish. I pinched and bit myself hard, trying to suppress my feelings for him.

With my mind made up, I consciously stayed away from Tan Qingqi. After a long time, I eventually was able to bring my turbulent emotions under control.

Half a month later, I ran into Tan Qingqi and Weiping chatting in the office. Before I could retreat, Tan Qingqi already invited me to join them. They were having a discussion about the "superfluous men" the Russian writers of the 19 century created.

At first, I remained quiet, not completely at ease near Tan Qingqi. But Tan Qingqi drew me into the conversation about Lermontov's *Hero of Our Time*, asking my opinions about the main character and the themes. Gazing afar, I gathered my thoughts and replied, not completely related to the book, "The times produce their heroes. It's a pity that a lot of brilliant men who were not born at the right time and the right place wasted their talents and idled away their lives like Pechorin that Lermontov created…"

"Long Qiru," eyes moist with embarrassment, Tan Qingqi interrupted me. "You're looking for heroes. This is reality. Perfect men exist only in fiction."

We fixed our eyes on each other. At this moment, we both realized that I had overcome my feelings for him.

Although many people in the factory were alienated from Tan Qingqi and me, due to Tan Qingqi's prestige gained through his expertise, his adroit maneuvering and socialization with them, we were left alone in this daring, unrealistic atmosphere we created for ourselves.

However, Wang Shumin, the one who was actively striving to be qualified for party membership, was a potential danger to us. Having a disadvantaged landlord family background, she must outdo others at all costs in order to advance herself. She had disavowed her parents. When the hospital notified her of their grave conditions, she refused to visit them. A girl with some cold-blooded snake-like qualities and a sinister edge, she was driven to trap and hurt people, and made no secret of her man-hunt. In her presence, people kept their mouths shut or just nodded ambiguously. Even Tan Qingqi had to defer to her. For some reason, she took extreme exception to Tan Qingqi and me as if we were some unreasonable rotten aliens. She was seldom around. But whenever she was present, she would prick up her ears. From the rolling of her eyeballs, I could tell that she was listening in and trying hard to digest whatever she overheard from us. With her eavesdropping and reporting on us constantly, trouble was not too far away.

One day, I arrived at work and noticed the unusual taut atmosphere and serious, dazed look on everyone's face, sensing something serious was taking place. I was shocked to learn that Tan Qingqi had been taken into solitary confinement to account for an affair he had with a divorced retired army woman working in the same factory and that he would be allowed to return home only on weekends.

Although we once noticed the scratch marks on Tan Qingqi's face, we didn't know his wife was driven clinically insane during the Cultural Revolution. With this information, his affair with that reed-thin, vixen-faced woman seemed to make some sense. How the affair began was unclear. We only learned that he had lived with her as a couple for quite some time in a room rented from a peasant in a rural area not too far from the factory. This was known by a few of his confidants at work. An informant got wind of it and reported it to the administrators. A trap was set up. Tan Qingqi's pal in the factory, a known loyal man's man who had helped Tan Qingqi with this lodging arrangement, was coerced to lead the group to their secret hideout. Tan Qingqi and his paramour were caught at bedtime.

At the administrators' threat of jail term, the woman panicked and instantly collapsed. She turned against Tan Qingqi, accusing him of "corrupting and seducing" her, a woman from a "good" family with a sound military background. Tan Qingqi was put in a perilous state.

One Sunday, Tan Qingqi unexpectedly showed up at my home to discuss his situation with me.

When my husband returned home from his weekend shift at night, I told him about Tan Qingqi's visit.

At this, his mood instantly darkened. Without a word, he began to examine the whole room over with probing eyes. When he discovered the cigarette butts in the dustbin, he squatted down and dug out every single one of them.

With the number of cigarette butts counted, he opened his mouth. "There are 23 of them," he said while scrutinizing me. "It takes five to six minutes to finish one cigarette. Assume he took them one after another. Twenty three of them, that's a good two hours. So, he was here for at least two to three hours. A man and a woman unrelated by marriage locking themselves behind a closed door in a tiny room for this long, how could there be anything good out of it?"

I was dumbfounded at what I saw and heard. It was the first time that I had a chance to glimpse and fathom the depth of his deviousness and his distrustfulness. I said to myself, with a mind like this, he can find fault in anything I do. Once he fixates on one, I will never be able to clear myself.

Living with my family, I was already more and more estranged from him. While I still went home with him when he picked me up Saturday afternoon, my heart was not with him anymore. Although I was alienated from him, I had never thought about divorce. Instead, I had braced myself to live the consequences of my folly and bear his deficiencies, and tried to educate him. But the lone world he lived in had left an indelible mark on him, making it impossible to even conduct a two-way conversation with him, let alone impart to his mind something that was beyond the scope of his interest and comprehension. Now at what I saw and heard, my hope of living with him in peace was dashed. It proved that my hope was but an illusion. Shattered and dismayed by the prospect, I yearned to be freed.

From then on, I found myself no longer confined by my sense of marital duty and returning home less and less.

One Sunday evening during Tan Qingqi's allowed home visit, he boldly visited me at my parents' home, evidently desperately needing my help. The appearance of a much older male associate of mine at the door of my parents' home was enough to raise Mother's alarm that resulted in her interference and supervision of our talk.

At Mother's righteous supervision and patronizing posture, Tan Qingqi was visibly rattled and flustered. There was a blackout that night, but the dim candlelight didn't help him very much. To calm himself, Tan Qingqi politely asked for permission to smoke. With a deep draw, he summoned up his courage and came straight to the

point. "I'm ashamed... to come here... and disturb you at home,"
he said. "I apologize for my bold act. I know I have no right to get
Qiru involved in my disgrace, but I have no other options... but
to resort to her help... I was caught red-handed in my extramarital
affair... By giving in to temptation... at a moment of weakness...
I found myself unable to extricate myself, but sliding along. I have
disgraced myself..."

Tan Qingqi faltered, unable to go on.

At the sight of a grizzle-haired man sweating with shame like a
wrongdoing boy, Mother softened her stance. She assuaged, "We all
have our own frailties. We are all fallible."

To make it easy for Tan Qingqi, I came straight to the point.
"Mr. Tan, do you want me to speak to Liu Jun?" I asked.

Liu Jun was the name of his paramour.

"Yes, please." Avidly, Tan Qingqi said, "Please speak to her and
try to arouse her conscience to be truthful. This way, the nature of
this case could be less severe."

Out of sense of justice, I made the promise to him. "Don't worry,
Mr. Tan." I said, "I will try my best. I think I can make Liu Jun
change her mind."

I was confident because Liu Jun and I shared an amiable relationship. With a pleasant manner and a pair of beautiful eyes brimming
full of love, longing and kindness, Liu Jun seemed to be a very nice
woman, humane and reasonable.

The next day, when I had a chance, I requested to speak to her.
She eagerly complied.

After we sat down in a private room next to her workshop, I
started cautiously, "Ms. Liu, you and Mr. Tan have been together for
years. I'm sure you still have some feelings for him. Now Mr. Tan is
in a perilous situation. You are the only one who can spare him serious harm. Will you please try to save him by telling the truth? If you
don't do something to extricate him from the predicament, I'm sure
you will regret it later on."

All the while, Liu Jun listened silently with a strange, crooked
smile on her lowered face, and didn't respond.

Waiting and extracting no response from her, I was a little impatient. I pressed further, trying to make her see the potential harm to Tan Qingqi, "Ms. Liu, if you don't do something to help him, Mr. Tan will end up in jail. Can you have a clear conscience while he is rotting in jail? Can you honestly say to yourself that he 'seduced' and 'corrupted' you? Please think again."

I waited, but there was still no response from her, except the same enigmatic smirk on her face. All of a sudden, she grabbed the three-fourth-empty oblate-shaped small alcohol burner from the table, drank the alcohol of about an ounce or so in it, and flung herself immediately onto the wood floors.

It set off a huge commotion in the factory. Liu Jun was carried on a stretcher to the factory's medical room.

The mission went awry. Things took a sudden turn and worked against us.

At the end of the day, an emergency meeting was convened. Party Secretary Liu, a retired army woman who was normally genial, looked visibly agitated and riled. "Comrades," she began her speech. "You have all learned what happened in the factory this morning. This incident is of a grave nature that warrants every revolutionary comrade's primary attention. Right in front of our eyes, class enemies have brazenly turned our proletarian front into a Beethoven (sic. Petofi) Club. Not only this, they dared to stir up trouble in our proletarian domain to interrupt our normal operation. This has shown how frenzied and desperate class enemies really are. It has proved the correctness of Chairman Mao's theory of class struggle and the necessity of carrying it on. As a matter of fact, class enemies are continuing with their attempts to sabotage our socialist front. We must heighten our vigilance and our awareness of class warfare, and continue to carry on class struggle. For those who dared to stir up trouble for us, we will deal them a swift and firm punishment!"

Her ominous words sealed Tan Qingqi's fate and mine. Right away, I felt the disdain and hostile glares coming from the masses, ostracized at once.

The following morning, I arrived at work only to be informed that this would be my last day of work here. I was to report to another neighborhood factory this afternoon. It was an applique factory in a slum area in Chaoyangmen. Tan Qingqi was also to be placed in another collective-owned matchbox-making factory in the same area as a tentative resolution, pending a formal verdict. With our group disbanded, Li Weiping, offspring of a low-grade Communist official, was faulted for her close association with us. She was sent down to a workshop. Her seemingly sure chance to be selected for college was gone.

Even before this, Li Weiping's brother, who, at the time had not met me, but had spotted some "exotic bourgeois creature" at the bus stop and "positively" identified her as me, had warned her against my "corrosive bourgeois influence". Not only this, Li Weiping's mother had gone to the factory administrators to request that her child be kept away from me so as to "save her from being led astray by a bourgeois young diehard".

At noon, on my way home, I found Tan Qingqi waiting for me somewhere. We decided to meet after lunch at a roadside eatery close to both of the new factories we were assigned to.

In the tiny, crowded dirty eatery, we met each other.

At my apologies for the failed mission, Tan Qingqi stopped me. "You don't owe me any apologies, Long Qiru." He said, "They've already decided to fault me. On the contrary, I should apologize to you for getting you into such a mess." With a deep draw of his lit cigarette, he continued, "Although I know Liu Jun is a cunning woman, capable of trickery, I never expected her to do such a thing as to drink the alcohol in the burner. I know her capacity. She can easily gulp down a bottle of liquor without even changing facial color. She deliberately created this scene to have you implicated. For what reason, I don't know. What she did was just too bizarre and incomprehensible. I guess she did it out of desperation, trying to drag one more soul down into this quagmire together with her. I'm sorry that I brought you into this mess." Pausing and looking me in the eye, he continued, "Long Qiru, I'm grateful for your help. Not many people would go out of their way to offer any help in a situation like this."

With the time to return to work approaching and not much more to say to each other, we parted.

From that day on, we never saw each other again. A few months later, Weiping informed me that Tan Qingqi had been sent to a reform-through-labor farm as a "bad element", serving a three-year sentence without a trial. Years later when his sentence was over, he remained working on the farm like all other convicts having served their terms. He was never returned to normal society again.

ANOTHER TRANSFER

few minutes' walk diagonally across from the eatery, I arrived at the factory I was transferred to. Repelled by the dirty, dilapidated, disorderly ghetto scene of this area, at the sight of the shabby, tawdry façade of the factory painted with vulgar red, green, pink and yellow flowers, I was even more revolted. At the thought of having to work in this repulsive environment with people I had little in common with at a job I was ill-suited for, I was in a bad mood. I tarried outside, hesitating about going in. But as the noon break was to be over in a minute, I toughened myself, walking resolutely toward the gate.

As I was passing through the cramped tiny yard, I noticed in exasperation that behind the windows of a room in the passageway swarmed with girls and women craning their necks to gape at me as if I were a zoo animal. Used to being gawked at, I ignored them and walked straight to the office.

The moment I stepped into the dim, musty small office that had tacky dirt floors, a rustic-looking old woman with a swarthy, leathery face sitting behind a desk stopped what she was doing and lifted her head, revealing a face scrawled with hatred. At the sight, I took a deep breath. I surmised she must be Party Secretary Li Er'e that I was supposed to report to.

Taking off her glasses, the woman sized me up. "Aha," with a sneer, she blabbered in a cracked coarse voice, "This must be Long Qiru, the creature nobody wants." Measuring me from head to toe again, she resumed sardonically, "You indeed look like a bourgeois creature and a troublemaker. The names serve you right."

Faced with a woman so full of unveiled malignancy at a stranger just by the way she looked and the class she was from, I sensed a tough future ahead.

As I was thinking, I heard her say, "I heard this is the second time you were kicked out from your job." Putting her glasses back on, she pulled out a half-inch-thick stack of papers from a 10x13 manila envelope in front of her and read, "This time it was because of your 'suspicious relationship with a bad element and acted as his accomplice to stir up trouble in our proletariat domain and interrupted normal operation'." Weighing the stack in her hand, she continued with a sneer, "Look, this stack of paper is all about your crap. Do you want me to go on and read more?"

It was the first time that I ever set eyes on my *dang'an*. I was unsettled by the thickness of it, wondering what was in there against me. But I didn't show my uneasiness. Instead, without looking at her, I answered flatly, "Just tell me where you want to place me."

"Huh," Li Er'e reviled. "This creature's indeed a brick in the latrine, hard and stinky! Listen carefully: Nobody wants you. We didn't volunteer to take you in. By doing so, we're doing you and society a favor. Let me make it clear beforehand: If you don't know where you are and dare to stir up trouble here, you'll see what you'll be dealt. Right now I'm busy. I don't have the time to deal with your shit. I'll take care of you later." Turning to the woman standing by her, she ordered, "Take her to the inspection shop."

Into the dank, squalid workshop crowded with female workers and housewives contracted to do the work for the factory, I found myself under relentless chilling stares of the whole room of women. Obviously, the way I looked caused their strong aversion. In no time, I heard some not too veiled whispers and snickers and found myself the gossiped object. Evidently, rumors about me had been spread throughout the factory even before my arrival. Having nothing in common with them anyway, I ignored them and settled in my assigned place, avoiding eye contact with any of them, and engaged myself in the work.

Just as I was unpacking a package to inspect the work, some biting remarks reached my ears.

"Do you see the porcelain doll over there?" a woman asked her partner.

With a twinkle in her eyes, the other woman darted a look at me, then looked away in her act, and then fixed her eyes on me again and asked, "Which one?"

"Over there," chin pointing to my direction, the first woman said. "The delicate porcelain doll over there. Take good care of her."

"What 'delicate porcelain doll'?" Merrily, the other responded, "I only see a worn-out shoe!"

At this, the whole shop erupted into hysterical laughter. All of them gloated at me.

At such unmistakable, unwarranted sexual affront, my lips trembled. Tears welled up in my eyes.

"The doll's cranky," staring at me, the first woman said slowly, with a tinge of pleasure in her voice. "Treat her nice and handle her gently."

"'Handle her gently'?" The other retorted in merriment, "Is she some nestling? She's nothing but a worn-out shoe! I bet you, in bed, she'll beg to be roughed!" This said, she began to howl like a cat in heat, "Harder, harder!" With something even filthier "whispered" into the other woman's ear loud enough for everyone to hear, the whole shop again was rocked with unruly guffaws.

I was unable to control my tears anymore. I wept and shivered in ire at such ruthless abuse and at my impotence to handle the abuse.

"You see? You see?" The first woman spoke again, "I told you to treat her nice. She's only a fledgling…"

"Pooh," merrily, the other responded. "A fledgling? Her hole has already been thrust loose and wide!"

At this outrageous, salacious crass remark, the whole shop hooted again.

I had never heard of anything as filthy as this in my entire life. I trembled and heaved uncontrollably. I wanted to dash out of this garbage dump at this instant and never return, but I could not. Knowing they would play and toy with me relentlessly if I showed my vulnerability, I tried to swallow back my tears. But I was simply unable to control them. They kept streaming down my cheeks.

The more I wept, the more vicious they became, relishing the fun of toying with me at their mercy incapable of responding. I clenched my teeth and tried to distract myself with busy work. Eventually, I was able to get hold of myself, but found tears still rolling down my cheeks from time to time.

Although I knew ghettos were fraught with low lives, I didn't expect a work place to be like this, so crass, so grossly indecent and so rampant with ruthless random malignancy ready to aim at anyone, including strangers who had done them no wrong.

At the bell sounding the end of the day, I heaved out a sigh of relief as if I were a released hostage. On my way, a ruddy-cheeked, middle-aged burly man from another workshop whom I later found out to be Lao Luo caught up with me.

While riding alongside of me, he said, "I heard you'd been roughed." At my nonresponse, he sighed, "'A downed phoenix is the sport of chickens'. You know what? Don't take them too seriously. This is the only way they know to talk. Before the Liberation (Communist term for their takeover), a lot of them were prostitutes dealing with pimps, madams, local riffraff and odd-job men. They were made rough." At my silence, he paused and then resumed, "I'm just a craftsman, with only a primary school education. I'm unable to understand lots of things and speak the way I want to. But I have traveled with a shadow puppet troupe and seen some of the world—low world, of course. I can tell you don't belong in this world."

I was grateful for his unexpected kindness and his perspective. Nevertheless, still in low spirit, I was tongue-tied, unable to express my gratitude or utter anything.

At the next intersection, Lao Luo bid me "good-bye". In return, I gave him a grateful look and a nod.

As a punishment, I was assigned to dig air-raid shelters and some-times to perform other outdoor dirty, heavy physical labor of the day, such as carting coal, together with three other females, working in bitter cold or in scorching sun. Gasping for a moment to breathe on my own, I was glad to be away from the filthy, soul-polluting indoor environment.

Among us four singled out was Chen Hanyuan, a sexy, viva-cious woman in her late 20s whose father was a Nationalist colonel handling military supplies. She was faulted for some "sex offenses". I had no idea what she had been through, but from the angry, bitter scowl on her originally joyful, beautiful face, I could tell that she had been through a lot and a lot worse than what I had been through. A jolly, carefree beautiful woman, she was dealt a situation where she had to claw out every inch of her existence. Nonetheless, no matter how hard they tried to break her spirit, she refused to bend, fiercely upholding her pride. The other two singled-outs, Xiao Bai and Wang Min, teenage girls faulted for having had sex with their boyfriend and had an abortion, were also spirited pretty girls from a background called "*genzheng miaohong* (red seedling with upright roots)". Growing up in this tough neighborhood and toughened at a young age, the two girls much younger than I was seemed totally unaffected by what they were going through. I was amazed by their toughness in handling the crap.

One morning, when we were working outdoors, our supervisor, a bald boy who left us completely alone, arrived. "Long Qiru," he said. "Secretary Li wants to see you."

I dropped my work and went with him, knowing it couldn't be anything good.

When I arrived at the office, I found Li Er'e, the old woman I met the first day, waiting for me at her desk. At my appearance, she asked, "Long Qiru, did you sell a flute lately?"

"Yes," I replied in befuddlement.

I sold it to *San Yang* (*Three Sheep*), a well-known secondhand store for expensive exotic commodities such as antiques, curios, jewelry, watches, clocks, carpets, furniture, fur coats, musical instruments and other rare, eye-opening domestic and imported goods that were acquired from customers. At a time when 6 million, three-fourths of the Beijing residents, had to leave or be prepared to leave on short notice for relocations and deployments, frills and treasured possessions that escaped Red Guards' looting were nothing but burdens to be dispossessed. That store thus acquired a load of rare stock that could cause one's jaw to drop but was unwanted by anyone at the time.

"Where did you get the flute?" Li Er'e continued with her inquiry.

"I bought it at the repair shop for musical instruments at Donghuamen," still clueless, I was cooperative and gave a detailed answer.

It was bought years ago when I was in low spirit with the monthly allowance I saved that Mother gave me. During the wave of national relocations and deployments, the vast majority of entertainment troupes had been disbanded and performers transferred to factories and other fields to be "reeducated" and "revolutionized". Their musical instruments and whatever professional possessions were thence no longer needed, and sold cheap. A good German brand upright of decent condition could be bought for 300 yuan, equivalent to 50 dollars then. But a piano or a violin was too beyond me. A flute was affordable. Its serene, solitary and ethereal sound suited my mental state then. In an emergency to treat my son's illness, I sold it to *San Yang*. At the time, the pawnshop employees were mandated to notify authorities of their acquisitions in order to verify their origins. I was thus turned in.

"Do you play the flute?" Li Er'e asked.

"No."

"Then why did you buy it?" with a sneer, she asked. Without waiting for my answer, she went on, "Are you sure you bought it, not stole it from somewhere?"

Exasperated by the insult, I challenged her, "Do you have any proof that I stole it?"

"We have plenty of proof!" Li Er'e claimed.

"Then prove it."

"When it's time, we will!" She growled, "Don't you think you can get away with your shit if you are not caught. By offering you a chance to confess, we are doing you a favor. You'd better be sensible and quit denying. Otherwise, we will not treat it leniently!"

"Go ahead. Do whatever you have to do."

At this point, her coercion had no effect on me at all. Only fury dominated me. Before she could stop me, I had dashed out of her office and slammed the door behind me.

When I returned to my teammates, I vented out.

At this, Chen Hanyun smiled. "Long Qiru," she said. "Don't let this bother you. It's nothing! I've been accused of worse things. Let them do what they need to do. If you don't give a damn, what can they do about you?" At my sullen look, she held up her thumb and forefinger an inch apart, and continued, "Look, Long Qiru. I have a *dang'an* this thick. The thicker, the better. What is my major offense? I give them a headache! They can do nothing about me, nothing at all! Look, I'm still alive and still kicking!" She started to cackle hysterically.

At her words, I smiled. Compared with what Chen Hanyun had to put up with and what I had been through, this was indeed nothing.

At the time, I had filed for divorce. Still hoping to make me change my mind about the divorce, my husband came to meet me at work every Saturday afternoon and followed me silently all the way to the outside of Mother's home despite my irritated rejections and spectators' jeers. Eventually softened by his persistency and his pitiable state, I decided to meet with him in Zhongshan Park the coming Sunday to discuss the problems between us and find out whether we could work out a compromise between us and save the marriage.

It was a fine, crisp winter afternoon. As we were sitting on a bench in a sunny, busy section, a policeman suddenly appeared in front of us and demanded, "Stand up! Come with me!"

Wondering what law we had broken, we followed him into the park's police precinct.

"Sit far away from each other!" he berated and left us there without any explanation.

Half an hour later, a policeman emerged from inside. Handing us a writing pad and two pens, he commanded abrasively, "Write down your offense in detail."

Clueless about what he meant, I protested, "What 'offense'? We didn't do anything wrong!"

"You didn't do anything wrong?" he disparaged. "How did you wind up here then? No more nonsense! Write down your self-criticism on your offense against public decency. Otherwise, you are going to stay here!"

At the sight of the policeman who detained us, I said, "Comrade Policeman, you saw us. We were just sitting on a bench talking. We didn't do anything wrong..."

"No more nonsense," he interrupted me and chided. "Someone reported that you two were engaged in an indecent act!"

Recalling a man walking past us while my husband was wrapping his winter coat around me, I shot back, "'Indecent act'? How ridiculous. We are husband and wife. We have a home. Why do we have to display ourselves in public?"

My husband and I both refused to cooperate, vehemently denying any wrongdoing. Unable to make us bend, they kept us there for several hours. At around eight o'clock at night, they finally let us go.

The next morning, I arrived at the factory, fully prepared for what was awaiting me. Hardly had I settled down when I was called into Li Er'e's office.

With a sneer on her face, Li Er'e scoffed, "Long Qiru, you sure keep us busy. With you around, not one day can we concentrate on our work and not deal with your shit. I guess a dog will never change its habit of eating shit. You're a living scandal, like the feces in a cesspool whose odor can be smelled from miles away. The scenes you created here weren't enough that you had to do it in public as well? Does it ever occur to you that you have a face to keep? I guess not. To tell you the truth, I am embarrassed for you. I guess you bourgeoisie don't know what decency means. One trouble after another, you are incorrigibly unrepentant! Just as Chairman Mao says, 'Class enemies will never change and will meet God with a granite-like skull carried on their shoulders'!"

At the unwarranted remarks, I screamed, "I didn't do anything wrong!"

"You didn't?" Li Er'e sneered, "Then why were you detained by the police? Why is it always you who were caught, but not anyone else?" Stiffening her body, she went on, "With your messy history and background, you are mandated to behave. Class enemies are not permitted to make mischief!"

Vexed by the groundless accusation, I turned around to leave, but Li Er'e stopped me. "You are not allowed to leave, you itchy cunt!"

I trembled in ire at this low, filthy curse that came out of an official's mouth. Unable to leave and knowing it was just the beginning of more filth, I furiously jammed my forefingers into my ears to block them from being polluted.

While Li Er'e continued with more soul-polluting filth, someone appeared at the door. I seized the moment and stormed out.

That summer, out of the need for educated people, the party opened up the door for more "college students". A great many youths with trusted backgrounds—Communist, worker, poor-peasant and army man of whatever education level were admitted. Even the small factory I was in of about 100 was allocated one nominee. Qin Shufang, a third grader and a foul-mouthed girl who unabashedly bragged she could "curse three days and three nights straight without repeating" herself, was chosen.

At the nomination meeting, Li Er'e gave a speech. "Comrades," she began. "Our great leader Chairman Mao has instructed us that 'the domination of our schools by bourgeois intellectuals should by no means be tolerated to continue any longer' and that 'the proletariat must build up our own army of intellectuals instead of relying on bourgeois ones'. It is an honor that Chairman Mao granted us. We have chosen Comrade Qin Shufang to represent our factory to carry out this glorious yet tough task entrusted to us proletariat." At these words, the workers applauded and cheered triumphantly. When the din was signaled to quiet down, Li Er'e continued, "Chairman Mao has also instructed us that 'the history that was dragged backward by the bourgeoisie should be reversed'. In the past, we were kept at the bottom. Now Chairman Mao has lifted us to the top. We must repay Chairman Mao's trust by carrying out his class line and class policies thoroughly, never giving the vile spawn of class enemies any chance. They are going to be kept at the bottom with a foot stamping on them to make sure they are never able to turn over!"

The workers now went wild and hysterical with obnoxious hurrahs while a few gloatingly stared at me, the implied "vile spawn" and the one known to be malcontented. I stared them back and forced them to look away. I said to myself, go ahead with your stupidity. What do I care? It's a nation for idiots anyway.

If in the past natural selection had been tilted toward those exposed to knowledge and those economically advantaged, with this drastic radical new policy, it would create a complete reversal. But very few of the selected that suited their agenda were capable of carrying out such task, for most of them were either brainless followers, unable to think on their own at all, or lacked broad rudimentary knowledge like people who were exposed to knowledge daily from early age on. By doing so, it would leave out the most knowledgeable and the most brilliant ones of the population. It was nothing but a farce and a guaranteed failure.

THE INSANITY CONTINUES

"Enemies" are forever needed in the Communist revolution. In the ever-escalating class warfare, the list of "enemies" was steadily and forever expanding with new additions. There was always a new campaign of some sort timely supplying the stock of "enemies". Having exhausted the "enemy" terms, now they launched a new campaign to "ferret out worms of every hue chewing off socialism". Public struggle sessions were frequently held to condemn those cast-outs with some inconsequential problems.

Ever since the Lin Biao Incident, the masses had lost their faith in Mao and the party. The thrill and the zeal to follow them had gone. Fatigued by years of unending campaigns, meetings, and struggle sessions, during those occasions, the workers paid little attention to what was going on but chattered, hollered and mumbled when occasions arose for slogan shouting. If the accused was experienced in political sports and had some sense of humor, able to detach himself from the proceeding, he could view the scene as a comedy and derive some fun out of the absurdity.

At the time, whenever there was a public struggle session, we four—Chen Hanyun, Xiao Bai, Wang Min and I—would be taken to a local stadium to be seated together with other miscellaneous "minor offenders" to be humiliated. Appearing in public as a disgraced person to be gawked at and taunted, I was incensed and ashamed, trying to stay as invisible as possible while Chen Hanyun would be her usual self, holding her head high defiantly, and Xiao Bai and Wang Min would whisper and titter all the while as if nothing unusual were taking place. Defined as a "worm surreptitiously chewing off socialism", I felt the dark sense of humor. But to be seen and humiliated in public, I was not in the mood to laugh it off. Instead, I was mad as hell. Seeing how my pals dealt with it, I tried to emulate them. But, no matter how hard I tried, I was still deeply hurt.

The first time we were taken to such an occasion, seen and taunted in public in front of perhaps a thousand spectators, including my fellow workers, as "garbage", "trollop", "worn-out shoe", "sodden goods", "rotten flesh" and other even more filthy names, I shivered in fury. When we were back to work from the struggle session, I was still smoldering while Xiao Bai and Wang Min were already talking about going to a movie at night with their boyfriend. Despite Chen Hanyun's claim of not letting anything affect her, I could tell that she was just as bitter and humiliated as I was.

After a while, Chen Hanyun got over her wrath. Noticing my mental state, she tapped me on the shoulder and coaxed, "Long Qiru, I know it's hard. But try not to take it too hard. The harder you take it, the more power you will give them." Seeing me still sulky, Chen Hanyun changed her tone, "Listen, Long Qiru. There's going to be more like this coming our way. If you don't learn to take it easy, you are going to kill yourself before they kill you. Do you want to be like those *yuansigui* (the wrongful dead) who were unable to take it any longer and killed themselves? Think about it. They do this purposely to break our spirit. Don't let them win. Lift up your head and keep it high and show them that they cannot defeat you!"

I had figured out the purpose why we four were treated like this, for in the same factory, there was another girl transferred from another factory for having had sex with a fellow worker and having had an abortion. But she was not punished as we four were because of her total submission and saccharine deference to them. I knew punishing the wrong-doers was not the purpose and that their ultimate goal was to break the spirit of the individuals until they became unconscious beings, with no personality, no will, no initiative, no feelings, and no thoughts of their own. Day in and day out working together with the three, their spirit had unknowingly rubbed off on me. "Don't worry about me," I smiled and said. "I'm not going to kill myself, and I'm not going to let them kill me either and let them win."

However, despite my effort, deep down, I still felt the effect of this public humiliation. The rest of my day was still overcast.

At the end of the day, I found Xiao Li, Xiao Cao and Xiao Feng, the three young girls who had befriended me in this factory, waiting for me at the gate as usual. At the sight, I felt an expansion in my chest. At a time when one had just been humiliated publicly, this gesture meant a lot. Touched by their wordless moral support and knowing they would stand by me against the world, I broke my mirthless state and flashed them a smile. Without a word, Xiao Li and Xiao Cao wrapped their arms around me, and walked me to the daycare center to pick up my son.

On our way, Xiao Li, a polio-impaired yet cheerful pretty girl so long having been walking with me in silence, broke the silence and said solemnly, "Long Qiru, your position in our hearts will never change no matter what they do to you."

Xiao Feng, a tall, slim, comely girl with a quiet, graceful demeanor and a scholarly look, eagerly concurred, "Yes. In our hearts, you are high above those who denigrate you."

"Long Qiru," with a coy smile on her face, Xiao Cao also joined the comments. "At first, we thought you were unapproachable, belonging to a different class. But when we got to know you, we found you a very nice, very special person. I don't think I could handle any of this garbage that is dumped on you..."

At their unexpected spontaneous words that revealed so much about my position in their hearts, I was choked full of gratitude for their appreciation of me and their unwavering support for me.

Throughout those years, it was their selfless devotion to me that made my life in that factory so much easier. They spent much of their spare time keeping me and my son company and bringing us much needed joy, comfort and companionship. Their total acceptance and camaraderie provided me with the much needed balanced new perspectives and a more positive outlook. Though I still could not consider myself to be one of them, I had learned that we were all human beings and that in this respect I was not much different from them. A reject and an outcast, I found my haven in them.

❧

By then, politics had faded out of my consciousness. Struggling to survive at the bottom, I no longer cared about politics. How to remain alive and have my son shielded from harm were my only obsessions.

One weekend, when I was home busy with chores, my son begged me to let him go downstairs to play. Tied up with work, I was unable to accompany him. At his promise of avoiding trouble, I let him go, thinking of joining him shortly.

In no time, came my son's wailing in the corridor. I rushed out and caught a shocking sight: My son's nose had turned into a bloody mess, broken both inside and outside. Blood was gushing out, dripping onto his clothes and trailing along his path.

"What happened?" I exclaimed hysterically while rushing to treat the wounds.

"Xiao Qiang destroyed my tricycle and hit me with a brick..." my son wailed louder, blood oozing out of the blood clotting herb powder and cotton swabs I put in his nostrils. The tricycle was my son's only toy, made by his father with great love.

"A brick?" Shocked and shaken at the cruelty of the crippled boy six years older than my son, I asked. "Why?"

"He said, 'I'll kill you, you counterrevolutionary dog whelp...'"

I was busy treating the broken surface and re-blocking his nostrils. At the name "dog whelp" I used to be called, I flew into a rage. "Why did you go down? I told you not to!" As I was screaming, my palm fell hard on his bottom.

It was the first time that I ever hit my son. The thought of exposing him to harm and injustice simply drove me insane. Seeing him hurt was like hurting myself a hundred times as much. My son cried again. I held him tightly, and we cried and huddled in each other's arms.

Mother couldn't stand it. She reproached me, "Why did you hit him? He's only 3-years old. He was just bullied by some urchin, and you hit him again? Why don't you go and see that boy's parents?"

"It's not our world," I cried. "We have nowhere to seek justice. If I hurt him first, no one else can hurt him anymore…"

"What logic," said Mother. "Stop crying and tidy yourself up. I'll go with you to see that boy's parents."

Mother and I went together to the boy's home in the next building occupied by the employees of the prestigious Foreign Trade Ministry. At the sight of us, the ones far below them and not protected by law, the man didn't respond to our complaint, but simply shoved his son away and slammed the door loudly in condescension only to see it reopened by his woman. "Get out of here!" She screeched, "You're not welcome!"

Mother was beside herself. On the way back, she coaxed my son gently, "Listen to your mom. Don't go down by yourself again. There're too many bad people out there."

Since then, I started hitting my son in the belief that I was immunizing and disillusioning him, making him invulnerable to hurt. I didn't realize by doing so, I would deprive him of his last sanctuary and destroy his very self, his childhood innocence and his faith in this world and human beings at such an early age. Later on, the anger caused by the never-ending injustice we experienced turned me into a monster. Whenever my son did something wrong, I would hit him, abusing him verbally and physically to release my long-suppressed anger and frustration. It became a habit. When he was a tenth grader, one night, he came home late again despite my repeated warnings. I had been repeatedly contacted by his teacher for him not doing his homework. In a fit of rage, I hit him in the head with a small, narrow stool. Although I had consciously reduced the force before it struck him, this incident left me a lifelong, deeply troubled guilty conscience and recurring nightmare to this day. I'm living with this guilt and regret.

In the summer of 1975, my husband was turned in to the police by his neighbor for having suspicious relationships with some women. His three-year sentence to reform-through-labor became a "legitimate ground" for my divorce that resulted in swift finalization.

One morning not long after I arrived at the factory, I was notified to go to the district court to receive the divorce certificate. In the afternoon, I returned to work.

Shortly after I settled in my place, a woman's comments to her partner reached my ears. It was the same duo who had mercilessly reduced me to tears when I just started my work here three years ago.

"This woman must be crazy," said she, looking at me disapprovingly. "She gave up everything, retroactive and future child supports. Isn't this foolish?"

Apparently, the workers had got wind of the details of the court verdict. With a smirk, the other woman responded, "Who knows why? She must have some scandalous secrets held by her now-ex that forced her to give up her legal rights. Anyway, who gives a hoot about this odd creature?" This said, a torrent of unnecessary obscene remarks spurted merrily out of her mouth, directed at me. They both cackled.

Since I left my husband, my son and I had lived solely on my meager income out of my own choice. Before my husband was sentenced and deprived of his wages, I had been granted monthly child support. But I turned it down. I didn't want to have anything to do with him. Besides, I would have a chance to remarry, but he wouldn't, with his background and now the sentence.

For years, I had borne my co-workers' misconception as someone that would do unethical things that they were likely to do, since I was from a "no-good" class. Everything I did was misconstrued as something done out of ulterior ill motive.

Three years of anger at their daily abuse and ill-conception of me had accumulated to the explosive point. Shivering uncontrollably, I blurted out a common curse equivalent to a voiceless "F" and a voiced "you" in English.

At my laughable attempt to curse, the whole workshop exploded into hooting, entertained by the hilarious scene of my fury and my inability to curse, mocking me as a "fledgling".

At their delight, I trembled helplessly, angry at the abuse, at my impotence to handle the abuse, at being compelled to cross the threshold, abandoning myself to the world that I had despised and defied for so long, and at giving in to my innocence extorters and my spirit grinders.

Since this incident, however, I found myself accepted by my coworkers. With my surrender, I gained their first and final approval. I also learned that most common folks didn't really hate us. Even for those fanned by the Communists, once they saw us knocked off the pedestal that we established for ourselves and placed ourselves on, and deign to speak their language and mingle with them as our equals, they would become receptive of us and be full of compassion for our unfortunate fate. In terms of warmth and generosity of the spirit, they were much better than my own people.

After years of stubbornly holding my ground, I found myself finally reaching the turning point in my life to start being assimilated into the masses. Once crossing the threshold, my transformation was like a cascade. From an innocent, vulnerable, defenseless lamb that anyone could leave his mark on, I saw myself turn into an alley cat fiercely fighting for my space to survive.

Disillusioned and angry at my lost innocence, I became cynical and irreverent. I no longer held any faith or conviction, no longer believed in truth and beauty, and no longer considered anything to be sacred or worthwhile. I no longer took myself seriously, no longer troubled my brain, and no longer kept my feelings and opinions to myself. Instead, I had acquired the masses' facile logic, crude demeanor and simple solutions to problems, mocking things and people, and screaming out when wronged. Worst of all, to my deepest regret, I no longer had a pure soul. The anger and frustration caused by years of mistreatments had made me cross the boundary to do unethical things and justified my acts as "returning wrongs with wrongs" like many of my coworkers.

Almost 10 years of the Cultural Revolution had fundamentally changed the nation. The national character was degenerated; the culture and the morals of the nation drastically declined. We were all righteously doing unethical things with justification and no shame. What is more, the concept of a citizen's rights and obligations vanished from our minds. Now everyone had virtually been assimilated into the masses—wearing the same drab mass-production outfit, speaking the same simple language about the same simple matters, having the same simple needs and worries, and leading the same minimal existence. If there had been undesirable families left unscathed by the earlier campaigns, after the Cultural Revolution, which was "to wring everyone's soul" and "to pound all and clean up all", few families were able to maintain their privileges and live an exclusive life above the masses anymore. The social strata were completely flipped, with the once rich and educated at the bottom, and the poor and uneducated elevated. Lording it over all, were the self-proclaimed most qualified "proletariat"—the Communists and their families.

Nineteen seventy-six was an inauspicious year. While Mao, the tyrant, was still clinging to life and his insane crusade, Zhou Enlai, a better Communist, passed away. At the death of the only sane one that mattered among those hell-bent leftist lunatics, the nation saw itself bereft of all hope. Large spontaneous mourning and demonstrations were held in many cities. When the police attempted to arrest people in Tiananmen Square, angry mourners beat up the police, overturned the police cars, and set afire the military barracks nearby. It led to a crackdown. Deng Xiaoping was expelled as "China's Nagy" in what was termed "Tiananmen Incident (April 5)". Tens of thousands were arrested; hundreds were beheaded; all residents were demanded to account for his or her whereabouts during those days of riot. I escaped their suspicion by denying being there. With all the detention centers packed full with the arrested, my friend, Zhang Huachen, a mid-rank army officer descendant, and thousands of others like him were shoved into the empty rooms in Zhongshan Park, with only squatting room and handcuffed from behind. When he was released half a year later due to the nephritis he contracted, his wrists had been grazed to bare bones. Booted from his job, he eked out a living as a self-employed repairman. With tightened-up rule and the leftist absurd, lunatic campaigns going on one after another, there was no end in sight for this hopeless life. As if we hadn't suffered enough, on July 28, we were hit with an unprecedented catastrophic earthquake.

That day, when dawn was still hours away, a prodigious force violently jolted us awake from our sound sleep. "Earthquake!" my brother Ciqing shouted out an alarm. In the dark, I scooped up my son. With a blanket wrapped around him, I dashed down the stairway frantically with my family and the terrified crowds. In the open lot, we found ourselves among our dazed neighbors who were either half naked, in night wear, bare-footed, or wrapped in a sheet or blanket, heatedly conjecturing the magnitude of the quake.

Since Beijing was situated on a fault line, we were used to quakes. We had never, however, experienced a quake of this magnitude. Given the likely aftershocks and the possible collapse of the buildings, going back inside was out of the question.

At daybreak, when things quieted down, one after another, we returned to our home to get our camping needs ready. With our cots, beddings and things of importance collected, food cooked, and kettle and thermos flask filled, we joined our neighbors in this camping army. Soon, the street was turned into an improvised tent city.

School and work were halted. In official news, the quake was reported like a weather forecast: An earthquake of 7.8 Richter Magnitude took place in Tangshan (an industrial city 96 miles east of Beijing), nothing much else. But some experts estimated it at as high as 8.2 Magnitude, which we believed to be closer to truth given that the Communists lied all the time to serve their needs. Some 16 hours later, we were hit by another powerful quake reported at 7.1 Magnitude.

Without official relief or attention, we were left to struggle on our own. To prevent the truth from leaking out, the Communists declined international aid, as usual—It wouldn't affect them anyway. Even in Beijing, the capital city, normal life was interrupted. Very often, we were without water, gas or electricity.

At this unprecedented catastrophe, media remained oddly quiet with no reports about the consequences and casualties, but continued to wage Mao's class warfare insanely as if nothing unusual were taking place and the colossal quake was worthy of only a one-time headline. What was worse, at the time of our hardships, media oddly raved that the situation was "excellent" and "becoming better and better". They published Mao's poem that depicted a peaceful and prosperous scene that "everywhere orioles sing and swallows dart" as if to celebrate our plight. Mao's speech was also released that declared "the Chinese are not afraid of death. Even if half of the population is gone, there'd still be another 600 million left".

At such official indiscretion and callousness, the Beijing residents were riled. Grievances, cries of wrath, and veiled antipathy against Mao and the party were heard all around. There were even private invocations for Mao's immediate death.

One day, upon hearing the droning of the official tune over his battery-powered radio again, Zhang Wenliang, a tall, big-hearted, outspoken man with a stentorian voice who was camping next to us and the chauffeur of Fang Yi, Minister of Foreign Economic Relations and Trade Ministry, initiated a talk with Mother. "Old Xu," with an incredible look on his face, he began in a sarcastic tone. "Do you hear what they say that the situation is 'excellent' and 'becoming better and better' and that 'everywhere orioles sing and swallows dart'?"

With a grin, Mother replied, "Who can miss it? It's propagated daily by the media."

At Mother's response, Zhang Wenliang continued animatedly, "Old Xu! On this sick land where falsehood is propagated and propelled daily as truth, no one dares to say anything that contains an iota of truth. I'm a party member and a veteran from a 'genzheng miaohong (red seedling with upright roots)' family. I'm not afraid. This is a pack of lies! Let the emperor come out of his palace and take a look at the common people. He must be in high fever and delirium!" With his emotions aroused by his own words, he proceeded with more effervescence, "'The Chinese are not afraid of death? With one half gone, there will still be another 600 million left'? What nonsense is that? Which half is he in? I bet he didn't count himself in the dead half. This is simply trifling with human lives!" Spitting out an expletive, he vented on, "How can we have any sane policies in a country ruled by a dying lunatic who refuses to give up power even on his death bed? In the hands of this perverse tyrant, the nation is but a toy that he trifles with. When he needed Deng Xiaoping, he reinstated him. When he felt threatened, he deposed him and unleashed his mad woman. Now that the 'White-Boned Demon' Jiang Qing is becoming the empress, there'll be no end of sufferings for us common people!"

Mother smiled at such unchecked open remarks against Mao. Nevertheless, she didn't have the same status, and couldn't afford to make such comments. Instead, she responded tactfully, "Our ancestors considered a natural calamity the wrath of heaven for the evils conducted on earth that would result in fundamental changes. Could this quake be the harbinger of change?"

"It may well be," contemplating the question, Zhang Wenliang answered. "If they persist in their perverse rule, the Communist rule is sure to come to its end soon. Even our Minister Fang said so."

By word of mouth, we learned that out of 1.6 million of the total population in Tangshan at the time, more than half a million perished in the quake while another half million were severely injured with missing limbs. The aftermath epidemics added more to the death toll. One of my co-workers' husband dispatched with his regiment for rescue efforts told her that the whole city was wiped out and that the stench from the decomposed bodies lasted for months and that many who survived had only their torsos left.

Truth leaked out from the angry posters posted at the State Bureau of Seismology. Scientists who had successfully prevented significant losses in the Haicheng earthquake a year before had predicted the advent of this monumental quake in the Tangshan area and reported their findings to the administration. However, to stay in Mao's favor, the administrators were busy waging Mao's class warfare and delayed handling this matter, which resulted in the leveling of the entire city, the colossal loss of lives and injuries, including the obliteration of the entire monitoring team of seismologists working there.

☙

One day, I was with my son at the bus stop on our way home. The moment I stepped into the bus, I heard a familiar hoarse female voice call out, "Long Qiru, is that you?"

I winced at being recognized by an old acquaintance in public. Since my downfall, I had severed all the old ties and avoided acquaintances, wishing to steer clear of the contrast and abasement. It was my former classmate and ex-friend Kong Xiuhua. Having nowhere to avoid her, I greeted her reluctantly, "Yeah, Kong Xiuhua."

"You have a son already?" she sounded surprised.

"Yeah," even more embarrassed, I answered dryly, praying she pose no more questions for me and make me a spotlight in public.

My concern turned out unnecessary. We didn't have much to say to each other, except remaining awkwardly silent. Apparently, neither of us forgot about her denunciation of me ten years ago.

Stung by the memories of my humiliating past and my present pitiable state, I couldn't wait to get off. When the bus reached my destination, I heaved out.

When I stood up to get off, Kong Xiuhua suddenly took out three ears of corn from her bag and thrust them to me. "Here," she said. "Take them!"

I thanked her and declined her offer. In our earlier relationship, I had been the giver. Now I had become the pitiable lesser. Although she didn't express any remorse explicitly for what she had done to me at my most wretched state, her gesture had revealed her remorseful moment.

When I was wishing desperately this encounter would never occur again, one afternoon, on my way to pick up my son at his kindergarten, I unexpectedly spotted my former teacher, Mr. Hong Jinlong. The moment I saw the uniquely nimble, graceful athletic gait and the straight, lithe figure, I recognized him and wanted to turn around. But it was too late. He already espied me.

"Long Qiru!" he exclaimed as he quickened to approach me. His keen, candid eyes and his fervent voice revealed his trust in me not reduced a bit by the wear and tear of the years.

At this familiar trusting, soul-revealing fervency, tears at once welled up in my eyes. It dredged up all of my shame and pain. They were the last things in this world that I wanted to remember. "Mr. Hong," I murmured my acknowledgement and subconsciously lowered my head.

"Long Qiru," I heard Mr. Hong say in a keen voice. "Listen. What happened to you in the past was not your fault. I had conveyed and emphasized this to the police when they came to our school to investigate you through me. I told them you were absolutely innocent and blameless!"

At his kind words and firm belief in me that did not contain any momentary doubt about me, tears poured out of my eyes.

Mr. Hong was stirred up by my tears. Having got hold of his emotions, he said to me firmly, "Listen, Long Qiru. It was the past. It happened a decade ago. It's over now. Don't be haunted by it. It's the future that matters. There's a long way ahead of you. Take good care of yourself and live well!"

With more tears waiting to spurt out, I nodded to him a grateful "good-bye" and made off.

THE END OF THE
CULTURAL REVOLUTION

Mao eventually died in September 1976. At the news, we were all stunned, unable to believe that the tyrant who had seemed to cling to his life and rule us forever finally kicked the bucket. Having been played and hoodwinked by Mao and the party for so long, we were simply skeptical of what we were told, surreptitiously exchanging our suspicions with one another about some possible ruse or trap laid behind it. There was no spontaneous sorrow or mourning as had been seen displayed at Zhou Enlai's death. Other than an eerie silence, the nation didn't seem to know how to react to and cope with it. For almost 30 years, Mao's shadow had haunted us without an end, now we found ourselves still haunted by him even after his death, by his ghost.

At the death of the tyrant, I quivered with a sense of liberation. I said to myself, the "immortal god", the one who had been hailed to have "a ten-thousand-year long life" at last expired! But who will be the successor? The answer is apparent: Whoever will be in power can't be any worse than he was since none of the widely-hated ultra-leftists has any real power. Although I couldn't wait to see changes take place, I couldn't demonstrate my true feelings. Instead, I loathingly put on a black armband as a mourning sign like everyone else.

Three days after his death, a nation-wide mourning ritual was held in Tiananmen Square and in every institution simultaneously. Before 3 p.m. that day, we lined up silently in front of the factory's black-and-white TV set for the simulcast. At the official announcement and the rise of the mourning music, the workers simultaneously lowered their heads and dutifully sobbed out in unison. A few even wailed while one "fainted". On this life-stage, we all had become excellent actors. Putting on a political show had melted into many people's blood and become part of their thinking and guideline. I wondered whether they themselves could tell what was real and what was for show. To protect myself, I rubbed my eyes hard to make them look red in my act of wiping off tears.

In the wake of Mao's death, the entire nation seemed to have come to a halt and appeared eerily calm as if knowing some secret pivotal move was in the making, about to take place. Just as we were waiting in presentiment, to our great astonishment and excitement, we learned that in a stealthy surprise move, the soft-liners arrested Mao's wife and her Shanghai clique Zhang Chunqiao[14], Yao Wenyuan[15] and Wang Hongwen and branded them the "Gang of Four" on the charge of plotting a coup d'état. At their arrests, the Shanghai gang and the million-member "Shanghai Workers' Militia" to be used in the Mao cult's farcical amateur coup after Mao's death surrendered without firing a shot.

The news plunged the entire nation into utmost ecstasy. People's spirits were never before as high. After living under Mao's tyrannical rule for almost 30 years, all were waiting for a thorough change. Everywhere, it was a scene of celebration for this liberation: bottles were emptied in every household; firecrackers were set off on every street. To mock the widely-hated Mao's wife Jiang Qing and her three male minions, shrewd grocery workers bundled up one female and three male crabs together to be sold, bellowing derisively, "Sangong yimu (three twits and a twat)! Sangong yimu!" In a few days, the usually unseasonable, undesirable male crabs were all sold out this way. No one wanted to miss out on the fun of symbolically eating up the much hated gang.

Every night, we were crammed in front of our small 15" black-and-white TV set Mother purchased recently with the ticket allocated by her institution, enthusiastically and attentively watching the trial of the "Gang of Four". What we saw, however, were only officially sanctioned segments. With no latitude allowed to link the "Gang of Four" to Mao in any way, the trial was nothing but a farce. All the evils were imputed to the "Gang of Four". Mao and the party were still "great, glorious and correct" as they had ever been.

❧

With Mao gone and key ultra-leftists arrested, the Cultural Revolution died down.

In August 1977, the Cultural Revolution was officially declared a "comprehensive victory" that "triumphantly ended for the time being" and that it was "mandated by Chairman Mao to be carried out every seven or eight years". There was no reference to the bankrupt economy, the millions of lives lost, and countless more lives ruined during those years. Instead, a mausoleum was to be built to keep the corpse of the mass murderer for public viewing at the cost of millions of dollars a year. As for Liu Shaoqi, for whom the Cultural Revolution was launched, there were simply no words on his state or his whereabouts.

We had no idea that Liu Shaoqi had passed away eight years before this declaration.

On January 13, 1967, Liu Shaoqi requested to resign from all of his positions and return to his homeland to become a farmer in order to end the disastrous Cultural Revolution. But Mao refused. He wanted nothing short of Liu's total destruction, perhaps physical annihilation as well. It was revealed years later by witnesses and depicted by Harrison Salisbury in his *New Emperors: China in the Era of Mao and Deng* that on his death bed, he was still tortured daily. Every time when the trusted military doctors and nurses arrived, they would shout, "Down with China's Khrushchev!" and hit him black and blue with a stethoscope and stabbed him with a needle that left no blood vessel good to put a needle in. They deliberately put him on the verge of death and revived him only to torture him more. Despite his paralytic state and bloody pus all over his body, he was strapped down to a bare stretcher, lying in his own wastes. On his seventieth birthday in 1968, Zhou Enlai, acting on Mao's devious order, dispatched Wang Dongxing[16] to deliver a transistor radio to him only for him to listen to the news deliberately released on that day about his being officially denounced and permanently expelled from the party. On Lin Biao's Order No.1, Liu Shaoqi, in high fever and grave conditions, lying naked under a blanket, was transferred to a basement cell of barred window with no glass in Kaifeng on October 17, 1969. Less than a month later, he succumbed. The former chairman of the state who had advocated being the party's "obedient instrument" finally rested in peace.

With the Mao-Era officially ending, things began to get better little by little. New policies were implemented: Many persecuted were rehabilitated and restored to positions and their confiscated properties returned; the remaining country settlers were allowed to return to the city; the chosen few "worker-peasant-soldier students" were sent abroad to catch up with the world; remedial courses were offered for the "worker-peasant-soldier college graduates" already in some positions to be qualified for the jobs; and examinations were in place to fill the urgent needs for qualified people.

With hope and opportunities dangling ahead, many youths began to equip themselves with knowledge. My friend and former coworker, Li Weiping, was engaged in learning Japanese.

At this trend, I felt secretly uneasy, but I was pessimistic. I said to myself, there's no point for you to advance your learning. With your background, there won't be any chance for you. Besides, as a 28-year-old, you would look pathetic to sit in the same classroom with teenagers in their rush to catch up. You already know what they don't know. I thus excluded myself from this trend.

One late afternoon, Weiping came for a visit.

Hardly had she sat down when she said excitedly, "Qiru! Guess what happened?"

"What?" I asked, hardly interested.

"My friend Xiao Tian has been taken into the Chinese Academy of Social Sciences, working under Li Zehou!"

Recalling a girl I once met at my parents' home who wasn't able to write coherently and grammatically in Chinese, at the news of her being taken in to work under a renowned philosopher at the highest social-sciences research institute, I was shocked. To make sure she was the one that Weiping was referring to, I asked, "Is that the girl you brought here to learn English from my father?"

"Yes," confirmed Weiping. "She has graduated from college as a 'worker-peasant-soldier student'."

Upon my inquiry about how she was taken in by Li Zehou, Weiping divulged that Xiao Tian herself acknowledged that she gained Li's favor by sleeping with him.

I wasn't surprised at what Weiping revealed about Xiao Tian. To get ahead, some ambitious people who were born poor would do whatever it takes. It was a prevalent female practice then to get out of a frustrating situation or get ahead. What shocked me was that I found the world moving on with me left far behind.

Disquieted by the news of being surpassed by people with no intellect, not even basic training, I was bitter. After a speechless moment, I said tartly, "This world is changed, taken over by people with below-average intelligence and training."

"Yes," in an emphatic tone, Weiping said. "The world *is* changed. These people may have below-average intelligence and training, but so what? The earth is still rotating! History is bound to cast aside relentlessly the ones who cannot change and adjust to the new era. Qiru! My friends and acquaintances are all busy advancing themselves while you, the one that I once admired, are left out. It's disheartening to see you like this. If you don't change and save yourself, I'm not coming anymore. What for?"

My heart sank. In her bleary eyes, I suddenly saw myself just a pitiable creature about to be discarded by the world, even by my friend Weiping. It was a shocking, revealing moment, a timely wake-up call.

Weiping left without staying for supper. Her departure left me a void and an even stronger feeling of being abandoned by the world.

For a long while, I was wallowing in self-pity, lamenting my fate and the fate of the gentry leftover in a changed society, wasting my life in self-exile and inured in my self-pitying state. With no future in sight and no challenging undertaking, I was idling away my time. In my eyes, nothing was worth the effort. Today or tomorrow, it made no difference. Days had lost their meanings and begun to blend in my mind. I had lost track of time.

Alarmed by my pathetic state, I decided to catch up. I took out some books I had read as a teenager but had since put aside and found in panic that my memory had deteriorated to the extent that I had no memories of the things I had learned and the books I had read, and that my mind was no longer sharp.

Frozen by 11 years' of knowledge vacuum, traumatized by the rape and its aftermath, and degenerated by years of banishment to the lowest rung of society, my mind had become a blank and a hope- less tangle. I was unable to organize any of my thoughts, much less to express or articulate them. Even writing a letter became a painful task. Words just refused to come out of my disorderly mind. Not only did my growth cease, but functioning and reacting normally were out of the question. Other than anger, which was easy to express—all I needed was to scream, I was unable to communicate with people or think clearly for myself.

Awakened from my self-destructive state, I ruminated for days. I said to myself, life has gone on without you. There are still years ahead of you. What can you do when the situation changes? What excuse can you offer for your being nothing? Persecuted? Life goes on. No one is going to stop his life to feel sorry for you and save you unless you help yourself and prove your worth. Life is short. You cannot afford self-pity and to be a loser. You cannot allow your mis- fortune to define you.

But, with my tainted, indelible past and my irreversible collec- tive-ownership status, it was apparent that no matter how hard I tried, I wouldn't benefit from the current political atmosphere. I wanted very much to leave the factory where I had worked for more than four years, but I saw no way out. I felt like a clipped bird, yearning to fly, but to no avail.

Not long after Weiping's visit, college entrance examinations were resumed after 11 years of interruption. It was said to be an "open opportunity" for anyone below the age of 30.

I knew it was the only opportunity to have my fate changed. But I had no illusion about my chance. The probability of having my life thus reversed was next to nothing. First of all, I had to take the politicized examinations by conforming to the political trend, which I definitely would not do, which would definitely disqualify me. What was worse, I would not pass the political screening. With my background, there was no way for them to choose me over someone politically desirable. To have my past dredged up and reexamined only to be rejected was the last thing I needed. My past was the last thing that I wanted to be unearthed.

But, urged by my parents, I was compelled to register for the upcoming national examinations. However, I had no confidence, knowing clearly that I was still an outcast and that society would not take me back. With hardly any preparation, I took the examinations and didn't do well. Subconsciously, I wanted to fail. As if making sure I would be failed, in the essay section of the Chinese examination, I called for Deng Xiaoping's reinstatement against the trend. As was expected, I was rejected. I felt relieved of the dread of having my stigmatized past dredged up again only to be dismissed.

One day, we were informed about getting back our properties confiscated 11 years ago on account of the new policy and Father's clearance of all charges. Eleven years is a long time in a person's life. However, so used to subsisting on the mercy of the Communists, at the news, we were jubilant.

As usual, my sister Qijuan was dispatched to handle this. She had been conscientiously handling almost all the family matters arising during the Cultural Revolution. The entire family benefited from her caring, her prudence and her deftness in dealing with the Communists. Now she willingly and selflessly went off for the task again.

Hours later, at the unusual loud, rhythmic bursting noises produced by a motor engine, we all jumped up in excitement, expecting a larger vehicle to be in tow soon. We rushed out to help unload. But, when we saw no other vehicle in sight except a lone motorcycle with my sister standing next to it, our hearts sank.

"What's going on?" Mother asked, "Where are the returned properties?"

Chin pointing toward the compartment at the passenger side of the motorcycle, in a subdued manner, my sister answered, "They are all here."

A close look revealed two wretched-looking alien objects lying pathetically at the bottom of the compartment: a hoe and a patch of brown felt-rug of foot-mat size.

When our properties were taken away from us, it was a mountain load piled up in two army-personnel trucks. Now what we received was just two unwanted objects that didn't even belong to us.

"Absurd," Mother uttered in disbelief. "These things are not ours!"

"They said they were ours."

"What about the other things? Where are they?"

"They said these were all we had," my sister answered sullenly as she took the objects out and carried them home.

Once inside, Mother pursued further, "Where's the jewelry?"

"They said the jewelry had been turned over to the state."

"What about the inventory list they left us after the ransacking?" Mother raised her voice.

"They took it back."

"How could you give it back to them while we received nothing on the list?"

"How could I not give it back to them?" so far having had her emotions in check, at Mother's blame, my sister lost her composure. "It would have been conceived as an affront to their authority and an attempt to square the accounts later. They had already warned me beforehand not to try to settle the old scores and that it won't be in our favor if we don't stay low-key. Don't forget the power they hold over us. They can do anything they want to do to us. They said that it was a correct action to ransack us in accordance with the party's policy then and that it is also in line with the party's policy to return the confiscated properties to us now. They also said we were treated leniently according to the party's policy, but it didn't mean we came out completely clean, which is true…"

"How could you accept what they said about us 'not being completely clean'?" Mother interrupted my sister and refuted. "Haven't we already been cleared of all of the accusations? If we weren't in the wrong then, why did they raid us and confiscate our properties? If we weren't completely clean, why did they return the properties? They can't have it both ways!"

"Sure they can. The party is always right." My sister said, "We can't claim to be completely clean. We were investigated, weren't we? Father's being investigated was by no means a mistake. There was good reason for it. They said it was the party's lenient policy that put Father's case to rest."

Mother went silent. At the anticlimactic ending, she was crestfallen. After a long speechless moment, she said resignedly, "Originally, I was going to give each of you a 24-karat gold chain and distribute the jewelry among you. There's no such trouble now. They are all gone."

Besides the jewelry, also gone were our half-moon shaped carved rosewood antique coffee table inlaid with a pink marble top, two Zeiss cameras and Father's collection of old watches—Rolex, Longines, Rado, Tissot, Omega, Movado and Breitling, not counting the furniture and other miscellaneous possessions such as costly clothing and bed sets. For our lush, expensive royal-purple wool-fleece Chuktu Persian blanket framed with rich royal-purple silk satin, we received a rotten patch of a felt-rug. The countless government bonds we were mandated to purchase monthly for a decade since the 1950's to "assist socialist construction" were automatically nullified. Uncle Six lost almost everything too, including his sofa set, furniture, government bonds, piano, refrigerator, TV, camera, watches and other things of value.

While the rehabilitated Communists were generously compensated for their losses, we were not. Save for accepting the reality, we could do nothing about it. As powerless masses, we had learned to live with reality, knowing all we had was ourselves.

Later on, a tiny sum of cash, equivalent to a couple of hundreds of dollars, a fraction of the real value of our jewelry, was given to us as compensation. Mother's 3-carat round ruby halo ring with diamond accents and her pair of 24-carat gold twist-rope bangles of a woman's index finger in diameter of hundreds of grams alone were worth of tens of hundreds of dollars today. Rumor had it that a portion of the jewelry was stolen by the peasant student who had angrily accused us of "committing crimes" during the ransacking. A large brick-walled yard with six large brick rooms in it was built in his village with questionable funds.

Countless looted invaluable Grade-A national treasures wound up in the hands of Kang Sheng, Chen Boda, Jiang Qing and countless other officials. With a coupon of 5 Yuan (equivalent to 70 cents) offered for something such as a bolt of silk or a sofa, the Communists also bought off the masses with the looted leftover pittance.

At around the time of college examinations, an acquaintance introduced me to a former high Communist official, Du Wenmin, the brother-in-law of Peng Zhen, the fifth-ranking official and the mayor of Beijing before the Cultural Revolution. Faulted together with Peng Zhen and arrested at the beginning of the Cultural Revolution, Du spent 10 years in Qincheng Prison on the outskirts of Beijing, where high-profile political prisoners were held. In jail, he was known to his jailors only by his assigned number. Mistreated with malnourishment and lack of medical attention, he had lost all his teeth and the ability to walk. He had also lost hearing in one ear to beatings. When he was released after Mao's death, he was put on a stretcher, taken directly from prison to Fuxing Hospital, where political prisoners were treated.

Although I was sympathetic with his ordeals, I was turned off by his shameless, lustful, suspicious and cynical looks. There was no spontaneity about him. His words and smile were insincere and calculated. He displayed no genuine emotions. A decade of prison life without any human contact but traps and enemies had turned him into a man incapable of love, trust and noble sentiment.

I rejected him. But, no matter what I did, whether it was my outright rejection or dealing him my frank opinions about him, he kept coming to our home every night. With me taking refuge in my bedroom refusing to see him, my parents were left to deal with him night after night. Many times late at night, I was awakened by their conversation and found him still there exhausting my parents.

At his persistent shameless act, I was exasperated, feeling like an object that he wanted and felt entitled to possess.

At the time, the match-maker was remorseful because of his colleagues' oblique curses of him, "Which son of a bitch did this vile thing by placing a flower on a pile of cow dung?" Tormented by his conscience, he eventually divulged to me the information he had withheld: After Du regained his health, he immediately began his wild chase of young women, many of whom were merely teenagers.

However, even with this new telling information about Du, Father would not change his mind. Not even the condemnation of him by his acquaintances for "bartering away" his own daughter could deter him. He disregarded the censure and went ahead with his plan of pressuring me to marry Du.

I used to be Father's favorite. He and Mother had placed enormous hope in me to help preserve the family, but my situation turned out the worst among the offspring. I not only shattered their hope, but rubbed salt into their wounds with my disgrace and failures. Intensely frustrated and unhappy with his own life, Father was made even more exasperated by my wretched state. With nowhere to vent his anger, I became his outlet. At my refusal to marry Du as the only possibility to have my own and the family's bad luck overturned, Father became vicious.

"Long Qiru," he snarled every day. "You have lived here long enough. 'A married daughter is dumped-water that cannot be taken back.' It's a charity that we allow you to stay. We don't plan to keep you here forever. We've brought you up and you haven't returned the favor. Instead, you burdened us with not only you but Wang Fusheng's vile spawn and plagued us with your disgrace. Marrying Du will give you a chance for redemption. Not only will you benefit from this, the entire family can be sheltered under this red umbrella. Since the situation has changed, it is foreseeable that Du will be restored to power. Even in his present low-ebb state, his past status still generates prestige. And he has wide connections that can work for him. But, if you refuse to marry him, I will push you right into the pit of hell. I mean it!"

I was wrathful at Father's heartless words, knowing everyone in the family wanted me to make the sacrifice and that no one in the family supported me morally or had my interests in mind; the need to survive had made everyone cynical. I yelled back, "I know I owe you my life. I will pay you back—all of you!"

Despite my adamant rejection, Du went ahead with his plan, presenting his request of marrying me to his party organization. At the warning of likely consequences that would result from marrying a woman like me, he was undeterred. After the investigation of my background, his superior met with him, and warned him that if he resolved to go ahead with his plan, a "demerit" would be added to his *dang'an*. But he still would not budge.

With all the barriers overcome, Du began zeroing in on me. One day, he arrived with a request to speak to me.

"Qiru," he said. "I know how frustrated you are with your current state and what you are up against. Without proper channels and right connections, you won't be able to move one step. I can do nothing to erase the adverse contents in your *dang'an*. I myself have one to deal with and am subjected to the party's discipline. But I can take you out of the factory and make you a secondary school teacher or an office worker. It's easy stuff, just a matter of a few phone calls. I have wide connections that can work for me."

Day in and day out, I was caught in the pincer movement from my own family and from Du, feeling like a cornered animal with nowhere to retreat. Father's constant angry carping simply made it impossible for me to live in peace with him under the same roof and maintain my sanity. At the shameless contract Du offered me for an exchange of my fate, I said to myself bitterly, what are you anyway? You are nothing but an object in Du's eyes and a tool and a pawn in the eyes of your own family. What is marriage to you? No one loves you anyway, not even your own family. No clear-headed man with some capital or political survival in mind will choose you as his marriage partner anyway.

In a fit of rage, at the age of 29, I married the Communist, 33 years my senior, at the end of 1978.

MY NEW LIFE

After working seven years in three different factories, at the end of 1978, I was lifted out and became a teacher. When I informed my friends of five years in the factory, they were very happy for me. They said that I "deserve this break" and that I "shouldn't be buried" there with them forever but "return to" where I "rightly belong". Knowing what they had meant in my difficult times, at their heartfelt happiness and sincere wishes for me, I was very touched and humbled, feeling indebted to them. Had it not been for them, my life would have been much harder. It was their support and kindness that boosted my spirit, balanced my outlook and added joy to my life. Ready to move on, I bid them farewell and left my past behind resolutely.

The day before the spring semester began, I reported to my new job. At the prospect of a more suitable job working with people more compatible in a far better working environment, I was in good spirits.

The school was originally built for the children of the Beijing Garrison. It had an army-barracks layout with rows of redbrick classrooms and staff dormitories alongside the campus. A properly centered U-shaped two-story redbrick staff building was set behind an overlapped running track and a soccer field, with a basketball court and a volleyball court along the side. At the neat, open layout, my sense of being a decent human being returned to me. Into the staff building overlaid with cherry finish hardwood floors, I felt this was a place where I could stay.

At the door that said "Principal's Office", I knocked. At the permission, I stepped in and found myself in a bright, neatly-arranged room. An upright-looking man in his 40s with a straight military man's posture and a no-nonsense demeanor, and a seemly, honest-looking, magnanimous woman in her 50s were sitting on burgundy-colored armchairs.

At my self-introduction, they both stood up to greet me sincerely and warmly. Looking me straight in the eye, the man shook my hand firmly and said, "Long Qiru, welcome to our school. I'm Xu Shengxiang, principal of this school." Turning to the woman, he introduced, "This is Party Secretary Chen Jin." Even before Chen Jin opened her mouth, her large, limpid eyes that conveyed candor, kindness and purity of the heart already spoke plenty. I shook her hand and greeted her. "Long Qiru," with a motherly air and tone, Chen Jin addressed me. "Welcome to our school!" Gesturing at the sofa set, she said, "Please be seated and make yourself at home."

When we were all seated, Xu Shengxiang said earnestly, "Long Qiru, we are pleased to have you here. From now on you are a member of our school. As we all know, teachers are 'soul engineers'. Teaching is a sacred and honorable profession. You have our trust. I'm sure you'll do fine here." Turning to Chen Jin, he asked, "Secretary Chen, do you intend to say something?"

"Of course," looking at me fondly, Chen Jin answered, her face and posture exuding the air of a kind mother. "Long Qiru, we can tell you'll do a fine job here. We have confidence in you. But, this said, if you have any problems at work, please don't hesitate to talk to people. We will all help you out."

Having been treated for years as a subhuman, at this easy, cordial reception, I was very pleased with the new environment, feeling quite at home. Buoyed by their sincere welcome, immediate acceptance and doubtless trust, I was optimistic about my future life here. A new horizon seemed to be unfolding in front of me.

They led me to the personnel office next door, and introduced me to a rustic, severe, and supercilious-looking woman, Yu Shi'e. At my greeting, Yu Shi'e didn't stir, but sat on her seat, coldly measuring me from head to toe. With Chen Jin and Xu Shengxiang excusing themselves, I was left to deal with this formidable woman alone.

At her relentless, inimical stares, I said to myself, Day One you are already treated like this. With your history and the power of personnel officers who can even make their superiors bow to them, it won't be as easy for your future life here as you thought.

Just as I was thinking, I heard Yu Shi'e's earthy accent. "Long Qiru," she said. "We know how you got here."

Already feeling like a subhuman by the demeaning reception, at this unexpected remark, I was startled. Hardly could I take in what she said when I heard her again, "You came from a collective-owned factory. That is where you rightly belong. You got here through marrying a high-ranking official."

At once, I found my newly gained confidence and enthusiasm about the new job gone.

"You came here through the backdoor," Yu Shi'e said again. "It is illegal."

God, I said to myself. Is she going to do something to reverse the result? It's highly unlikely. Illegal deeds like this and worse than this are prevalent. The pursuit will only expose how rampant the corruption within the party is and end up with tracing to their own people—Things like this can only be accomplished by their own kind.

"Since you are new here," I heard Yu Shi'e again. "I'll make it clear beforehand: This is proletariat's educational domain. We do not allow any bourgeois influence to poison our youngsters."

At her words, I said to myself, despite your marriage to a Communist, you are still not accepted and still viewed as a quasi-class-enemy even in this Post-Mao era. Prepare yourself. The next thing she'll bring up will be your past.

As I was bracing myself for her remarks about my past, I heard her say, "You look very different from the masses. Why do you wear your hair this way?"

I never took much care of my appearance. I had no inkling what she meant. "Why," I murmured in bafflement while my eyes couldn't help being drawn to her varnished stiff, stylish hair. "I never went to a hair-dresser. I cut it myself. I didn't do anything special to style it. It's just …natural."

"You carry yourself," Yu She'e continued. "It shows your bourgeois class origin and bourgeois taste."

Heck, I said to myself. My "crime" is again due to my bearing and my background. This is the way I was brought up. I have different taste. I won't apologize for it.

"Long Qiru," Yu Shi'e spoke again. "We know your history. We know what's in your *dang'an*. As early as secondary school, you have been caught messing around with men. You don't want new material to be added to your record, do you? Mind your conduct. Your behavior will not escape the masses' supervision!"

Ouch. Having my past mercilessly brought up in a grossly distorted, hurtful way in the place I just arrived at, I toughened myself. Threatening one with adverse material in his *dang'an* could usually effectively put him in his place. But in this situation, it didn't produce the intended effect on me. I said to myself, OK. Since you'll never get a fair judgment and are not allowed to live out of the shadow of your past, bring it on.

To my surprise, this was the end of it. I was let go to report to my assigned office.

Into my assigned office, at my self-introduction, the whole room of teachers stood up to greet me. My mood was at once lifted by the sight. There were older teachers who survived the Cultural Revolution, younger worker-peasant-soldier college graduates and youngsters who were freshly out of high school, a common phenomenon seen everywhere after the Cultural Revolution.

Not long after I settled at my designated desk, a balding, bespectacled middle-aged man pushed the door open and walked straight toward me. With a broad smile and an outstretched hand, he addressed me warmly, "Long Qiru, welcome, welcome! I'm Lu Jialiang, a chemistry teacher. Welcome to our school!"

I shook his hand, surprised he had learned my name already.

Noticing my wonderment, Lu Jialiang explained with a smile, "We've heard a lot about you even before your arrival. Never mind. It's all claptrap. By the way, if you need any help, just let me know. My office is right next door. Actually, after work, we can go home together. You ride eastward, right?"

In the presence of other people in the office, Lu Jialiang acted as if I were the only one that deserved his attention. Sensing my colleagues' reactions to this, I felt awkward. By his inappropriate act, I had been excluded from other people. Although I wasn't comfortable at this undue friendliness, I couldn't fault a friendly gesture and reject friendship.

At my nod, Lu Jialing said, "All right. I'll see you after work."

The day began with a meeting and ended up with teachers' preparation. As I requested, I was assigned to teach the seventh grade in order to be familiarized with the curriculum grade by grade and brush up my long-forgotten very basic English and learn the language at the same time. The day went by smoothly.

At the end of the day, Lu Jialiang came to my office to look for me. We rode home together. On our way, Lu Jialing informed me of the situation in the school.

"Beware of Yu Shi'e," he alerted me. "She's an ultra-leftist. She loves hunting people. She can make your life hell."

I nodded my head and said, "I already had a taste of it this morning upon my arrival."

With a chortle, Lu Jialiang continued, "Having a husband of naval lieutenant-general rank, she regards herself unexcelled in this world although she's only a semi-literate peasant woman. If it were not for her husband, she would still be a peasant, which would suit her and everyone around her better."

Lu Jialiang's words reminded me of Li Er'e. I chuckled and responded, "I'm very familiar with those women."

Since the communist takeover, wives of Communist officials, often semi-literate peasants like their husbands, were inserted into different levels of leadership positions. Meteorically placed in positions of power, they lost their humility and became unbearably imperious. With no reference point and no exposure to or understanding of urban society where people were more sophisticated, things were more complicated and problems required more painstaking, discriminatory handling, they created tons of trouble for everyone with their high-handed dogmatic way of dealing with people and things.

As I was brooding, I heard Lu Jialiang say, "There's nothing wrong with being peasants. It's just that they can't be put in a leadership position."

"I agree." I concurred. "With no exposure to complex situations and sophisticated viewpoints, once they are put in position, they'll make a mess of everything."

"They certainly do," said Lu Jialiang. "By the way, Chen Jin's husband is also a high-ranking official, at a higher rank than Yu Shi'e's. Her husband is a colonel general. But she doesn't act any differently because she's educated, from the big city of Nanjing. She's well-liked by staff members."

I nodded, not surprised at her popularity.

"Principal Xu Shengxiang is a decent human being too," said Lu Jialiang. "He has a strict working-class upbringing and a military background. Although he doesn't have much education, he was born and raised in Beijing, exposed to people and things. He respects education and defers to teachers."

I nodded my head, recalling Xu Shengxiang's straight body posture and blunt demeanor.

At an intersection, we bid each other good-bye.

My work at school went well. My students were crazy about me. For my earnestness with my job and my candor, I was well-accepted by many of my colleagues as well.

In my office, I formed friendships with three young girls, Ye Lei, Shen Xiangxiang and Zhang Xiaomi, who newly graduated from high school. Growing up in educated, upright Communist families in the Post-Mao era exposed to horrendous stories that occurred during the Cultural Revolution and made aware of the consequences caused by leftist policies and having a job among common folks, they were closely in touch with reality and had a healthy outlook, open-minded to truth and knowledge. Young and idealistic, the girls found easy resonance in my non-conforming behavior, my fierce independence and my truthfulness. But, coming from a Communist family imbued with party discipline, they withheld their opinions publicly. Although they never joined me in my public comments, in private, they shared every bit of my opinions and were thrilled by my daring pointedness.

Once after lunch, they suggested a walk in the campus.

It turned out that they had something to say to me in private. They informed me that Yu Shi'e had admonished them to "watch out against" my "bourgeois corrosion" and asked them to report on me. They also alerted me of the wide spread rumors about the "abnormal relationship" between Lu Jialiang and me.

At their words, a sense of dark humor rose in me. There was nothing new about the accusation of my so-called "bourgeois corrosion". And the rumors about me and Lu Jialiang's "abnormal relationship" were simply laughable. But I was vexed by so soon having become a gossip subject.

As a matter of fact, Lu Jialiang did accompany me home almost every day, and often went beyond his own destination to treat his hair loss. He was raised as a Christian, a decent man. He never initiated or suggested anything inappropriate. Besides, it made my long ride seem shorter. There was no reason to be alarmed. I took him for a friend.

At my reaction, Ye Lei corresponded in exasperation, "It's sheer nonsense. They have nothing else to do but gossip about people."

"Just laugh it off," Shen Xiangxiang added benevolently. "There's no merit in whatever they say. Don't pay any attention to it."

In her usual proper, serious manner, Zhang Xiaomi opined, "Those small-minded people judge others by their own worth. But we know you better. Your mind is not set for this. Don't even give it a thought. It's not worth it."

At their understanding and trust, I laughed it off.

In defiance, I continued to ride home with Lu Jialiang.

One day, Yu Shi'e called me into her office.

"Long Qiru," she said. "We are not happy with your conduct. Not long after you came here, you have already shown your true colors and caused a scandal. We have noticed the abnormal relationship between you and Lu Jialiang. Many people saw you and him together after school. I'm obliged to remind you again of your wanton history and warn you not to repeat your past offenses of seducing men and breaking up other people's family. Lu Jialiang is married with a son."

At these untrue and groundless accusations, I shot back, "Breaking up his family? It's an unwarranted accusation. How is it my fault? I'm just a recipient of a friendship!"

"Don't deny it," Yu Shi'e roared. "You don't want to carry the name of a 'recidivist', do you? Behave yourself!" Pausing, she then resumed, "Not only this, we've also taken notice of your bourgeois corrosive influence on your colleagues. Zhang Xiaomi, Shen Xiangxiang and Ye Lei are revolutionary offspring. Desist from spreading your bourgeois liberal ideas and poisoning their minds. Otherwise, we will not take it lightly!"

Annoyed and feeling funny at the groundless accusation of "seducing men", at her laughable claim of "poisoning" other people's minds, I saw no point in arguing with her anymore.

On my way back to my office, I said to myself, to hell with the rumors. Is my friendship with Lu Jialiang against the law? The more they gossip, the more defiance I will show.

I continued to ride home with Lu Jialiang. By doing so, I unexpectedly found the topic no longer gossiped about. Just as the saying goes, "Face the apparition with no fears, the apparition disappears."

But a few days later, something that happened in my class worried me.

That day, at some students' lack of initiative and dedication to their studies, in a moment of frustration, I blurted out, "Socialism is harming you!"

My words instantly turned the classroom into a soundproof vacuum. The students were all astounded at my shocking statement. And I myself was horrified at my slip of the tongue. I said to myself, this is just what Yu Shi'e needs to get at you. Your stupid tongue provided her just the opportunity to catch you. If one of the students reports you, you'll be doomed.

As I was fidgety, desperately racking my brain to find a way to save myself, a boy objected, "Isn't this anti-party, anti-socialism?"

At his words, I immediately apologized and came up with an explanation. "I, I apologize for what I said," I hastened to say. "I didn't mean it. What I meant is that you shouldn't feel complacent upon the security guaranteed by the socialist system. I was just… trying to persuade you… to work harder. I'm terribly sorry about this miscommunication."

To my advantage, I was their beloved teacher. No one had the heart to ruin me. I escaped.

At home, it didn't take long for me to find out how wide the gap between Du Wenmin and me was. At first, I was his novelty, and he was impressed by my broad-based knowledge and pointed views. But after he was exonerated and restored to power, he immediately aligned his political stance with the official line. The gap between us widened by the day.

Du was born into a wealthy landlord family in Hebei Province. His paternal uncle, Zhang Bi, was the puppet Police Commissioner of Beijing during the Japanese Invasion. When the Japanese invaded Northeast China, Du was a tenth-grader in a prominent secondary school in Beijing. At the time, the Communists were widely recruiting peasants and students on the pretext of fighting the Japanese invasion. Du's Anti-Japanese activities caught the attention of underground Communists on campus. They drew him into their circle and their ideology. At that impressionable age, he was easily beguiled by the grand picture of communism and their propaganda that Chiang Kai-shek was "non-resistant" toward Japanese aggression, believing the Communists were the only hope in saving China. At the age of 16, he was inducted into the Communist Party by an older underground Communist schoolmate. A year later in 1934, disguised as a peasant under the alias of "Du Wenmin", which remained his name to this day, he was sent to Yan'an, the Communist base, to be groomed. At the age of 18, he was dispatched to a military region with a position equivalent to a brigadier general to conduct guerrilla warfare in the Jin-Cha-Ji region (Shanxi Province and what is now part of Liaoning Province and Hebei Province). When the Communists took over the Northeast at the end of 1948, he was put in charge of the industrial city of Fushun, which held the lifeline of coal and gasoline. In the 1950s, for an attempted rape of his domestic servant, he was demoted by three grades and transferred to Beijing as a bureau chief in charge of the development of nuclear bombs in the Second Ministry of Machine Building. When the Cultural Revolution began, he fell victim along with his brother-in-law Peng Zhen. He was jailed for 10 years in Qincheng Prison, where Peng Zhen, Wang Guangmei and other high-profile political prisoners were held to exact information against Liu Shaoqi.

Years of prison life subjected to intense brain wash and tortures beyond imagination can leave a deep mark on anyone. An example was Zheng Tingji, a family friend and a Nationalist lieutenant general who was jailed for 13 years for being a "war criminal". Deemed to have been effectively brain washed, he was released on Liu Shaoqi's amnesty in 1961. He held no grudge for his long imprisonment but was sincerely thankful for "being granted a new life". David Crook, an English Communist born to Jewish immigrant parents from East End, London, was another example. Like other foreign Communists living in a privileged walled compound, he was clueless about the reality of China. Despite his diehard loyalty to the Chinese Communists, they incarcerated him in 1967 on the charge of being a "spy". When he was released five years later, he still whole-heartedly embraced Mao's hard line, like other incarcerated and released foreign Communists—Sidney Rittenberg, Israel Epstein, Elsie Fairfax-Cholmeley, Rewi Alley, Michael Shapiro... When the Cultural Revolution was repudiated later, David Crook vehemently defended it and demanded that the policies return to Mao's hard line, and advocated the resumption of Mao's "*kaimen banxue*" (open-door college admission to workers, peasants and soldiers, regardless of their educational backgrounds).

Du Wenmin was another story. Ten years of prison life made him a suspicious man. Each time I shopped, he would measure the groceries with a scale and keep itemized accounts of every single *fen* (equivalent to cent) I spent. Even more bizarre, this so-called "Communist" and "proletarian" declared by Marx to "have nothing but chains to lose" and to "deliver the entire mankind to an egalitarian class-less, state-less world" kept his bank account a secret and his suitcases at home locked. Not only this, he locked the TV set every night before he went to bed as well. He even slept with his keys and wallet under his pillow.

Knowing how distrustful he was and what possessions meant to him, when people from his ancestral home arrived at our home with the returned jewelry confiscated from his mother during the Cultural Revolution intending to leave it with me, I declined and directed them to his work place. But when Du returned home, he didn't mention a word of it but simply locked the jewelry in one of his suitcases and took it to his office the following day.

Du was so stingy that he couldn't even spare any mercy on a child. At the time, my son was at the tender age of five. However, he was not allowed to be a child. In Du's presence, he wasn't allowed to make noise or speak without his permission. He wasn't even allowed to have a second helping from the same dish without his permission. Cruelly deprived of any joy of living, my son was turned into a prisoner in his own home without any freedom or his own wish, however small that might be.

Added to the unpleasantness were the insults from his two biased daughters. Perceiving me as the obstacle in their inheritance of their father's 10-years' retroactive pay, they constantly harassed me, accusing me of "coveting" their father's wealth in their attempts to drive me out.

Living with Du, I felt as if I were serving out a labor-capital contract for the favor he did for me. My relationship with him took a sudden turn for the worse when Deng Xiaoping turned back on his own words of "seeking truth from facts", arresting people who had pushed for his return to power and advocated freedom and democracy during the Beijing Spring movement (1977-1978). Not only this, he also raised *Four Sticking-Tos*—sticking to proletariat dictatorship, Communist leadership, Marxism-Leninism and Mao-Thoughts, and socialist road.

At the changed political atmosphere, I couldn't help lamenting over the missed historical opportunity to have China turned into a healthy, democratic society by allowing freedom and adopting democracy.

At my comments, Du exploded, "Rubbish! These are ultra-counterrevolutionary ideas! How dare you oppose the Communist leadership? You should be imprisoned for your ultra-counterrevolutionary ideas!"

Taken aback by his sudden change of stance against his previous claim, I asked him in bewilderment, "Wasn't this what you and I agreed upon early on when we just met? Now you're shifting position. Which is your true belief?"

"How dare you concoct a story to vilify a veteran revolutionary?" Du roared, "This is another counterrevolutionary crime you committed!"

At the time, contradicting an individual Communist official was still categorized as a "counterrevolutionary crime". From his reactions, I realized that he had already closed off his mind and counted me as his enemy and that it would be futile and dangerous for me to continue arguing with him.

Since then, we had stopped talking to each other. Except sharing the dining table at night, we had nothing else to do with each other anymore.

Although my colleague Wu Zuxin had long dismissed my marriage to Du as a "farce" and advised me to simply end it, I was not prepared for a divorce since I was just married. Not believing in love anymore, I decided to turn a blind eye to reality.

But one day within a year of our marriage, Party Secretary Chen Jin called me into her office. "Long Qiru," she said. "Your husband Du Wenmin has filed for divorce. Do you want to fight him? If you do, we will assist you."

"What?" Shocked and feeling comical at the same time, I scoffed at once, "How absurd this whole thing is. Even a man as ancient as he is thinks he's a bargain. What am I afraid of? What do I have to lose but a decrepit? I welcome it!"

"Long Qiru," said Chen Jin. "I'm outraged by his behavior. He's not a real Communist, but a corrupt, power-abusing bureaucrat. If you need help, let us know. You have our sympathy and support."

I thanked her for her support and understanding, and returned to my office.

One afternoon when I returned home from work, I found the TV set gone. Du had moved out without any notice. Since then, every once in a while when I returned home, I would notice a piece of furniture missing. Piece by piece, Du moved all the things that had some value to an undisclosed location that was allocated to him at his restoration to power. I couldn't wait for him to move out completely. One day when several young engineers showed up with his order to move all his possessions out, I eagerly helped them clear out everything that was Du's, except a twin bed, a full bed, a desk, and two chairs.

Having Du completely purged from my life, I was glad to have the apartment for myself. For the first time in my life, I felt that I had a place of my own. I enjoyed the life of living on my own. This was a period when I felt I belonged to myself and lived for myself.

Before long, Chen Jin called me into her office again.

"Long Qiru," she inquired. "Is it true that your husband took almost everything with him, leaving you an empty apartment and that he's dating a woman 37 years his junior?"

Apparently, she had got wind of what I had told my colleagues during my chitchats with them. Upon my confirmation, Chen Jin was outraged. "Is this a Communist?" She exclaimed, "Shame on him! I'll fight him to the end!"

Seeing no benefit in doing this, I tried to stop her. "Secretary Chen," I said. "It's not worth it. I'm much happier now. I don't need that aggravation."

Chen Jin looked surprised. "It is your right, Long Qiru," she corrected me. "You are entitled to it. I'll fight for you!"

Unable to stop her, I left the matter up to her.

Within half a year, the marriage was dissolved. At Chen Jin's insistence, the local civil organization arbitrated that the old man fork over 1,000 yuan ($125), equivalent to the price of the color TV he took with him, out of his tens of thousands of yuan as the divorce settlement to compensate for the marital possessions he took away.

One afternoon, Du and I were summoned to the local civil organization for the finalization.

Before handing out the divorce certificate, the woman in charge of the matter made a speech. "Comrade Du Wenmin and Comrade Long Qiru," she said. "I think you both should learn a lesson from this." Turning to Du, she went on, "Comrade Du, you lost your sense in front of a younger woman, cheated and used. The financial loss is trivial in comparison with your tarnished reputation as an esteemed veteran revolutionary because of this. Long Qiru is not the right person you can rely on as a revolutionary companion for the rest of your life. You should marry someone who shares the same values and moral standards." Turning to me, the woman switched to a scornful tone, berating, "As for Comrade Long Qiru, your life style is undesirable and irresponsible, rooted deeply in your bourgeois family background. Your conduct is despicable. It is impudent and immoral, inconsistent with the party's teaching and should be condemned by society!"

What she said was preposterous. But I was not in the mood to laugh. I said to myself impatiently, say whatever you have to say. Just give me the damn paper and let me go.

When I finally got hold of the paper, I trotted out while Du remained there, resuming the role of a "victim".

On my way home, the woman's words began to sink in. Riled by this distorted picture, I said to myself, for the price of a color TV, you are accused of "cheating" and "using" Du. Du's no victim. It was he who pursued you, not the other way around. He has a history of chasing teenage girls and he's dating someone 37 years his junior now. The more I thought about it, the more roiled I became. I turned my bicycle around, riding back to wrangle with the woman.

On my way there, I thought better of it. I said to myself, do you stand a chance to make the woman change her opinion about you and your class? Absolutely not. She and you are different species and will never see things eye-to-eye. In the eyes of people like her, you and your class are the incarnation of everything evil. So why bother? Having Du off your back is worth any price.

I resolved on moving on and putting a period to that phase of my life.

AROUND FATHER'S DEATH

With the leftists still in place impeding the implementation of new policies, in 1980, the campaign to "clean up the remnants of the 'Gang of Four'" began. We found Yu Shi'e, the personnel officer who had actively hit out at people, pulling in her horns, looking deflated. We soon learned that her husband was under investigation for his connections with the "Gang of Four". Before long, he was stripped of all of his positions, expelled from the party, charged with rape as well, and arrested. Overnight, Yu Shi'e and her family lost all of their power and privileges. They were evicted from the exclusive, Western-style, general-grade-only building in the prestigious naval compound and moved into a tiny, crude two-room dormitory in the humble school staff's living quarters. Yu Shi'e promptly filed for divorce. A series of adversities ensued: Yu Shi'e lost the position as a much feared personnel officer; one of her daughters was sentenced for sleeping with foreigners; the other was shipped back by her newly-wed Japanese merchant husband who now had no use for her and filed for divorce; and her son was incarcerated for "hooliganism". As a result of her extreme leftist style of work, no one was sympathetic to her. But no one treated her the way she had treated them.

One day, I came across Yu Shi'e in the hallway. Hit and trounced by the series of misfortunes, the arrogant, insufferable Yu had changed. There was no trace left of her former formidable person-nel officer image. As I was nodding past, much to my surprise, she stopped me. It was the first time that she ever deigned to acknowl-edge me as an equal human being. I surmised that she must have thought that an underdog like me was more likely to be receptive of her and sympathetic to her misfortunes.

"Long Qiru," tartly, Yu Shi'e opened her mouth. "Now I've learned life is unpredictable. You never know what's going to happen to you. Your life can change overnight."

Looking at her morose, pathetic face, I nodded understandingly, hoping she would truly learn something from her own misfortunes.

As the purge of the remnants of the "Gang of Four" went on, the ultra-leftists gradually lost their grip on power. Their ultra-leftist policies also lost momentum. Well into my 30s and having a son of my own, I found myself a *"keyi jiaoyuhao de zinu* (offspring of undesirable background showing probability of redemption)", "glo-riously" ascending from a borderline class enemy to a quasi-member of "the people" range, wearing another grotesque and not-too-flat-tering label.

As the nation moved further away from Mao's hard line, it saw the urgent need for more qualified people to fill the gaps and vacan-cies left in every field caused by the 10 years' Cultural Revolution. Courses were offered for those who missed the opportunity of a col-lege education.

In 1983, a once-in-a-lifetime occasion arrived. Along with other colleges, Beijing Foreign Studies University provided an opportunity for secondary school English teachers to make up for their missed chance for a college education. The number allocated to Beijing was 36. With many schools allotted one nominee, there would be hun-dreds of teachers contending for this rare opportunity.

At the time, legions of people had left China. My friends Jennifer, Lynn and their family had settled in America. Weng Rulian and Chen Ting had departed too. Many of my acquaintances and schoolmates fortunate to have received a helping hand or were offered a chance to study abroad had also taken off.

The wave of exodus and the news about those succeeding in their adopted country already made me very uneasy at being left far behind. At this chance, I said to myself, you are approaching 34. This may be your only occasion for self-realization. If you see this hard-to-come-by opening pass you by, it'll mean you'll be stuck where you are, forever. You cannot allow this to happen. But, with a fellow English teacher also attempting to take advantage of this opportunity to upgrade his worker-peasant-soldier college-graduate status, the possibility for me to be nominated was slim since his working class background was far more favorable than mine. Despite the de-emphasis of class background in school enrollment and job employment, in reality, those having a favorable background still had the advantage over people like me. Nevertheless, I told myself, you must not give up this opportunity without a good fight. You must try your best to be nominated.

To my surprise and advantage, at the last minute, this teacher withdrew his name of his own accord thanks to his apprehension of the examination. I became the nominee by default.

After the examination, I was admitted to the university as one of the 36, ranking number six. With this anticipated college degree, I would be closer to freedom and redemption. At the financial feasibility of becoming a graduate student in America, my dream of going to America began to rekindle.

Around the time of my college enrollment, Father's illness took a drastic turn for the worse. The cancerous cells diagnosed in his colon area surgically removed and treated nine years ago had metastasized to his liver. Common sense told us that he would have about half a year's life left.

Father became weaker and weaker, but he remained very calm as if he was ready to give himself up to God's will. Faced with his final stage, Father at last demonstrated his poise, wisdom and human dignity.

A brilliant man who skipped grades along the way, in 1928 Father entered the renowned British-run Customs College in Beijing taught exclusively in English as the number-one candidate and made history as the first and the only 15-year-old ever to be accepted into this college. He completed the four-year course study in three years and graduated at the age of 18, proficient in English, French, German, Russian, Spanish and Japanese with specialties that included international law, tariff law, appraisal, and accounting. He was the chess champion year after year at the Customs, where many Oxford and Harvard graduates and well-known foreign nationals of the time served. He was nicknamed "Omnipotent Expert" by his colleagues for his broad-range of knowledge. But, under the Communists' capricious, tyrannical rule, his specialties, knowledge and talents were wasted. He did not enjoy his existence. He did not even live like himself. Death might be a welcome release for this intensely tormented soul.

Back then, I was unable to understand Father, not knowing how he was haunted by his background. Having been through so many hazardous campaigns, investigated and interrogated so many times and witnessed so many perish in year after year of Communist campaigns, Father lived in constant fear. And he knew in no ambiguous terms that his life was held in the hands of those empowered workers and peasants. To survive, he swallowed his pride and dignity and turned himself into a caricature.

During his hospitalization, each time we visited him, he would dismiss us and urge us to go back to work. "Don't waste time staying with me," he would say. "There's nothing much you can do here. I've lived my life, and I'm at the end of my journey. But you still have yours ahead of you."

Father's ultimate concern was me. Even in his semi-conscious state, he would repeatedly urge me, "Leave, Qiru. Go to America. Instead of being held down here, you can achieve something in a free country. You can make it there."

The hope for me to go to America was so dim then that I didn't know this was my last phase in China.

A smaller version of Father in terms of breadth and depth of intellect, curiosity and capability, I had been his darling daughter and the hope of his shattered, bleak life. For my potential, he had poured his heart out, heavily investing his time to nurture me, hoping to have the declined family revived, the blaze of his life rekindled, and the guilt he had for the family relieved through me. But my disgrace and string of failures crushed his only hope and added more pain and insult to his wretched existence. Terribly disappointed, he turned sour, channeling all his anger and frustration into relentless bashing of me. I don't blame him. Nothing I did could gladden his old heart and relieve him of his guilt of failing to carry on the family line and resurrect the family. After all, it was I who failed him and rubbed salt in his wounds. To make his displeasure amply palpable to me, he had deliberately fawned on my sister, Qijuan, a party member now, heaped with honors, awards and promotions. But I knew I was still the one that occupied the deep recesses of his heart and mind.

One night, Father's final moment arrived. As the only one at his bedside, I witnessed his life disappear bit by bit in a state of unconsciousness and shortness of breath. Gurgling with his last breath, Father was finally delivered out of his more than 30 years of ordeals living under a Communist regime and rested in peace.

One quiet Sunday afternoon, there were knocks on my door. I opened it and saw a young man in his late 20s with a pair of close-set eyes and small shoulders standing there. The man introduced himself, "I am Wang Jue, your neighbor from the next building. We came across each other a few times."

With my mind always preoccupied with something, I never paid much attention to people passing by me unless there was something special about them. I didn't recall ever seeing this quite ordinary, pretentious man.

At my puzzled, impatient look, he explained, "I am here to have a word with your son."

"Did he do something wrong?" I asked.

"Not really," said he. "He threw a tomato stem from the balcony, nothing serious. Don't worry."

I let him in. He approached my son and told him to listen to me and not to cause any trouble for me. Before he left, he stopped at the door and said, "By the way, I have heard some things about you. If you ever need any assistance, please let me know."

I thanked him for his kindness, wondering what he had heard about me.

The following afternoon, he came again with a brand new soccer ball. Handing it to my son, he said, "The ball is yours."

My son beamed. Uneasy about receiving something from a stranger, I immediately offered him money. But he declined, insisting the ball didn't cost him anything. At Wang's suggestion, my son went out to play soccer with him. It was just what my son needed—a boy's game and a father figure that he lacked.

They returned at dinnertime. Out of decorum, I invited Wang to join us for dinner. He readily accepted.

During the meal, without being asked, he told me that he had been a catcher for the Beijing Baseball Team and now he taught in Beijing Medical College No. 2. I knew he said this to impress me. But, coming from a family with a long line of scholars and achievers, I wasn't easily impressed. In general, sportsmen were looked down upon by Chinese society. I wasn't impressed by his claimed college-teaching position either—It was a well-known fact that very few of the worker-peasant-soldier college-graduates placed in positions were able to function. From his half-raw look and the content and diction of his talk that revealed his education level and family background, I assumed he was one of them.

After dinner, Wang stayed on and continued with his tiresome monologue for hours. Although bored to death, I remained polite and bore his rambling. From my son's disapproving facial expression and the shaking of his head, I could tell that even my 10-year-old son was impatient with his long-winded, far-fetched twaddle. My first impression of him was pretty negative. His non-stopping balderdash only made it worse. With my silence and suppressed yawning, he should have got the hint and left. But, so full of himself, he was oblivious to or unwilling to acknowledge the signals.

As I was wondering when this incoherence was going to end, I heard him say, "I believe once equals a hundred times. True love should last forever like Qiong Yao's love stories."

From my students, I had heard of Qiong Yao, a Taiwanese writer whose love stories attracted mainly a teenage following.

However reluctantly, I could not pretend not to see the obvious anymore. At his odd, bold declaration of love out of nowhere to a woman he just met, I instantly rebelled inwardly, resenting his brazen trespass of my inner world and his bumptious, offensive assumption that I already fell for him. I had no idea how my silence could give rise to such a remark and be construed as a sign of encouragement and consent. Nevertheless, brought up in an unfailingly polite world, I remained silent and hoped my silence would send him a clear signal how I truly felt about him and that he would pick it up and go away. But he didn't.

Ever since then, he had become a frequent visitor, using my son as an excuse. Almost every night, he would come and check my son's homework and play with him. Later on, he would arrive with groceries and start to cook as if he lived here. Before I realized it, he had already inserted himself into our life.

Although I didn't like him, he made me feel that I was still living among normal human beings, cared for and protected. Humbled by life and desperate to shed the image of being an anomaly, I said to myself, you were already thrown out of that lofty world. This is where you belong now. Take what you can get, or you miss out on life. By holding onto your ideals, you are paying a price that leaves your son and yourself forsaken by the world. Half-heartedly, I accepted him and settled for reality. Although I was never drawn to his version of paradise, I decided to close my eyes and "live like other common folks" as he demanded of me instead of stubbornly holding onto my ideals.

One Sunday after lunch when we were relaxing, there came slow, but persistent and demanding knocks on the door. The person kept knocking as if he had an unsettled score or a rightful claim.

"Who's this?" highly alarmed, I asked from behind the door.

"It's me," came the familiar sickening mumble.

At once I recognized the voice of the rapist. Having vanished from my life for 17 years, he again found out where I lived and re-emerged like a haunting ghost. I couldn't believe that after 17 years of living in the ruins caused by him, the pervert still would not let me go. Stunned and shaky, I trembled with rage and fright.

At Wang Jue's inquiry, I cried in hysteria, "It's him!" At his incomprehension, I screamed in exasperation, "The rapist!"

"Open the door," Wang Jue said and strode to the door.

"No!" Dreading seeing the ruffian again, I leapt ahead of Wang and blocked his way. Crying frantically, I pushed him back to the living room.

Outraged by this brazen blackmail, Wang Jue tried to persuade me to confront him. "Long Qiru," he said. "You can't avoid him. He's sensing his power over you and will remain overpowering you for the rest of your life. You can't give in to this blackmail. Go and open the door!"

"No!" Frantically, I rejected. In no way would I entertain this idea.

"Listen. He's playing on your fear. The only way to stop him is to stand up for yourself and confront him."

Wang Jue tried in vain to persuade me to open the door. A long time had passed, but the villain was still there, flagrantly and persistently knocking on the door. Evidently, he had no intention of leaving.

"Long Qiru!" Wang Jue yelled at me, "Not answering the door is not the solution. He will not be deterred. On the contrary, sensing that you fear him, he will only become even more brazen. This encounter is inevitable. It's better to confront him when I'm here!"

This said, before I was able to stop him, he had shoved me aside and stridden to the door and hurled it open, leaving me just about enough time to escape to my son's room and take refuge there.

From behind the closed door, I could hear the thumping and Wang Jue's fuming shouts, "You bastard, coward! What are you here for? You want to trash Long Qiru again?"

"Lemme speak, lemme speak," I heard the miscreant bellow. "I went to jail for her! I went to jail for her!"

In no time, I heard a loud hurling of the door slamming against the wall, followed by heart-palpitating frenzied footsteps racing and leaping down the stairway, and the dastard's bawling all the way to downstairs, "Long Qiru and I were lovers 17 years ago! Long Qiru and I were lovers 17 years ago!"

The loud commotion led all the way into the neighborhood, with many neighbors coming out to watch this wild chase.

The commotion eventually died down.

As I was wondering what was going on, I heard some knocking on my door. It was Xiao Li, the local policeman in charge of our neighborhood, with Wang Jue behind him. Xiao Li told me to go to the police precinct with him.

Once there, I found myself taken into a room to give my account with Wang Jue left out of the scene.

Unlike many policemen of the previous generation, Xiao Li was a nice, handsome young man brought up in the Post-Mao era, when class hatred was not taught. But, having to expose my ignominious past to a much younger, unmarried man, I was mortified. I cried irrepressibly. Xiao Li listened intently, visibly stirred up by my intense account and bursting emotions.

When I finally finished and gradually calmed down, Xiao Li said, "The Cultural Revolution was a horrible era. Tens of millions were victimized by the extreme circumstances." Pausing, he then resumed, "I'm sorry about your situation. But laws can do nothing to stop this harassment. All I can do is to warn him that if he comes again, he will be subject to arrest. But then he'll be released and do this again. He's an outlaw, already giving no regard to whatsoever."

Having had to go through the humiliation all over again only to be informed that I was on my own, I panicked, feeling helplessly forsaken. The disturbing scenario of being left to my own devices to deal with a hardened criminal made me intensely aware of my vulnerability as a woman who was not even adequate to deal with normal men's harassment.

Returning home, I immediately blocked the doorway with pieces of heavy furniture, hoping this would at least gain me some time at his potential break-in.

At night, I was unable to sleep, pricking up my ears and frightened by any slightest noise.

The next day, on our way to and back from school, I was all nerves, constantly looking back and watching out at every turn and every corner.

Not long after we returned home, a phone call came from the urban residents committee where the phone service was provided. Instinct told me it was from the convict. He was playing the same old trick of stalking me again. I ignored it. But the phone calls kept coming. Distraught and terribly agitated by this harassment, I was unable to think clearly and figure out the right solution to it, but to go by what I thought as the solution at the moment. I went down to the neighborhood committee to answer the call.

With all the ears and eyes there trained on me, I was uncomfortable even to whisper in public. But I was there to have the problem resolved once and for all. I toughened myself, overcame my inhibition and concern for decorum, and managed to raise my voice over the phone and hung up on him.

But the moment I returned home, the phone call came again. With the messenger arriving again and again, shouting out my name from downstairs so loud that the entire neighborhood could hear, I had to go down to answer the call again and again.

This continued for days, several times a day, with no end in sight. Although Wang Jue checked in on us every day, it was impossible to protect my son and myself this way. I couldn't live like this. Frightful and furious, I felt utterly defenseless, ruthlessly played by a hardened criminal at his will.

As strange and inexplicable as his resurfacing was, after a whole week of harassment, the felon mysteriously disappeared. Wang Jue surmised that his allowed home-visiting time was over and that he had returned to the reform-through-labor farm.

༺ஐ༻

Life regained its routine.

By then, Wang Jue had felt secure enough to divulge his need to pass the high school equivalency test. It was this divulgence that made me finally figure out that he was not a college graduate and not a teacher but an autopsy technician dissecting and demonstrating the anatomy to students. There were countless knife cuts and cigarette burns on his legs and arms, and a word "love" formed by big, ugly welts burnt on his chest. As time went on, more bizarre things about him were spilled out: With a baseball bat, he beat a pickpocket into a paraplegic; he was also in deep debt. Before he met me, he borrowed money equivalent to more than 13 years of his earnings to purchase two motorcycles only to find the man he trusted his borrowed money with absconding without a trace…

At more things about him done beyond normal range that I found out, I was even more repelled, wary of my future life with him. However, already a fait accompli, I decided to keep one eye open and see his good side only. After so many setbacks, I was willing to compromise. For his sake, I curbed my drive and gave up all my upward attempts in order to make him feel more secure. Meanwhile, I tried yielding to his wishes by living the life of his version of happiness by "just being a woman like everyone else".

Nevertheless, it was impossible to please him. He was insecure and suspicious. Nothing could escape him. Any subtle changes in our thoughts or mood would be caught on by him and relentlessly pursued, leaving us no room to think or feel on our own. No matter how hard I tried to bend myself, he still perceived challenge. Whenever this notion was in place, he would start a prolonged ugly fight and insult me as "a twice-divorced woman no man wants". But, when I challenged him to let me go, he would threaten to kill himself right in my presence by crossing one leg over the concrete enclosure of the balcony, reaching for the switch, or grabbing the kitchen knife. Countless days and nights were exhausted in this vulgar drama. What was worse, his solution to deal with perceived challenge was violence. No actions of his were allowed to be questioned, or I would meet with a head-on blow. Once, he slapped me and my son in the face with full force and beat my son savagely, forcing him to admit to wrongs he did not do. My son was so afraid of his brutality that his nose twitched for years. Coming from a family whose parents never raised their voices, I had never been exposed to anything remotely close to this. His behavior simply turned me averse.

No matter what I convinced myself of, I couldn't help but admit to myself that I had gone a full circle only to land at the very same place where I started. Wang Jue was no better than my son's father.

One evening, when Wang Jue was in my home, Weiping came for a visit. After dinner, we retired to the living room.

"Weiping," Wang Jue said. "Can I talk to you?"

At Weiping's consent, Wang Jue began, "Weiping, I feel exhausted in this relationship. You know how hard it is to remold Qiru. She's not pure and innocent anymore. She has her own mind about everything. It's impossible to return her to her original innocent state and lead her to the ultimate happiness. She's incapable of leading a simple life and being a simple woman like everyone else."

Whenever my family members and friends visited me, Wang Jue would seize the opportunity to get his side of the story out. He had won over my family. They all thought he was a fine young man who broke through traditions and bias, involved with an older, divorced woman and her baggage. Now he was doing this again.

I was uncomfortable with my personal affair being discussed by others and criticized again. Having been repeatedly told that I was "no good", "distinctly different from other people", I had tried hard to repress my consciousness and closed my eyes to be led by him to the "utmost happiness" of his desire by metamorphosing myself, adopting his tastes and "living like a simple, ordinary woman" as he told me to. What else does he want? I asked myself.

"Wang Jue," I heard Weiping's calm voice. "Since you are getting me involved in your private affair, forgive me for speaking bluntly. I've known you and observed the relationship for years. In my opinion, you are looking for a route of decent retreat."

"What are you talking about?" Enmeshed in a web of his own spinning, Wang Jue looked and sounded taken aback, unable to vindicate himself.

Looking at Wang intently, Weiping went on, "I think you are trying to build up your image and win sympathy so that when you leave Qiru, you won't get the blame."

So used to having his opinions imposed on me and to convincing other people, Wang Jue was struck by Weiping's candor. Having had his painstakingly built-up image ripped off in front of me in a second, he looked flustered, attempting to contest.

But Weiping would have none of it. "Let me finish," she went on calmly. "You are fascinated by Qiru, someone very different from the people in your social circle. By this association, your ego is flattered. You envision yourself a hero in this life drama and fancy yourself Qiru's savior. But in reality, you are still what you are. You don't have the ability to live up to this life of your fantasy. By positioning yourself in this impossible 'savior' position, you torment yourself and the people around you."

"It's your opinion. I don't have to accept this." Despite Wang's unmoved show, his trailing-off voice betrayed him.

Enlightened by Weiping's insight and ashamed to have someone much younger to defend me, I didn't know what to say, except remaining silent.

"Qiru," Weiping said. "I have to go. I'm not coming any time soon until you sort things out. You have to take care of yourself."

I nodded, touched by her selfless act.

When I came back from seeing Weiping off, Wang Jue had overcome his embarrassment. "'Looking for a route of decent retreat'," in an angry mocking tone, he mimicked Weiping. "What right does your stupid, conceited, pretentious friend have to judge me? And you allowed someone else to meddle with your own business and slight me? I feel sorry for you. You have betrayed me and yourself. Here's the key. Take it back. I'm not coming back anymore!" He flung the key at me, slammed the door violently, and bolted down the stairs as he always did after a fight.

When I was trying to make sense of the whole thing, someone tapped on my door. It was my next-door neighbor, Old Wang, a retired air force officer. Obviously, our fight had disturbed our neighbors. I uneasily apologized for the disturbance.

"Never mind," said Old Wang. "My wife has been nudging me to speak to you. I've thought about doing so for a while." Pausing, he went on, "You know, we don't mean to interfere with your private life, but this man is too excessive, coming and going at his will, taking advantage of a single woman. My wife and I are peeved at his blatant behavior. I think the guy is controlling you. I don't think he's sincere enough to marry you. Isn't this obvious? You've been with him for about… three years? If he were sincere, he would have committed a long time ago. You have to watch out for your own interest and not be duped."

Surprised at what I heard, I was touched by his unexpected kindness and sense of justice. I had thought I was perceived as a loose woman and some strange creature whose welfare was beyond their consideration. I thanked him earnestly and promised him that I would seriously consider his advice.

It didn't take long to dawn on me that it was I who was actually saving Wang. With my savings, he was free of the debt that had troubled him for eight years. I couldn't figure out what he truly wanted from me. Leaving him or staying with him, neither seemed to suit him. What bothered me more was his mother's accusation of me "seducing youngster". As usual, I didn't make any effort to reconcile with him. Subconsciously, I was about ready to end this hopeless, suffocating relationship.

Months later, against his own words, Wang Jue knocked on my door again one day. At his sight, I immediately positioned myself at the partially opened doorway.

At my silent message, Wang sensed the change in me. For a moment, he seemed to have accepted the reality, nodding his head and snorting. But before he went away, he bridled, spitting out bitterly, "I should have known better about the people from your class. You are cold and merciless."

Clearly, he meant the clear-cut determination he saw in me.

Since very young, I had been taught to always be honest, principled, and own up to the consequences of our words and deeds, and never do things that violate the trust. We thought other people hold the same standards. Once finding our trust is violated, we cut them off. But in this case, I had allowed myself to be untrue to my standard and lapsed into a world where the line is blurred and ambiguity is a way of life that I was unaccustomed to and allowed this behavior to happen over and again.

The next day, Xiao Du, an inconspicuous-looking girl who frequently visited me together with Wang Jue appeared at my door with a middle-aged man behind her.

At my bewilderment, the man introduced himself, "I'm Xiao Du's father. I'm here to let you know that my daughter is another woman Wang Jue 'saved'! She has lived with him in his home for eight years as a de-facto wife. But he refused to make the commitment. Yesterday after he returned from your apartment, he picked a huge fight with her."

I was shocked by this revelation, recalling the frequent visits made by Xiao Du and another girl named Lin, who often came here to demand to know Wang's whereabouts. Honest and trusting by nature, I never suspected that Wang Jue and Xiao Du had a sexual relationship and that he had been living a double life that was hidden from me. I couldn't believe that he had been lying all the time even till the last minute of our relationship. The extent of deceit and the degree of duplicity were simply too beyond me.

It took me three years to finally act upon my initial intuition and end the relationship that I was dragged into.

One day, several months after Xiao Du's visit, there were knocks on my door. It was Wang Jue standing there with a crazed, feverish and pitiable look. Evidently, he was counting on me to pity his illness and take him back again as I had done in the past after a fight.

Without a word, I stopped him right there. Looking over my shoulder finding the furniture setting changed and the disappearance of the hideous crude cabinet unit designed by him and built by a peasant carpenter that I privately hated, he realized his chance was gone.

He left without a word and never came back again.

DETERMINED TO LEAVE

At the time, my school was at the bottom of the District Board of Education's list, among those that rarely had college admittance. Such a reputation would not bring any motivated students here. To turn things around, the school assigned the best teachers to teach the senior classes. I was the English teacher of the team. With students almost entirely of uneducated peasant stock from the nearby commune and the Beijing Garrison, whose servicemen were also of peasant origin, it was very hard to turn things around. After each normal day's work, we had to stay for two extra hours with no extra pay to teach the selected promising students. With the trust placed on us and the noble goal in mind, no one had any cynical thought about having to stay beyond the normal work day and not getting paid. All were single-mindedly devoted to turning the school around. At the end of the school year, our concerted hard work sent some students to college. We made it to the District Board's commended-schools list.

At the end of the term, a school award for teachers was to be held. I was one of the nominees for this honor. The day before the award ceremony, I was called into Chen Jin's office.

"Long Qiru," said Chen Jin. "I called you in to have you briefed in advance about the result of the nomination process." Pausing, she then resumed, "Everyone acknowledges that you are the hard-est-working and the most caring teacher of our school and that your achievements are the most remarkable of all. Together with Hu Hong, Wu Zuxin and Lu Jialiang, you have turned the school around, lifting it onto the district's honors list. Everyone recognizes your special attributes, such as strong work ethic, strong sense of jus-tice and high integrity. You don't evade truth or mince your words. You tell things as they are. But this truthfulness is not appreciated in this land. The Chinese are not honest with themselves. They don't want to see the true ugly image of themselves. They prefer glossing over things. Your outspokenness and uncompromising personality have offended some people. Your integrity works against you in this land where truth is often purposely blurred and half-truth is told and accepted as the whole truth. People that are good at dancing around truth are the most popular ones here. Your individuality also puts you at a disadvantage. The Chinese culture is not an individualist culture, but a collective culture deriving from its agrarian mode of society. People rely on each other to survive. But you are a 'one-man army'. You don't ally with anyone like the other people. By being so, you offended their sensitivity and made them feel inferior and jealous of you. Moreover, there are some misgivings about your back-ground. In a word, your nomination has caused some controversy. In my opinion, you don't care about such superficial things, do you?"

I smiled at her understanding and high opinion of me. But I couldn't say I was not a bit bothered by this. I knew all too well that rectitude was not welcomed in this land. Working honestly would not get one anywhere; knowing how to play the game would. Besides, with Mao's class line still influencing many people's think-ing, my background would be in the way of everything. I would not get anywhere anyway. But I said to myself, as long as you have a clean conscience, what do you care? You'll be able to laugh it off.

Without giving this more thought, I worked as hard as ever. Nevertheless, despite my even higher achievements in the students' college enrollment examinations the following year, I was again left out of the symbolic acknowledgement—the award. Not only this, there were no words of comfort from anyone this time, not even from the fair, thoughtful Chen Jin. At being taken for granted and at less caring and less competent teachers awarded, I was embittered.

However, notwithstanding my bitterness, I worked just as hard. It was in my nature. I never took one day off to accompany my son on Children's Day or when he was sick, always putting the students' interest ahead of my own son's.

It snowed heavily that New Year's Eve, and it was bitterly cold. As usual, I stayed late, pressured by the time frame of reviewing and teaching six years' contents in a year. In a gratifying session, I forgot about time until a note was passed to me. It was from Yang Xiaofan, my best student who was later admitted into a top college, Beijing Aeronautics College. He wished me, his "most beloved teacher" a "very happy New Year". Touched by the utmost reward, I smiled and raised my head and met his fond, smiling eyes. He reminded me that it was already nine o'clock. There was no one else around except me and my students.

With the last student gone, I rushed to the staff building only to find the entire building pitch dark and chilled out like a huge refrigerator. Not knowing where my son was, I groped my way out as quickly as possible in the hallway. At the turn, one lone dim light came from my office. I was shocked and ached to find my son there alone, whimpering with fear and hunger in the frigid cold. The fire in the stove was put out four hours ago at the end of the school day.

With aching guilt, I held my son tightly in my arms, kissing and comforting him and warming up his cold cheeks and hands with my hands and warm breath. Having my son assuaged, I turned off the only light and led him downstairs out of the building in complete darkness.

Outside, the freezing temperature had refrozen the heavily-trafficked thick snow and ice melted during the day and turned them into hard, bumpy, slippery lumps and ruts. Watching my son riding his little bike struggling to maintain his balance on the treacherous frozen ice and snow, I ached, full of regrets and bitter thoughts. I said to myself, you never had any cynical thought, not even on New Year's Eve when everyone rushed home to be with his family. While you were taking care of other people's children, who was thinking of doing the same for your son? For other people's children, you sacrificed your time and your own son's interest. You are acknowledged as the most caring and the hardest-working teacher, but what is the reward? Your son was neglected and you were even begrudged a small symbolic honor, a mug. Not only this, your son is discriminated against because of your political status.

Once after work, I was called in by my son's teacher, a short, rusty-cheeked and pear-shaped woman at the elementary section of the school.

"Long Qiru," she began in a contemptuous tone. "Your son is out of control. He beat a poor peasant boy and broke the blackboard. Since he's still young, I won't *shanggang shangxian*, raising his act to a higher plane and categorizing it as an act of class retaliation or class hatred, but I do think his behavior comes from the influence of his family background. This kind of child should be sent to a *gong-du xuexiao* (work-study boarding schools for 'buliang shaonian'—'dishonorable juveniles'). Considering you are a single mother, I've decided leniently that you and the boy's parents equally split the cost of replacement."

During the Mao years, in Beijing alone, there were several such high-walled, high-wired work-study boarding schools and as many juvenile delinquent centers run by the police with youngsters as young as 7-years old taken in for some one-time misdemeanor such as pilfering or fighting. Even cursing, habitual lying, contradicting teacher, disrupting class, breaking glass or blackboard or showing interest in sex at an "inappropriate age" could land him in such a place.

I couldn't believe that in the Post-Mao era when class warfare was put to an end and the hideous children's work-study schools that destroyed the lives of tens of millions were dying out, seemingly on their way to the dustbin of history, there were still people clinging onto Mao's totalitarian rule and draconian means. Although Mao's class line had been abolished at the time, many people still refused to let it go, for it was the only thing they could hold onto that would make them feel superior to others. As one who benefited from Mao's class line and felt superior solely on the ground of her working-class origin and her husband's being chosen for the South Pole surveying team, and nothing much else, the teacher could hardly contain herself. She persisted in judging people by class line. In her mind, one's worth was solely decided by his birth. Once one was born with an "undesirable" background, he was "innately no good".

At her words of sending my son to a work-study school, I was beside myself at our no-win status and at the vast overt and covert discrimination we were experiencing.

I had heard the story from my son: The unruly peasant boy goaded my son into a fight, beat him with a stick and broke the blackboard accidentally. Having managed to suppress my trembling rage, I said to her sharply, "If my son beat him and broke the blackboard, then we should be solely responsible for this. Why do we have to split?"

In a fluster, she quibbled, "Well, it happened in a fight between them. So I figured both of them should pay a price for it."

"They are poor peasants, having the law on their side. Do you think they would swallow this injustice?" Seeing her speechless, I pressed further, "Who broke the blackboard, my son or the other boy?"

"The other boy did," reluctantly, she admitted.

"Then why should we be held responsible for the damage?"

"The boy's parents said their boy was hurt by your son…"

"If they claimed he was hurt," I interrupted her and asserted. "I will cover his medical expenses. But I'm not responsible for the broken blackboard, not even a single cent!"

Unable to advance any further arguments to justify her position, the teacher was compelled to concede to my terms. Though I beat the odds in this incident, I was very frustrated by the continuous injustice my son and I experienced.

Despite being hurt not only by urchins but by some small-hearted adults as well, my son remained intact, as kind, gentle and open-hearted as he had ever been, and gave whatever he had. Whenever he saw an elderly woman in the neighborhood, he would reach out to help by carrying the load for her, supporting her with his tender shoulders, keeping her company or running small errands for her.

There was a poor old woman who lived downstairs from us who couldn't afford to use propane. My son came up with the idea of collecting starter wood for her and had been doing this ever since he was 5-years old. In a scanty society, everything was put to use. There was hardly anything spared. Whenever my son spotted any wood, be it a broken stick or a fragmented plank, he would pick it up and carry it home for me to chop it into pieces to bring them downstairs to the old woman.

Once he hauled a huge tree stump of about 10" x 12" x 10" up to our fifth-floor apartment step-by-step. At his sweaty face and labored breath, my heart ached and swelled with pride. Although I knew the knotty stump was not igniting material and that it was impossible to chop off any of it with the rusty ax we had, I didn't want to disappoint him and decided to give it a try anyway. While chopping, I accidently cut my finger, causing profuse bleeding and emergent medical treatment.

Embittered and feeling wronged, I decided to do something to change our fate. The only way out at the time was to change my job. Thanks to the shortage of qualified personnel of the time, employment opportunities were gradually opened up to the public. Having waited for a thorough change for too long but little had taken place, many disappointed educated people had turned to different directions. The shrewd ones had abandoned their academic work, joining the trend to make fast money while others switched to a more profitable job. There was a steady outflow of the teaching ranks in secondary schools and colleges in search of a better life. Determined to explore the opportunities, when Radio Beijing, the official overseas broadcasting station, put up a newspaper advertisement to recruit staff members for its English Department, I seized the opportunity and registered for the examination.

With me passing the written examination and ranking number nine, I became one of the three-dozen candidates for the next round of the tests of oral fluency in English. As I was getting closer to altering my fate at the slim chance, I became uneasy, anxious about political screening.

Consumed by worries, during the oral examination, I was unnerved, unable to control myself, and shook uncontrollably. At my seemingly ridiculous extreme nerves and trembling voice, the chief examiner Zhang Jianxin, a well-known young anchorman of the time, asked me jokingly whether I was a weightlifter, apparently attempting to relax me. But even this casualness couldn't put me at ease. With my mind preoccupied and overwhelmed with concerns, when I was asked to say something about the situation in the Gulf countries, all I could come up with at the moment was "They fight each other". Waiting and seeing no further responses, Zhang Jianxin proceeded to ask me to read aloud a piece of news in English about the Indian Prime Minister Rajiv Gandhi. Although I was fluent, my tremulous voice gave me away.

After I walked out, I was angry at myself. I was well abreast of world affairs and knew quite a bit about the Gulf situation—the oil controversy caused by the measures taken by OPEC, the religious conflicts between the Shiites and the Sunnis, and the war between Iran and Iraq… But at the moment, my mind was frozen by anxiety. No other words came out of my mouth.

Just as I thought my chance was gone, I unexpectedly received a notice from Radio Beijing a week later, informing me to go through the final interview.

I was interviewed by a middle-aged, prominent-looking tall woman, Ms. Li, a well-known anchorwoman for her posh English whose name I now forgot. At her easy manner and the informal setting, I was able to relax and chat with her in simple English.

At the end of the interview, the man who took me into the building arrived to escort me out of the building as a security measure. Upon my inquiry about my chance, the man answered evasively, "We need to employ a dozen or so qualified people out of the three dozens. As long as you can get the permission to leave the school system, we'll take you in."

At his non-committal attitude, I was very disheartened. By the time I applied for this job, a new rule had been in place to forbid the outflow from secondary schools in order to stabilize the teaching ranks. No state-owned institutions were allowed to take in teachers.

Nevertheless, in a corrupt country like China where power equals everything, rules and regulations always bend to power. I wasn't from the privileged class and had no such connections to make the rule bend. With my stained history, Radio Beijing wouldn't be enthusiastic about going through the trouble on my behalf. Without their commitment, there was no way for me to bypass the rule. I knew my chance to get into Radio Beijing was as good as gone.

As I was on my way out of the complex, a calm, mellow contralto voice called out to me from behind. Wondering who in this prestigious place would know me, a person who didn't belong here, I turned around and saw a short, rotund, middle-aged woman with a smile on her face advancing toward me.

"Long Qiru," she again called out calmly. "Don't you remember me?"

From the kind, confident yet a little patronizing demeanor, smile, and tone, I could tell this was someone who was in some position and was highly satisfied with her life. I searched my memory, but I was clueless. I shook my head in embarrassment.

"I'm Zhang Gui…"

"Oh, Zhang Guihua," I cried out before she could finish, recognizing the trace of the same timbre of my classmate at Beijing Foreign Languages School, a kind-hearted, hard-working girl with a working-class background nicknamed "Little Teapot" for her New Year's performance and her large middle section.

"Zhang Guizhen," winking coaxingly, she coolly corrected me.

I immediately apologized, feeling like a fool. How could you mess up with her name? I asked myself. You've learned from Wang Qian that Zhang Guizhen has become the chief anchorwoman going by the name "Li Jiang" in the Central People's Broadcasting Station, which is under the same administration as Radio Beijing in the same complex. Who doesn't know Li Jiang, the number-one voice of the nation at the time?

In front of my former classmate who knew all about my past and who was well-established and looked properly matured owing to the responsibilities and position placed on her, I was very conscious of my ridiculously girlish image and my own pitiable situation, caught for still seeking a place for myself in this world at this age. Feeling inferior, I became tongue-tied.

"What are you doing here?" surprised to see me here, Zhang Guizhen inquired in a tone of a charitable elder or a superior, making me even more aware of the distance between us and my own status.

Uneasily, I told her I just had an interview at Radio Beijing.

At my answer, Zhang Guizhen sincerely wished me luck with all the good intentions of someone who was a success himself. Glancing at her watch, she uttered apologetically, "Oh, I'm sorry. I've got to rush to pick up my son at his kindergarten. Good-bye!"

Without exchanging contact information, she hurriedly ended this encounter and mounted on her bicycle, vanishing into the departing crowds.

I felt relieved. After all, what do we have in common? I said to myself, who needs to be associated with a useless person like you anyway?

Despite this setback, I went on with my pursuit, hoping I would be eventually taken in by some institution willing to overlook my history and tackle and bypass the rule on my behalf. I passed the English examinations at the official All-China Workers' Union, ranking number three; and a few non-state-owned foreign-trade companies not restricted by the policy, including CITIC (China International Trust and Investment Corporation), the largest foreign trade company in China headed by the "Red Capitalist" Rong Yiren[17]. But it was all to no avail. I was rejected by them as well. As a matter of fact, all of the non-state-owned foreign trade companies were established by and packed with elite offspring using their profitable connections to do business with foreigners. Evidently, I was of no use to them. My pursuit turned out futile.

While ordinary people were frustrated at every step with every likely exit blocked, the road for elite offspring was wide open. They either were directly involved in businesses making big money or were in some profitable position that would bring them the windfall. Ding Xiaoming, my former classmate, a handsome, gentle boy whose father was the chief of the Film Bureau and who stood out for his athleticism, now became a vice minister at the Foreign Trade Ministry, a powerful high-ranking official himself.

With no such connections, I found myself denied every opportunity I could get, unable to move one step like other people confined by rules and their backgrounds.

⁓

At the time, there was a wide-spread saying: "Exiting the door of China is easier than exiting the door of one's institution". In a country where one's fate was decided by his family background, the only way for the powerless and disadvantaged to live up to their potential was to leave China. Going to a free country where one can largely control his own fate became a fever that caused huge bustles and resonance in the nation. All that everyone was talking about was leaving. It was compared to the frenzied exodus on the eve of the communist takeover when millions fled.

Although leaving the country where I would never have a fair chance and going to a country like America where everyone has a chance to succeed had long been in my dream, with no known close relatives abroad to sponsor me and no hard currencies, my desire of leaving was but an unrealizable dream.

One day, my friend, Li Qing, came for a visit. Fed up with the situation in China large and small, Li Qing was also looking for a way out. For this purpose, he had piled up tens of thousands of English vocabulary words in his brain. Mutual dream, similar mindset and straightforward personality had turned us into close friends.

"Qiru," Li Qing exclaimed. "My cousin is leaving for America soon. She's admitted to a university in Hawaii as a graduate student!"

"Good for her," I answered.

At the time, stories about going abroad were legion; everyone around was doing something to get out. Without the needed American currency to take the TOEFL (Test of English as a Foreign Language), the very first step for me to get out, I just didn't see any possibility of my leaving.

"Qiru," urged Li Qing. "Your English is far better than my cousin's. She's only a worker-peasant-soldier college-graduate. What are you waiting for? The ship is sinking. Everyone is fleeing. There will be no future for us here!"

"It's not that I don't want to leave," I said. "But that I don't have the needed American currency to even begin the procedures…"

"Then go out and find a way to get it!" Li Qing screamed at me, "Waiting for our fair chance here is like waiting for Godot. It will never arrive! As long as we keep knocking, one day the door is going to open for us. I have never seen anyone who truly wants to leave get stuck here."

Like a fresh breeze, Li Qing's words cleared away all of my doubts.

With Li Qing's prodding and supervision all the way, I purchased TOEFL study material and began to practice the tests and look for ways to get out.

What happened shortly after Li Qing's visit only strengthened my determination to leave.

That day on my way home for lunch during the noon break, I stopped by the market to pick up some groceries at a busy section in Sanlihe, where many government ministries, a police precinct, a market, restaurants and stores were located.

As I was walking toward the market, a crowd caught my attention. Within the wall formed by spectators, a peasant girl was crying while several thuggish vendors were taunting and gibing at her.

"What's going on?" I asked people around.

"Those thugs took her eggs without paying," someone in the crowd informed me.

At what happened in a major section in the capital city in broad daylight and at no men coming to the poor girl's aid, I was riled. Without thinking, I approached the gang and demanded, "Give the eggs back to her."

Interrupted from their fun, the thugs all turned to me, swearing while swiftly closing in on me. "Fuck," the one taking the lead swore. "You old bitch, stinky cunt! Who do you think you are that you dare to stick your fucking nose into our business? Do you know who we are? Are you looking for trouble? That's easy. You need to be screwed? Come here!" He began to unzip his fly while moving closer to me.

At the tightened up physical threat, all the spectators remained watching intently and motionlessly. Knowing no men would come to my aid should something really bad happen, I trembled with ire and trepidation. At having to extricate myself, I softened my stance and murmured that they should either pay for the eggs or return them to the girl, and managed a swift, inglorious exit.

Returning home, I burst out into loud crying for a long time, humiliated by the scene I brought upon myself for attempting to stop an injustice, a move not one single man present attempted to make. I swore to myself I would try at all costs to leave this lawless and spineless nation that allowed thugs to rule.

From then on, leaving China became the sole purpose of my existence. Many of my friends and acquaintances had left. Many of my college mates had also departed. Li Qing was in the process of being admitted to Georgia Tech. All of this only enhanced my determination to leave.

MY FINAL DAYS IN CHINA

All at once, things began to take a turn for the better. After Father's death, his friend and middle-school classmate, Dr. Wen-Ping Lee, a celebrated dynamite engineer, took upon himself the avuncular role, extending his fatherly care to me and helping me out every way he could.

Uncle Lee had known me and been very fond of me since I was a preadolescent. Having a son my age, he understood too well the frustration of my generation who never had a chance to take off and fulfill our ambition and potential. He and Professor Yin Yifu, his former fellow inmate at a notorious labor camp in Xingkaihu, Heilongjiang Province, tried every way to foster me, helping me out with opportunities of translation work for the Chinese Academy of Sciences and tutoring for extra income. A man of few words, Uncle Lee's boundless mercy however could be felt by his kind, beaming gaze.

Uncle Lee attended the same missionary school with Father at Tianjin Huiwen Secondary School, a school that fostered a galaxy of distinguished men. After graduation, they parted ways. While Father proceeded to the prestigious Customs College, Uncle Lee entered the renowned Tangshan Transportation & Communications University. He then went on to the University of Michigan and received his doctorate in Transportation Engineering.

During World War II, Uncle Lee was chosen as the engineer-in-chief over the construction of the Ledo Road on the China section, an alternative route of supply to replace the Burma Road cut off by the Japanese. His work brought him into contact with Joseph Stilwell, Claire Lee Chennault, Dean Rusk, and many prominent Nationalist figures and commanders, Sun Liren, Du Yuming and Wei Lihuang. Together with the air route over the Hump, the completion of the Ledo Road made it possible for war supplies to be continuously transported to the Chinese Nationalist troops, which pinned down a million Japanese troops and contributed significantly to the victory in the Pacific battlefield. For his work, Truman awarded him a Presidential Medal of Freedom in 1946, which he was unable to receive until 1986.

Uncle Lee was caught in the Anti-Rightist campaign because of his matter-of-fact scientist's uprightness, nothing to do with presenting a political challenge, but pure academic dispute contradicting the Communists' arbitrary orders. For a dinner he attended and the list of attendees he prepared, Uncle Lee was linked to Zhang Bojun[18], the number-one "rightist", and was exiled to Xingkaihu as a "principal rightist". Luckily, his expertise was put to use there and earned him an early release in 1962, thanks to Liu Shaoqi's lenient policy. His "rightist" label was removed. He was returned to Beijing.

However, when the Cultural Revolution arrived, he found his real ordeals just began. His background unavoidably led to the ransacking of his home. When the Red Guards discovered the citations he received from Chiang Kai-shek and the Americans, the photos he took with the Americans and the Nationalist figures during the construction of the Ledo Road, and his training in America, they were infuriated at this "vicious four-fold enemy"—an "unrepentant rightist", a "hidden American imperialist spy", a "hidden Nationalist agent" and a "counterrevolutionary dreaming of restoring the Chiang Kai-shek regime". They beat him to unconsciousness and poured water on him to revive him only to torture him more. They threw him onto a pile of glass shards, forcing him to kneel there for hours. While he was in excruciating pain from the lashes, the laceration, and the tiny glass slivers embedded in his flesh, they pulled him up and paraded him in the streets with a dunce cap on his head and a heavy wooden board around his neck fastened with a metal cable that cut into his flesh. However, he survived. Perhaps his faith in one day being able to clear himself of all the false accusations helped him sustain and live on.

After the death of Mao, in 1979, he saw his "rightist" case overturned. He was exonerated together with half a million others. The other charges against him were also dropped. To silence criticism, the Communists conferred upon him the title of a consultant in the rubber stamp political advisory organization—the People's Political Consultative Conference. Albeit a symbolic position, he took his new role seriously, doing whatever he could for the right cause.

Keenly aware of my frustration and discontentment, Uncle Lee took upon himself to look for ways to help me out. With his help, prospects for me gradually brightened up.

Through his referral, I became the English tutor to the grandson of his fellow consultant, Uncle Li Ximi, the son of Li Genyuan, who also served under President Li Yuanhong like my grandfather and who was a leader of one of the uprisings in the Xinhai Revolution (1911), which ended 2,000 years of imperial rule and greeted in the republican era.

This unexpected relatedness naturally inclined me toward Uncle Li Ximi. What made me feel even closer to him was that everything about him reminded me of the long-lost past. Impeccably and unfailingly gracious, he was the incarnation of the bygone gentlemen that I was familiar with. Even his home in the dormitory for members of the State Council and their families at Xibianmen evoked in me the dream-like memory of my childhood home in the Customs compound in Haikou—same serenity and same vastness. Although Uncle Li Ximi was a man of few words, I found it very easy to communicate with him. He grasped the concept and nature of things instantly. With him, I felt that I was finally home, returning to my own long-lost kin, no longer frustrated by misunderstanding caused by my dislocation trapped among people who didn't have a similar mentality and outlook. His understanding of me and respect for me were abundantly conveyed through his wordless actions and mannerism toward me—He even bowed to me, his junior by one generation.

Upon learning about my goal of leaving China, his refined, handsome, brilliant-looking son-in-law generously and voluntarily paid me for my service with his precious American currency. With the American money I earned, I was able to take the TOEFL test, which, at the time, cost $26, and meet the very first requirement of getting out of China.

One Sunday afternoon in the late summer of 1986, I received a phone call from Uncle Wen-Ping Lee. He told me to go to his home with my college transcripts right away.

When I arrived there, I found Professor Yin Yifu also there.

"Qiru," Uncle Lee said. "Go to the Friendship Hotel with Professor Yin to meet with Dr. Jevons Lee."

From them, I had heard about Dr. Jevons Lee, a professor then from the Wharton School of Business who was lecturing in China. In my mind's eye, Dr. Lee was a kind elderly of Father's generation who fled China on the eve of the communist takeover.

We were on our way.

Before long, we were at the gate of the hotel. "Qiru," Professor Yin said. "I have some other commitment that I have to see to. Go in by yourself. Dr. Lee is expecting you."

Places like this were out of bounds for ordinary Chinese. At Professor Yin's abrupt departure, I found myself alone at the entrance, intimidated by the foreign-visitors-only place, worried about surveillance camera and uneasy about bringing myself to the door of a complete stranger for the purpose of getting help. But, well-acquainted with the two elderlies' quaintness and whims, knowing that they only had my best interest in mind and that they had solicited Dr. Jevons Lee to help me out, and with the kind elderly image of Dr. Lee in my mind, I braced myself and proceeded to the building to meet with him.

When a vibrant, handsome, brilliant-looking man not much older than I appeared at the door of his room, I was startled and uneasy. At his astonished look, I was even more uneasy, assuming he was turned off by the way I looked.

Led to an armchair, I sat down. Rattled by the real image of Dr. Lee, a successful man from a promising land, I was very conscious of my pitiable state. I wouldn't feel bad about receiving a helping hand from someone my father's generation who fled the Communists and understood what the Mainlanders left behind had been through, ready to help out the one that he deemed deserving the help. But, getting help from a proud, successful young man, I was very ashamed. While Dr. Jevons Lee had left a trail of sparkling records behind him, at 37, I was still struggling to find my place in this world. I said to myself, by putting yourself in this awkward, pitiable position, you have humiliated yourself.

When I was regretting coming here, I heard Dr. Lee say, "Qiru, show me your transcripts."

In embarrassment, I took them out and handed them to him. They were not earned from rigorous four-year college education, but from a highly condensed, rushed two-year remedial program.

As I was feeling bad about my transcripts, I heard Dr. Lee say, "Straight As, very impressive."

I blushed. Compared with what he had accomplished, this was nothing but a joke.

"Qiru," I heard Dr. Lee speak again. "Tell me something about yourself."

I was even more disconcerted and felt unworthy. I had nothing to brag about. However, obliged to say something, I replied hesitantly and diffidently, "I have nothing much to say about myself. I didn't accomplish anything. I didn't even have a formal education. Before the Cultural Revolution, I was a tenth grader at Beijing Foreign Languages School. Then I went to the countryside as a peasant. After a leg injury, I was returned to Beijing and spent seven years as a factory worker. In the early 1980s', I attended a remedial program offered by Beijing Foreign Studies University and obtained this worthless degree. I teach in a secondary school now." All the while, I kept my eyes downcast, ashamed of my own vacant resume.

Just as I was very uneasy and thinking of seizing the right moment to flee, I heard Dr. Lee say, "Qiru, the university you attended is a highly esteemed one. The degree you earned is not worthless.

Although you didn't say much about yourself, from the way you look and the few minutes of talk with you, I've learned quite a bit about you. And I've heard plenty of good things about you from Dr. Wen-Ping Lee and Professor Yin Yifu." Pausing as if tracing his own thoughts, he then resumed, "I've been in China many times. I have some basic idea what happened during the Cultural Revolution and what that ten-year nationwide disaster caused for the nation and individuals like you. I've spent a great deal of time studying it, reading literature, seeing movies, watching TV, and speaking to people about that era. I feel fortunate that my family left for Taiwan with the Nationalists on the eve of the communist takeover and escaped the kind of life you and many others have been through. We are able to have a normal life and pursue our dreams. But many talented and ambitious people are unfortunately stuck here, wasting their lives under the Communist goons." Pausing again, he continued, "I intend to do something in return for my good fortune and help deserving people out. Qiru, I can tell you have a lot of pride, dignity and intelligence. You won't fail me. Although I'm not sure how much actual help I can offer you, I will definitely look into graduate schools for you."

This was totally unexpected. But I wasn't sure whether he meant it or was just caught in the moment. Even if he meant it, he had so many responsibilities and commitments, and he lived so far away. Once he was gone, he would forget about it. So used to schemers and prowlers whose promises didn't mean anything unless you invest, and even then, very often, you wouldn't see the return, I didn't think this momentary crossing of our paths would result in anything.

Nevertheless, within two months of his return, I received three application forms sent by him. Knowing I couldn't afford to study in the most prestigious universities abroad like those sponsored by the government, he chose the most feasible and least expensive ones for me. Overjoyed at receiving the forms, I immediately plunged myself into the task of leaving.

With the American currency I earned, I was just about able to pay for one application fee of $35 to the least expensive school among the three options. It was Jersey City State University. Once having this out of the way, I set about meeting the requirements step by step. With Dr. Lee's selfless help all the way through, I was able to satisfy all the requirements.

In November 1987, I received the school's admission for spring 1988. With only two months left before the semester began, it was impossible to complete all the procedures in time—getting the permission to leave from the notoriously slow Chinese bureaucracy, the District Board of Education and the Beijing Municipal Public Security Bureau, and obtaining a visa from the American Embassy. I called the school to request an extension of the admission for the fall semester. My request was granted. Half a month later, I received the new admission.

With this new admission, I went to Chen Jin to request the permission to study abroad.

At this, Chen Jin responded eagerly, "Long Qiru, I know you are restless and frustrated here. You deserve a break. We won't hold you back. I'll see to it and make sure you get the permission and get it as soon as possible."

As Chen Jin promised, within three days, my school gave me the permission to leave and turned my application in to the District Board of Education. Two months later in January 1988, I received the permission from the Board.

Losing no time, the following day, I submitted my application for a passport to the Beijing Public Security Bureau. Four months later in late May, I was granted the passport.

Now I had come to the last juncture—acquiring a visa from the American Embassy.

The American embassy was right next to Mother's building, separated only by a wall and a street. Every day there was a long line of scores of applicants there, but only several of the lucky ones came out of the compound with a broad smile. Knowing the rejection rate was extremely high, I didn't join the line right away. Since there was enough time left for me to attend school on time, I decided to go there to observe, listen and inquire first.

Accustomed to bad luck and setbacks at every step along my way for so long, I didn't dare to envision that fortune would smile at me. I wasn't sure I would be granted a visa. I was so anxious that I went to a man who was said to possess the ability to tell one's future. However, even at his accurate observation about my bumpy past and his assurance of my smooth future, I was still doubtful about my success at the American Embassy.

On July 6, 1988, I decided to go to the American Embassy to try my luck.

At noontime, the winding line outside and inside finally led me to a petite American woman. After I struggled to finish answering her questions in English, she smiled and said, "You speak good British English. You don't need to study in America."

I knew she confused learning English as a second language with teaching English as a second language. But, before I was able to say anything, she already stamped on the last page of my passport and dated it. At the rejection, I was terribly disappointed—Many Communists concealing their true identities were granted the visa.

I had waited years just for this day. Now when the only chance arrived, it was within sight but one step beyond my reach. I burned with anxiety. I was three months shy of reaching 39. This might be my last opportunity ever. Having already lost my youth—the most productive years in one's life, I could not afford to see this chance slip away. I could not afford to fail.

Day by day, a determination was growing out of my frustration and desperation.

Two weeks later, I headed for the embassy again. This time, I didn't speak to any applicants in the waiting line. I didn't need to seek assurance. I was determined to win.

At my turn, a tall woman bearing the image of fortitude and capability called me out. At the typical image of an assertive American woman, I drew a deep breath. I braced myself and brought myself to her window. Upon her inquiry, I stated the reason why I wanted to study in America. After asking me some routine questions, she granted me the visa.

I was transported with rapture and ecstasy.

Once out of the embassy, I at once found myself surrounded by applicants, eagerly answering their inquiries.

I couldn't wait to get back home to share the good news with my family, but no one was home. With so many things to be taken care of, I wasted no time and left home right away. I needed to reserve an airplane ticket, to purchase needed things, to have my Beijing residence revoked, to exchange the permitted allowance of 30 dollars at Bank of China, to gather important documents and belongings and hand them over to Mother and Son, to make arrangements for my son's life in the case of my absence, and to say good-bye to friends and acquaintances. On my way, I arranged my routes in order to get things done in a most effective and economic way.

I stopped by China Airline first and was told the tickets to arrive in America on time were sold out. Having already gone this far, I was unfazed by this little hiccup and proceeded to Xicheng District to my bank to close my account and to revoke my resident status at the police precinct. Then, I headed back to Dongcheng District to Bank of China to exchange for the allowed amount of American currency. On my way home, I decided to drop in on my former colleague, Wu Zuxin, my on-and-off ally in the school theatrics who had transferred to the China Association for Promoting Democracy with the help of his fellow writer friend, the head of the organization.

At my appearance, Wu Zuxin was pleasantly surprised. It was about lunchtime. He treated me to lunch in his cafeteria.

"Well," after we sat down in his office with our lunch, Wu Zuxin asked. "What wind brought you here, Long Qiru?"

I smiled and said, "I'm leaving for America."

"Wow, finally!" eyebrow rising, Wu Zuxin exclaimed. "I knew in my heart that sooner or later, you were going to leave. A restless soul like you is not going to settle for the ordinary. Good for you!"

I thanked him and asked him about his new job. He said, "I'm a section chief now. It's a leisurely job, not much to do here. Well, we each have our own destiny. While I remain and continue with my dull life here, I'll wait and see you continue with your journey with the next chapter!"

"Please," I chuckled at his words, begging him to stop. "According to Confucius, one establishes himself in his 30s. By the time he reaches his 40s, he already reaches the free stage, no longer perplexed by anything. I'm a few months shy of reaching 39, approaching the free stage, yet I'm just about to begin my baby steps."

At my words, Wu Zuxin turned serious. "It's a cruel joke that fate played on us," he said. "But look at it this way: The vast majority of your generation simply capsized—Here we are talking about a hundred million. You are one of the very few who managed to emerge and get back on track again!"

I flashed him a sad smile.

Wu Zuxin had a sharp mind. But, born to a father of a Nationalist major general who passed away in a Communist prison, he was unable to apply his talents but turned to writing harmless children's books, which he dismissed as "a means of paying rent". Bored with this humdrum life and endowed with a writer's eye, he was more like an observer looking to draw entertainment from other people's daring unconventional acts and derive some satisfaction this way.

When Wu Zuxin learned that I was unable to obtain a ticket in time for school, he voluntarily called his friend at China Airline and arranged a ticket for me. With this help, I would be able to arrive in America in time for school.

Before my departure, Wu Zuxin bade me to help his son out once I took root in America. But, to my regret, I never did. After I came to America, I was busy working to establish myself here. By the time I was finally able to get around to look into it, I had lost his address in the move.

After bidding each other good-bye, I mounted on my bike and headed for China Airline to get the ticket.

At night, the whole family gathered at Mother's home for the news from me was elated at the good news.

In gratification, Mother said, "Qiru, I'm so happy for you. After so many years of living low, you finally got the break you deserve and become free at last. It gladdens my old heart. It's too bad your father didn't live to see this day. But, if spirits do exist, I'm sure he'll know it and feel gratified. Qiru, with you studying in America, you are going to redeem my missed opportunity and accomplish something that I failed to."

When Mother was studying in Fujen University, she was chosen to study in America. But Father stopped her for fear of losing her. It was a misstep that Mother forever regretted.

"It's a good beginning," Ciqing said excitedly. "One by one, we will all leave!"

Like all the male descendants in my family clan, my two poor brothers were held back by their birth, deprived of the opportunity to realize their potential. Both Tiemin and Ciqing became laborers. My going to America perhaps could provide them an opportunity to live out of their disappointment to some extent.

"What about you, Peining?" Turning to our niece, Tiemin inquired. "When are you going to start the procedures? You've been tinkering with leaving long before your aunt Qiru."

"Don't tempt her!" My sister screamed in panic, "Peining is not Qiru. She's vulnerable. There's no reason for her to run the risk and suffer needlessly. She has a good job and we have a good life here. The most important for us is that the entire family stays together!" This said, she became hysterical and started whimpering.

"Come on! Not again!" Mother groaned, throwing up her hands and rolling her eyes, "Everyone is tired of you. Each time this topic is brought up, you become hysterical. Didn't you see so many people leave and survive and succeed? Everyone takes it as a God-given opportunity for a better life. How have you become like this—a short-sighted, security-craving pitiable woman?"

"Sister has changed," Ciqing concurred good-naturedly.

Indeed, my once confident, adventurous sister had been reduced to a shadow of her former self. She had remolded herself to fit into the prescribed life—following, not initiating. Under the Communists, generations of people were bent out of their natural shape, not allowed to be themselves and chase their own destinies.

The next day when I returned to work, I informed the school of my imminent departure.

My colleagues were all excited and congratulated me. Some even bade me to help them out after I got my own footing abroad. The disillusion with the Communists and the reality had driven many to stake all they had in order to get out of China, legally and illegally.

The news of my leaving for America reached the home of my brother-in-law's parents in Tianjin. My brother-in-law's father, Guo Delong, an eminent pulmonologist and Father's classmate at Huiwen Secondary School at the time in his 70s who lived to see the death of Mao, the arrests of the ultra-leftists and his own release from prison, made a special trip to Beijing to congratulate me.

We held a dinner party at home.

After a few glasses of wine, Guo Delong exulted. "Qiru," eyes shining and with a broad smile, he said. "He who laughs last laughs the best. We two are the ultimate victors. We not only survived the Cultural Revolution, we live to see this day. Mao, the bloody murderer, kicked the bucket himself. I'm still here, alive and going strong! You, after being held down for decades, finally got a chance to take off! Qiru, you earned your chance to study in America. It is well deserved. As long as you keep this spirit, nothing can ever hold you down. I never have any doubt about you and know deep down that one day you'll make it to the top again. America provides just this opportunity for the ones determined to succeed and excel. I'm sure you will accomplish something there!"

Humbled by his trust of me, I felt the weight on my shoulders. Uncle Six and Uncle Ke had both expressed the same faith in me. Knowing everyone placed his high hope on me, with the $300 in total, exchanged at the bank and contributed by Mother from her life-savings for me to carry to America as an insurance—a big sum in the eye of us at the time and the blind trust placed on me, I vowed to myself, I will not let them down.

For half a year, my school administrators had kept my anticipated departure a secret from my students lest it might produce a devastating effect on them. With guilt and all sorts of emotions held inside, during my last stage of teaching, I tried with all my heart to instill knowledge and values in my students.

On the last day for students, near the end of the period, I had come to the juncture when I had to reveal the secret to them.

"Classmates," I said. "I have an announcement to make."

The class immediately quieted down in an expectant mood.

At the students' trustful look, I felt guilty, having trouble bringing up the subject. In our daily life, they had come to see me as a mother, a sister, a friend and even an idol, all looking up to me to guide them through the difficult teenage years. By leaving them half way, I felt-as if I were cheating on them. Mustering up my resolve, I spilled it out, "I, I'm leaving for America."

At once, the whole class erupted into a shocked, disbelieving and disappointed uproar.

At such an outburst, I was shaken with guilt. But, driven by my long-cherished dream, I was destined to meet my fate. Guilty as I still feel, I had no other alternatives. With a troubled conscience, I exhorted them one last time, bidding them no matter what happened in their future lives, they were not allowed to give up on themselves.

The following day, at the end of school, some parents arrived to say good-bye to me.

At this unexpected visit and their gracious, sincere congratulations and wishes, I was again overwhelmed by guilty emotions. They entrusted their children to my care, hoping that I could make a difference in their lives, but I'm leaving them without seeing them through to the next stage of their lives.

Experiencing the Communist follies on a daily basis themselves, they understood my frustration too well. At my reactions, all of them comforted me, assuring me that it was the Communists that were to blame for this outflow and that if they had the chance, they would do the same.

The news of my departure not only affected people around my school, but also caused a stir in the place where I was moonlighting at the time. At my unexpected announcement, Lin Yizuo, bureau chief of the State Bureau of Cooperatives and an educated man who attended the English class I taught there, was shocked, expressing his deep regret for not being able to make proper use of "quality people" but losing them to foreign countries, causing "bleeding" and "steady brain drain". As a gesture of his appreciation of me, he held a farewell dinner party for a non-employee in a reserved room of a top restaurant and personally presented me a huge basket of fresh mandarins, a tin of expensive tea, a pen and some other memorabilia.

At so much unexpected shower of attention and genuine respect and understanding, I became even more grateful, comforted by the appreciation.

The last day of the scholastic year and the last day of my work at my school, I was summoned into Chen Jin's office and found Shen Yu, the current principal and the even-handed new personnel officer, Ms. Wang, also present.

"Long Qiru," Chen Jin greeted me with a warm smile, saying sincerely. "Congratulations! Your departure is a great loss for our school. But we understand your desire and support your pursuits nonetheless. We are very happy that you have a chance to further your studies in America. We wish you every success and return to the motherland to contribute more!"

All of them began to heap up good words about me. I was warmed up by this unanticipated, sincere last-minute acknowledgement. But returning to the cage I'm about to flee? Hell, no. Never.

"Long Qiru," Chen Jin went on. "You may have been mistreated at some point in your life. We hope you won't hold any grudge. A mother is always a mother, no matter what wrongs she has done to you. We hope that you can propagate the bright side of your motherland and carry the positive image of your own people."

I chuckled at her words. In the Communists' mind, the Communist Party *is* the nation. Therefore, "propagating the bright side" of the motherland meant not to say anything negative about the party. I said to myself, isn't it too late to try to convert me to becoming the party's vehicle and entrust me with its mission?

At the end of the day, after saying good-bye to everyone, I got on my bike, heading for Mother's home to spend my last few days with her and the family.

Outside the gate of the school, I unexpectedly found a dozen or so of my students led by Lin Chuan and Hao Jin waiting there, looking dejected and subdued. Obviously, they came to say good-bye to me.

At the sight, a lump rose to my throat. I got off my bike and greeted them. We walked together.

While they remained silent all the way, I bade them collectively and individually, again and again, to overcome any difficulties on their way to strive for their own future. We walked league after league, for hours. At each intersection, I stopped and urged them to go home, but they stayed on.

Eventually, we arrived at Fuxingmen. There, I firmly insisted that they stop. I got onto my bike and rode off, not daring to look back.

As the day of the departure was drawing near, I became more and more attached to Mother and Son. At my imminent departure, I was unsettled and heartbroken. But we live only once. Remaining here would mean witnessing my entire life wasted in endless frustration. Having in mind the picture of a possible future for all of us rendered the temporary separation and hardship necessary and worthwhile.

The last day of my stay finally arrived. The whole family got up at 4 a.m. There would be a long drive to the airport. At the time, my brother-in-law Guo Ming had been transferred out of the factory and promoted to a section chief in Norinco, a company notorious for selling AK-47s abroad. He had a driver at his disposal. Mother, Son and my brother-in-law went with me.

On mid-morning, we arrived at the airport and saw a long line ahead of us to get into the waiting room. Moving along the line, we soon found ourselves within the gigantic waiting room. Before we knew it, we were already at the foot of an escalator. Mother and Son were stopped there.

It was too late to realize this was where we were to part. Pushed from behind and carried away by the forward moving crowd, in panic, I saw myself helplessly step onto the escalator. There was no way for me to come down. Desperate at losing the chance to say farewell to my dear mother and son since no one knew when we would ever be able to see each other again, I cried out to Mother and Son. They burst out crying too.

Once upstairs, I immediately stepped out of the line, crying out to Mother and Son across from the vast, voice-drowning space, bidding them a truncated, distant good-bye. I had no idea that this would be the last time that I ever saw my dear mother.

I had fought Mother fiercely. With the insight gained from rearing my own son, I had reconciled with Mother. The reconciliation brought out the closeness between us and my deep appreciation for her, and my gratitude for being her daughter. If there is anything special about me that pulled me through my ordeals and pushed me upward steadfastly, I owe it to Mother. It was her blood that runs in me that eventually became a dominant trait and turned me into a smaller version of her spirit and fortitude.

With heart-breaking regret, I was led toward a checkpoint. Here my brother-in-law had to stop. His pass was invalid beyond this point.

At this, I immediately panicked, knowing from this point on, all my familiarities and security would be gone. I would be entering into an unknown world all alone with no one knowing me but the $300 carried on my shoulder and the address, phone number, and the name of Brian Lee, Jevons Lee's friend that I had never met. At the thought of having to knock on a total stranger's door and nothing but $300 to live on, let alone the overwhelming amount of tuitions, I was even more apprehensive. Tears welled up in my eyes. When I cried out "Good-bye" to my brother-in-law, to my surprise, I found his eyes brimming with tears too. Heart melting, eyes blurred, I walked toward my own destiny.

EPILOGUE

When the plane finally took off, I breathed out a sigh of relief. Keep going, I prayed. Don't turn back. Once over the Pacific Ocean, I said to myself, you are almost on the loose. The moment the plane touched down in San Francisco for refueling, the whole plane of passengers immediately cheered and hurrahed loudly and shook hands to congratulate one another. For the first time in our lives, we could finally breathe like a free man! I felt like getting out and prostrating to kiss and embrace the soil—the "land of the free and the home of the brave". The euphoria was soon replaced by a new, calm, wonderful, soul-cleansing feeling that we had never experienced in China. We saw ourselves instantly transformed into kind, decent and dignified human beings harboring only good will toward one another and sharing the human bond.

When the plane was above New York City, it was nighttime. At the magnificent night view brilliantly illuminated by countless electric lights from the buildings and from the vehicle processions coming and going orderly along their lanes, I was in awe of the wonder. It felt like we were reaching outer-space. At the prosperity of America, I rued for the bleak life we had in China. Inside the JFK Airport, I again marveled at America's modernity, orderliness, efficiency, and civility.

Once out of the Customs, reality set in. I was alone among passengers cheerfully departing with people picking them up. Upon learning about my situation, Jin Feng, a dignified Taiwanese-American there to pick up my seatmate, took me to Brian Lee's home without demur. Coming from a country where civility and kindness were castigated and abandoned, and words like "thank you", "excuse me" and "please" disappeared from our lexicon ever since the Cultural Revolution, I was overwhelmed by this unfamiliar pure kindness. Miserable at my inferior position and my uncertain future, arriving at Brian Lee's home, I didn't even have the confidence to say "Thank you" to Jing Feng but regretfully saw him drive away.

Mrs. Lee was waiting for me outside. It was almost midnight, but the whole family was wide-awake for my arrival. They took me, a total stranger, in, and provided me the initially needed room and board and security. They were in the midst of moving to Long Island. Knowing I should do something in return for their generosity, the next day, I cleaned up their large dusty basement until it became spic and span, and hauled up bags of debris and discards and carried heavy lumber up to the curbside. That evening, they treated me to an expensive restaurant. During the meal, I was awed by the information that the whole large round table of food could be earned in one minute by some people.

The third day, with the direction of the workers working at the Lees' home, I went to Chinatown. Along my way to the employment agency, I again was awed by the prosperity and the amazing purchasing power of ordinary people. In the agency, at $80's cost, I got a shop-assistant job in a general store in the Bronx. Lin Weiran, a student from Eastman School of Music who was also there looking for a summer job, treated me to McDonald, and gave me $30, which was probably a month of his food supply. Out of concern for the tough subway ride into a tough neighborhood, he accompanied me to the store. In the store, I felt like a fool. I couldn't even comprehend colloquial English, let alone contextual English. At the end of the day, I was fired with a free supper and $2 for subway fare.

From that day on, I seldom had any free time off, always working, sometimes two to three jobs a day, very often 15 to 16 hours a day, working in whatever conditions in dangerous neighborhoods, behind double-fenced takeout restaurant like a caged animal, with customers pounding the fence and cursing, sleeping on chairs in the wide open in a basement with rats scurrying around and once on the shelf in a small, airless closet. I had worked as baby-sitter, busgirl, waitress, food-deliverer, and as housekeeper for a rich family in a five-story building on Park Avenue.

Carefully saving every dollar I made, approaching my school day, I was still far short of my tuition and living expenses. I was worried sick. At my fellow worker's decision of quitting school and losing his legal status just to make money to have some security, I was even more apprehensive. But I knew I had to stick to my goal. A day before my classes began, Brian Lee withdrew $3,000 for my tuition and gave me $50 as pocket money. At their blind trust, I was deeply touched. After thinking it over, I decided to work my own way out, and returned the money for my tuition. Half a year later, I finally made enough money for the scholastic year and then some, ending my marginal existence. Out of appreciation and respect, at my departure, my boss, Mr. Dai, a kind, hardworking three-restaurant owner, generously gave me $100.

With no time to lose and much to be accomplished, I devoted my entire waking time to studying and working. In one year, I obtained a master's degree. In another year, I accumulated half of the course requirement credits for a PhD in Linguistics at CUNY's Graduate Center. At my son's arrival from China, I placed my pursuit on hold and became a high school English teacher in NYC to provide financial and emotional support for him, which then, by a twist of fate, became my means of livelihood for the next 22 years.

In my difficult times, Nino Altamura, my landlord and a big-hearted man, and his nice family provided an ear and a shoulder for me to cry out my bottled-up troubles. On my wedding day, his daughter Loridana brought me an armful of bouquet of pink gladiolus and a generous wedding gift.

❧

In 1993, my son arrived in the US. The following year, I swore in as an American citizen in a solemn ceremony and became a tenured teacher. That same year, we bought our very first house. It was a charming little house, no big deal in America. At that time, 75% of Americans owned a house. But for us, it was a wild dream coming true. We were simply intoxicated by first time owning something in our lives.

In 1996, two years after I became an American citizen, I exercised my sacred citizen's right for the first time in my life. I spoke up at a town meeting against government encroachment. We won. This is impossible in China, where we have no say in whatever the government decides to do. There is no town meeting there. That same year, I exercised another sacred right as an American citizen. I voted for the first time in my life. In China, elections are a joke. They are rarely held, subject to the party's arbitrary suspension. Officials are party members appointed by the party. We can only vote for insignificant non-legislative positions and "people's representatives" into the so-called "People's Congress", which has no real power, but is a rubber-stamp organization and a mouthpiece for the party.

Mao's Cultural Revolution is history now, but the scars left from those years remain with us last survivors of Mao's ultimate revolution. This part of history remains with us and lives on in us.

The ordeals my family and I experienced during those years were quite ordinary. With stories by far more horrendous than ours untold, I told our stories by default.

For decades, I was a prisoner of my past. After coming to America, I began tasting what normal life was like for a human being. The dignified life here brought out my seething anger at the kind of life we had been through in China and compelled me to look back and confront my painful past, and relive that nightmarish life. This then turned into a nagging need to understand myself. I began by writing down the most painful memories. At first, my past was a hopelessly entangled jumble in my mind because I had tried hard to forget it all. I struggled for almost two decades to recall the buried memories, to research and study the history of the related eras so as to sequence events out, and to understand the nature of the events and myself. My retirement from work and from worldly concerns finally brought me the needed peace of mind and a clear view, the closure of my slow healing process, and the completion of this work.

The evil force turned China into a Communist country with class theory. The evil force is trying to turn the free world into another China with race theory. Class theory or race theory, the purpose remains the same—divide and rule. Do not fall into the trap and allow them to divide us. Together, we win. I hope my story can serve as a cautionary tale.

ACKNOWLEDGEMENTS

When I was still in China, my friend Jennifer and I vowed to tell the story. But I was only able to do so after I came to America—the land of the free. Without access to the needed information that can only be obtained in a free country, and the healing and perspectives that can only be acquired through time, distance and living among free-thinking, free-spirited people, telling the story would remain but a dream.

I'm indebted to many people who made it possible for me to tell the story.

My first and foremost thanks go to Dr. Jevons Lee, whose selfless, generous act brought me out of China, the huge spiritual prison, to live in this free land. It allowed me to take up this project and look at China from a completely different angle. Without this first step, I would still be frustrated in China, my angle of looking at things would remain the same, and my goal would never be accomplished.

Next, I should thank Wei Zheng, my acquaintance and a high Communist descendant who generously enlisted the help of his father, who was in charge of China's national archives. With the one-page biography of my grandfather that his father printed out for me, it made it possible for me to piece together the information I have of my ancestors and understand them better.

My gratitude no doubt goes to my family. Their support for my project and precious recollections of family history and of certain family members facilitated my effort to tell the stories. I owe my special thanks to my two brothers, Tiemin and Ciqing, for the information they provided and for allowing me to tell their stories. I especially thank my late maternal uncle Xu Ke, the lone survivor

in the family from the older generation whose rich, precious historical knowledge, insight, perspectives and memories of certain family
events and family members enabled me to connect the dots and tell
the story more accurately.

My special thanks and permanent apologies go to my son, who
was discriminated against ever since his birth because of my unfortunate background. Not only was I unable to provide the life and
protection a mother should provide for her son, I caused and added
pain to his young existence. I am most guilty of substantially weak-
ening his faith in human beings at his young age. I am living with
this guilt. It is comforting to see that despite the pain caused by me
and the Communist society, my son triumphed over his pain and
turned out to be a fine human being. He completely forgave me and
encouraged me to tell the stories.

I should especially thank Dr. Robert Bickers, co-director of British
Inter-university China Center and history professor at the University
of Bristol specializing in modern Chinese history and the history
of the British Empire at the time overseeing the research project on
the British-run Chinese Maritime Customs. When the information
about the Chinese Maritime Customs gradually became available
online, I contacted him to obtain more information. Throughout the
years, Dr. Bickers generously facilitated my writing project in every
way he could. He sent me by mail a free copy of more than 100 pages
of the 1948 Service List of the Chinese Maritime Customs Service
and enlisted his student Felix Boecking, who, at the time was doing
research in China on this project, to spare his precious time and
allowance restricted by the Chinese government to photocopy the
needed material for me. Dr. Bickers also sent me his research work,
The Chinese Maritime Customs at War, 1941-1945, which brought to
light what my father and other Customs' coastal employees had been
through during the Japanese occupation of the Customs and allowed
me to assess the situation properly. It was during this contact that
it dawned on me about the very root cause of my father's and the
family's woes, which in turn made my research and understanding
fall into place and elevated my understanding of the larger picture of
the Mao years. The Customs project site and Dr. Bickers' book *Out*

of China provided substantial invaluable information for my understanding of the history of an era and the functions and importance
of the Chinese Maritime Customs Service at the time. The research
works *The Making of New Chinese Bureaucrats: The Customs College
and the Chinese Maritime Customs Staff, 1908-1949* and *Modern
China's Customs Service: A Brief Introduction* by Dr. Chiyun Chang
published at the site supplied valuable information about this part
of the history and put my understanding in perspective. To help me
understand the situation better, Dr. Bickers linked me directly with
Dr. Chang, who graciously assisted me by clarifying my inquiries
and providing additional information. To make me understand how
wartime impacted the Customs and what the Customs' employees
went through after the war, Dr. Chang forwarded me his research
works *The Chinese Maritime Customs in 1949: The Investigation and
Postwar Rehabilitation of the Chinese Maritime Customs Employees* and
The Employees Left Behind. His book *Government, Imperialism and
Nationalism in China* furnished abundant material, sophisticated
analysis and insightful views, which enabled me to adequately assess
the situation the Customs' employees were in during the wartime.
Without this work, it was virtually impossible for me to understand
what employees like my father had been through. I owe my deep
gratitude to both Dr. Bickers and Dr. Chang.

Stephane Courtois et al's *Black Book of Communism*, George
Orwell's *1984*, and L. P. Hartley's *Facial Justice* deepened my understanding of totalitarianism and helped me recall what life was really
like during the Mao years. They became key sources of my background material and helped me accurately depict life during the
Mao era. The information in Johnathan Spence's *Search for Modern
China* about the Qing Dynasty, the Republic era, the Second Sino-
Japanese War and the Customs enabled me to piece together the
events that took place in my family during those eras, and see them
in historical context. The works done by those dogged democracy
fighters, such as Zhou Liangxiao and Gu Juying, Ding Shu, Wang
Youqin, Song Yongyi, and Hu Pengchi, and individuals' recollec-
tions such as Zhong Weiguang's and Song Bolin's published at
Virtual Museum of the Cultural Revolution at www.cnd.org, helped

me sequence things and tell the stories that occurred during the Cultural Revolution as precisely as possible. I'm indebted to them. I'm also thankful to Wikipedia, which provided valuable information about the Chinese Maritime Customs Service and other important data about China. It was this site that I visited whenever I needed to fact-check certain historical or political figures and certain historical events.

I owe my gratitude to the following people who took time to read my work or a section of it and affirmed its values: Jay Walder, the late Dr. Larry Secrest, Dr. Gary Haber, Barry Sarkisian, and Adam Trooskin. Grace Castagnetta, a former concert pianist and my late piano teacher at the time an octogenarian, read my very first draft in one breath without sleeping, honestly pointed out that I needed to "learn English first". Frank Derato generously edited my very first draft and wrote a seven-page-long affirmation, suggestions and encouragement. Wil Schuemann proofread a version of it, and pinpointed the gaps in my timeline. John Luce, after reading a chapter of my later version and recognizing its value, contemplated having his octogenarian mother to do the editing for me. Harry Atkins proofread a portion of a draft and confirmed the values of my work. Dr. Sal Restivo, upon reading a chapter, at once affirmed its values. Vaughn Jacobs read the current version and corresponded with me from time to time with bits of his feedback.

I especially need to thank Ed Tomas, who selflessly offered to read and pass along my original uncut long manuscript to his family, his friends and his colleague. He tirelessly advocated my work and contacted M.J., his friend and his CIA colleague specializing in totalitarian regimes and a total stranger to me, to further confirm and evaluate the worth of my work. Like Ed Tomas, M. J. sacrificed his precious time to read my long manuscript in his busy life. Without solicitation, he wrote an extolling book review any author can ever expect that accorded the work with the highest possible recognition that included all the essences and merits of the work. I should also thank Jennifer and Lynn for allowing me to tell their stories and for providing more information about themselves and family members.

My husband served as my daily sounding board, taking pains to deal with my frequently revised manuscript and my erratic computer, build my website and handle all the matters related to the book.

To my regret, due to the length of this book, I had no choice but to cut off my descriptions of those who had helped me along the way. But the memories of each one of them will be etched and preserved in my memory and cherished forever. I hope one day their generosity will be bountifully returned and rewarded in some way.

ENDNOTES

1. Peng Zhen (1902-1997): Fifth-ranking official and Mayor of Beijing before the Cultural Revolution. As Liu Shaoqi's right-hand man, he took Mao's ax first during the Cultural Revolution.

2. Liu Shaoqi (1898-1969): Orthodox Communist and second-ranking official before the Cultural Revolution. Before the communist takeover, Liu was organizing workers' movements within the legal range while Mao was organizing peasants' armed riots against landlords. When Liu's prestige rose above Mao, Mao decided to permanently rid himself of his long-term rival with the means of a cultural revolution. Liu Shaoqi died from horrible tortures.

3. Zhou Enlai (1898-1976): Premier. A skilled diplomat and a capable hand in state affairs, he was widely respected and beloved for his pragmatism and his humanity. However, his need to survive outweighed his conscience. He was the executor and architect of many of Mao's policies.

4. Chen Boda (1904-1989): The party's principal theorist and Mao's close associate who rose to power during the Cultural Revolution but soon was banished for siding with Lin Biao on separating power between the state and the party in order to check Mao's absolute power.

5. Kang Sheng (1998-1975): A widely-hated leftist figure and China's Beria (Stalin's accomplice and architect of terror) overseeing the work of the party's internal security and intelligence apparatus. Mao promoted him during the Cultural Revolution for his usefulness.

6. Jiang Qing (1914-1991): Mao's wife, a despised, notorious woman and an ultra-leftist who served as an important emissary for Mao in the early stages of the Cultural Revolution and played a significant role all through. After Mao's death, she was arrested and tried together with the other three members, known as the "Gang of Four".

7. Lin Biao (1907-1971): A marshal pivotal in the Communist victory against the Nationalists. To stay afloat, he stayed low-key and went along with Mao. He was chosen by Mao to replace Peng Dehuai as the defense minister and then as the vice chairman of the Communist Party. He promoted Mao's personality cult. But Mao eventually became suspicious of his loyalty. He died in a suspicious plane crash.

[8] Xie Fuzhi (1909-1972): Chief of Police, Mao's flunkey and China's Dzerzhinsky (Head of secret police, Stalin's henchman) who facilitated Red Guards' violence during the Cultural Revolution and turned their wild actions into institutionalized state-sponsored terror.

[9] Liang Shuming (1893-1968): A philosopher and teacher known for his unbending character and truthfulness, and for his role in the rural reconstruction movement during the early Republican era.

[10] He Siyuan (1896-1982): A western-trained economist-turned mayor of Beijing during the Nationalist era.

[11] Zhang Dongxun (1886-1973): A public intellectual.

[12] Wang Hongwen (1935-1992): A worker who headed a large rebel organization during the Cultural Revolution. He was promoted and used by Jiang Qing. After the death of Mao in 1976, he was arrested and tried together with the other three members of the "Gang".

[13] Wang Guangmei (1921-2006): Liu Shaoqi's wife. She had served as an interpreter during the truce negotiation between the Nationalist government and the Communist rebels brokered by George Marshall. During the Cultural Revolution, she was accused of being an American spy and arrested to implicate Liu Shaoqi. After Mao's death, she was released and rehabilitated.

[14] Zhang Chunqiao (1917-2005): An ultra-leftist party theorist who served an important role in Mao's launching of the Cultural Revolution. As a result, he was promoted to v ice premier and other key positions. After Mao's death, he was arrested and tried as a key member of the Maoist gang.

[15] Yao Wenyuan (1931-2005): A notorious leftist literary critic who was chosen in Mao's conspiracy by attacking Wu Han, a historian and deputy mayor of Beijing, in order to lead to Mayor Peng Zhen, and finally to Liu Shaoqi. He was arrested and tried as a member of the "Gang".

[16] Wang Dongxing (1916-2015): Mao's diehard loyalist. Military commander and the chief of Mao's personal bodyguard force, the 9th Bureau of the Ministry of Public Security, which included the 8341 Special Regiment.

[17] Rong Yiren (1916-2005): A wealthy capitalist who availed himself to the Communist Party.

[18] Zhang Bojun (1895-1969): A western-trained, left-leaning politician and intellectual who was incorporated into the Communist government. But when he criticized the party, he was branded "number-one rightist" and removed from his symbolic ministerial position.

CPSIA information can be obtained
at www.ICGtesting.com
Printed in the USA
BVHW090558301221
625026BV00003B/10